Characteristics of Effective Early Learning

Characteristics of Effective Early Learning

Helping young children become learners for life

Second edition

Edited by Helen Moylett

Open University Press

Open University Press
McGraw Hill
8th Floor, 338 Euston Road
London
England
NW1 3BH

email: enquiries@openup.co.uk
world wide web: www.openup.co.uk

First edition published 2022

A catalogue record of this book is available from the British Library

Executive Editor: Eleanor Christie
Editorial Assistant: Zoe Osman
Content Product Manager: Ali Davis

ISBN-13: 9780335248544
ISBN-10: 0335248544
eISBN: 9780335248551

Library of Congress Cataloging-in-Publication Data
CIP data applied for

Typeset by Transforma Pvt. Ltd., Chennai, India

Praise page

"This timely second edition reminds us all that the Characteristics of Effective Early Learning are powerful yardsticks against which the highest quality early years provision and practice can be judged. When young learners play and explore, develop positive attitudes to learning and display their creative, critical thinking we see how powerful and exceptional their learning can be. Chapter 1 should be read by all student early childhood educators, as well as those of us whose current experiences may be challenging long cherished values and beliefs. This chapter, and the chapters that follow – each a master-class in itself - offer the rationale and research to justify the Characteristics and to give us the will to keep them there."

Professor Julie Fisher, Early Years Adviser & Visiting Professor,
Oxford Brookes University, UK

"The revised edition of this valuable textbook is timely and welcome. Contributors reflect on the latest research evidence and the bearing of wider developments on early years practice such. These include the impact of COVID-19 on all aspects of children's early learning and development and the challenges presented to the sector and practitioners from the Black Lives Matter movement. Chapters also consider the wider social and policy challenges that practitioners face as they strive to provide the best learning support for young children. The publication provides academic evidence, practical guidance and support for undergraduates and the general reader."

Michael Freeston, Director of Quality Improvement, Early Years Alliance

"This second edition of Characteristics of Effective Early Learning *is refreshing, relevant and much-needed within the context of Early Childhood Education and Care (ECEC). This book continues to celebrate children's advocacy and child-centred practice consistently throughout each chapter. Helen's expert way of guiding the reader through these vital principles, alongside the Characteristics of Effective Learning, is enhanced with the crucial focus on how children learn, which somehow seems to get lost within UK policy and various government initiatives.*

There are two new fascinating chapters focused on the importance of essential relationships, attachment, well-being and affirmative parenting. Such a wonderful range of chapter contributors ensures that this book remains essential reading for students and professionals at all levels, reminding us that children are skilful learners from birth. I particularly valued the sections on the effectiveness of educational

*interventions and the centrality of a well-researched play-based peda-
gogy throughout. Each chapter also includes a 'key messages'
section – perfect prompts for us all."*

Dr Karen Boardman, Head of Early Years Education,
Edge Hill University, UK

*"Rarely have I read a book that so completely aligns with my own
philosophy, thinking and outlook on early education. This book offers
a wide-ranging overview of all aspects of effective early learning.
Expertly combining theory, research, case studies, examples and
practical ideas, it is a 'must-read' for all practitioners, teachers and
leaders working in the early years. From the vital role of self-regulation
to the importance of play and active learning; from ways to get children
thinking critically and creatively, to ideas for developing talk and
language, the book helps put the characteristics of effective learning
into context, in the most practical way. Whatever kind of early years
setting you work in, this book is sure to inform, inspire and enthuse
you and your staff. Not only is it easy to read and full of the best kinds
of common sense, but it will also encourage you to read more widely
among early years theorists, to expand your thinking and knowledge."*

Sue Cowley, Early Years Teacher, Author, Presenter and Trainer

Contents

List of Figures and Tables by chapter

Acknowledgements

As the editor I am very grateful to all the contributors for their enthusiasm in getting involved in sharing their expertise and to the publishing team for their support with this second edition. We are all particularly indebted to the many children and practitioners whose ideas and experiences bring our writing to life and without whom this book would not have been written.

This edition is dedicated to the memory of our colleague David Whitebread (1948–2021) whose chapter on self-regulation is one of many professional memorials to his commitment to children's learning and development and his years of dedicated research with practitioners.

Contributors

Elaine Bennett began her career as a nursery nurse. She is firmly based in practice as an Early Years Leader and Reception teacher at Friars Primary School and Nursery in Southend, Essex. The story of how she led the continuation of the early years learning journey into Year 1 forms part of her chapter in this book. Alongside teaching she writes, trains and campaigns for the very best, pedagogically responsible and respectful start for all children. She is the founder of the hugely popular 'Keeping Early Years Unique' movement which began life on Facebook.

Professor Tony Bertram is a Director of the Centre for Research in Early Childhood (CREC) and a Director of Amber Publications and Training Ltd (APT). He is co-Founder of the European Early Childhood Education Research Association (EECERA) and was its elected President from 1992 to 2007. He holds honorary academic posts at Wolverhampton University and currently is Professor at Birmingham City University. A member of several UK Government EY advisory groups and working parties, Tony has also worked extensively abroad for the British Council and the Organisation for Economic Co-operation and Development (OECD).

Di Chilvers is an advisory consultant, author and trainer in early childhood education, having worked in the early years sector for over 40 years. Her work focuses on children's creative and critical thinking and following children's interests, ideas and fascinations through observing children, understanding their development and *how* they learn and think. Visits to Reggio Emilia, Denmark, New Zealand, Oman, Ghana and India have all influenced Di's thinking and philosophy. Professional development initiatives include Talk for Maths Mastery, Talk for Reading, Sustained Shared Thinking, Assessment for Learning and Leading Learning, an observational approach. Di has created an assessment tool called the Development Map – an holistic, child-centred approach based on observation.

Clare Crowther is the Head of Atelier Nurseries in Bath and Chippenham. Clare's professional background in early years includes leading a large children's centre, the co-ordination of forest schools, and the training and continuing professional development of the early years workforce to level 7. Clare has written several publications, and until recently wrote monthly articles for a leading nursery magazine.

Judith Dancer (formerly Stevens) is a retired independent writer, consultant and trainer. She worked widely in the private and voluntary sectors in addition to holding numerous roles in primary education. Following a long career in local authority advisory posts, Judith took on leadership roles in national programmes including Every Child a Talker. Her many maths books include: *Foundations of Mathematics: An Active Approach to Number, Shape and Measures in the Early Years* (2013, with Carole Skinner), and several maths titles in the Featherstone *Little Books* series. She continues to have an interest in all aspects of mathematics, particularly maths outdoors and through stories, rhymes and role play.

Helen Moylett is an independent early years consultant. Early in her career she worked in schools as a teacher, an adviser and then in early years and primary education at Manchester Metropolitan University. In 2000 she became head of an early years centre. As a head teacher Helen was a Birth to Three Matters trainer and researcher. From 2004 to 2011 she worked for the National Strategies and was centrally involved in developing the Early Years Foundation Stage (EYFS) and led the Every Child a Talker programme. She was an expert adviser to the Tickell EYFS review and co-authored *Development Matters* (2012). Helen has written and edited several early years books. She tutors at the Centre for Research in Early Childhood in Birmingham and is a Vice President of Early Education. She received a Nursery World Lifetime Achievement Award in 2019.

Professor Christine Pascal OBE is Director of the Centre for Research in Early Childhood (CREC), based at the St Thomas Children's Centre in Birmingham and Director of Amber Publications and Training. She is a co-founder and President of the European Early Childhood Education Research Association and a Vice President of Early Education. She has been an Early Years Specialist Adviser to the House of Commons Select Committee on Education. She has written extensively on early childhood development and the quality of early education services and was awarded an OBE in 2001 and a Nursery World Lifetime Achievement Award in 2012.

Kim Porter has a long and diverse career in early years and primary education, teaching across Nursery to Year 6 prior to a successful headship in Calderdale. In addition to teaching, leadership and headship, Kim has extensive experience of supporting and improving pedagogy across maintained and non-maintained sectors, as an English Adviser, Literacy Consultant and Early Years lead in a local authority.

Kim led the Every Child A Talker (ECAT) programme in the North of England. Between 2013 and 2018 Kim worked in school improvement in Leeds. Kim's current role is with the charity Teach First, working as an achievement partner on the *Leading Together* programme. This programme focuses on supporting leaders in challenging circumstances through coaching and mentoring.

Professor Sue Rogers is based at the at the UCL Institute of Education, London, where she is currently Director (interim). Her research interests include play, curriculum and pedagogy in early childhood, young children's perspectives and professional learning in the early years workforce. She has published widely in the field of early childhood education and professional learning approaches, including three books: *Inside Role Play in Early Childhood Education: Researching Children's Perspectives* (2008, with Julie Evans); an edited collection on play pedagogy entitled *Rethinking Play and Pedagogy: Concepts, Contexts and Cultures* (2011) and *Adult Roles in the Early Years* (2012, with Janet Rose). She is currently researching children's agency in relation to climate change and environmental education.

Dr Shabana Roscoe is a research assistant and associate lecturer based at Manchester Metropolitan University's Psychology Department. Her PhD was a year-long ethnographic exploration in an English reception class, looking at 4- to 5-year-olds' agential navigations of adult-formulated rules in the context of self-initiated play. Her research interests span children's lived experiences in their everyday contexts, play in early years education and care settings, primary education, adult and child relations, and qualitative research methods, as well as the ethical aspects of conducting real-world research with young people. At MMU, she is contributing a service evaluation of how a group adolescent psychotherapy treatment can enhance and be enhanced through a trauma-informed provider.

Nancy Stewart is an independent early years consultant. She worked with children and families in the private and voluntary sector, as well as teaching and leading early years in schools before becoming a local authority advisor. She has lectured on foundation degree courses and been an Early Years Professional Status assessor. While working for the National Strategies leading Every Child a Talker, Nancy developed training materials on communication and language, play and assessment. She has also written and contributed to books on parenting and health and is author of *How Children Learn: The Characteristics of Effective Early Learning* (2011) and (with Helen Moylett) *Understanding the Revised EYFS* (2012). Nancy was Project Lead in the development of *Birth to Five Matters* (2021) and is a Vice President of Early Education.

Dr David Whitebread was Founding Director of the Play in Education, Development and Learning (PEDAL) research centre at the Faculty of Education, University of Cambridge. He taught in early years and primary schools for 12 years and during his first 17 years at Cambridge worked in early years teacher training. His research focused on self-regulation in young children, and the roles of play and oral language in its development. His work was published in many academic journals and he edited and wrote a number of influential reports and books, including *The Sage Handbook of Developmental Psychology and Early Childhood Education* (Sage, 2019), *Quality in Early Childhood Education – an International Review and Guide for Policy Makers* (WISE, 2015), *Teaching and Learning in the Early Years* (Routledge, 4th edn., 2015), *Developmental Psychology and Early Childhood Education* (Sage, 2012) and *The importance of play: a report on the value of children's play with a series of policy recommendations* (Toys Industries for Europe, 2012).

How young children learn: introduction and overview

Helen Moylett

Introduction

This is the second edition of a book which emphasises putting the child at the centre of provision and practice, at a time when that message has never been more relevant. The coronavirus pandemic may have changed young children's homes, their early years settings and schools; they may have endured grief, domestic turbulence or other changes in their family life: but the fundamental ways in which they learn have remained the same. However, the pandemic has caused many settings and schools to reflect on their provision and practice in new ways (Solly 2020; Yates 2020) and Black Lives Matter has prompted widespread reflection and action on racism as well as other forms of discrimination and injustice. The UK is reportedly the sixth richest country in the world and yet we went into the pandemic in what has been called 'a state of disastrous social fragility' (Harris 2020). After ten years of austerity many young children were already vulnerable to poor health, insecure attachment, developmental delay, educational underachievement and trauma. Many of these and other problems are caused or exacerbated by poverty which has increased steadily and unmercifully and affects some groups disproportionately.

Early years settings and schools cannot end poverty; but they can ensure that they recognise and value all families and are actively promoting inclusion and breaking down barriers to belonging and participation (see, for example, Henry-Allain and Lloyd-Rose 2021). The writers of this book believe that an emphasis on how children learn supports practitioners to provide the very best child-centred curriculum which acknowledges the power and depth of putting well-being first and supporting and extending children's interests through 'loving pedagogy' (Grimmer 2021). Every chapter emphasises the importance of getting to know children and their families, tuning into their experience and supporting their well-being because positive relationships with attentive, loving adults are so powerful in supporting children's emotional and cognitive development and learning. Their learning journeys are all unique and all fascinating.

All the chapters have been updated and we have added new ones covering two important themes which are present throughout the book: language and interaction and affirmative parenting. There are inevitably other important areas that could have been further explored but we hope that readers will find much that is inspiring and challenging as well as familiar about how children learn. The rest of this chapter is an overview of the characteristics and a summary of the chapters which follow.

Overview

All the authors believe that children are born ready, able and eager to learn. We are passionate in our commitment to children's entitlement to become skilled, enthusiastic learners, whatever their personal or family circumstances, and believe that the best early years pedagogy rests on deep understanding of child development. This book explores some aspects of how our habits of mind are formed as our brains and bodies develop and we come to understand ourselves as learners. The role of adults in this process is key. Young children left to their own devices will learn through playing and exploring but it is through the active intervention, guidance and support of a skilled adult that children make the most progress in their learning. This does not mean pushing children too far or too fast, but instead meeting children where they are emotionally and intellectually. It means being a partner with children, enjoying with them the power of their curiosity and the 'skill, will and thrill' of finding out what they can do.

The 'skill, will and thrill' represent the characteristics of effective early learning:

- playing and exploring – the *skill* to get engaged;
- active learning – the *will* to keep going;
- thinking creatively and critically – the *thrill* of discovery.

Readers in England will recognise these characteristics as specifically Early Years Foundation Stage (EYFS) terminology. The Statutory Framework (DfE 2021 1.15) requires practitioners to reflect them in their practice and explains them as:

- **playing and exploring** – children investigate and experience things, and 'have a go';
- **active learning** – children concentrate and keep on trying if they encounter difficulties, and enjoy achievements; and
- **creating and thinking critically** – children have and develop their own ideas, make links between ideas and develop strategies for doing things.

It would be easy to miss the importance of this brief statement which makes it mandatory for practitioners to respond not just to *what* children learn but also to *how* they learn.

Of course, these ideas about how children learn are not new and nor are they confined to children learning in England. The EYFS itself has been influenced by research and practice from across the world including Reggio Emilia, New Zealand and the United States. The writers of this book draw on many traditions and their own wide experience, as well as the non-statutory guidance which expands and explains the characteristics and the areas of learning (the how and what children learn) in practice. We are writing in England, and therefore drawing largely on English practice and guidance, but we believe that the learning power of children is universal as demonstrated in their play and exploration, active learning and creative and critical thinking.

Under 'A Unique Child', *Development Matters* (Early Education 2012) and the updated version, *Birth to 5 Matters* (Early Education 2021), set out what one might expect to see children doing when playing and exploring, being active in their learning and thinking creatively and critically. (In both documents there are further columns with suggestions for 'Positive Relationships: What adults might do' and 'Enabling Environments: what adults might provide'.)

Table 1.1   A Unique Child: Observing how a child is learning

A Unique Child: observing how a child is learning
Playing and exploring – engagement
Finding out and exploring
• Showing curiosity about objects, events and people • Using senses to explore the world around them • Engaging in open-ended activity • Showing particular interests
Playing with what they know
• Pretending objects are things from their experience • Representing their experiences in play • Taking on a role in their play • Acting out experiences with other people
Being willing to 'have a go'
• Initiating activities • Seeking challenge • Showing a 'can do' attitude • Taking a risk, engaging in new experiences, and learning from trial and error
Active learning – motivation
Being involved and concentrating
• Showing a deep drive to know more about people and their world • Maintaining focus on their activity for a period of time • Showing high levels of involvement, energy, fascination • Not easily distracted • Paying attention to details
Keeping on trying
• Persisting with an activity or toward their goal when challenges occur • Showing a belief that more effort or a different approach will pay off and that their skills will grow and develop (growth mindset) • Bouncing back after difficulties

(Continued)

Table 1.1 (Continued)

Enjoying achieving what they set out to do
- Showing satisfaction in meeting their own goals *(I can!)*
- Being proud of how they accomplished something – not just the end result
- Enjoying meeting challenges for their own sake rather than external rewards or praise (intrinsic motivation)

Thinking creatively and critically – thinking

Having their own ideas (creative thinking)
- Thinking of ideas that are new and meaningful to the child
- Playing with possibilities *(What if? What else?)*
- Visualising and imagining options
- Finding new ways to do things

Making links (building theories)
- Making links and noticing patterns in their experience
- Making predictions
- Testing their ideas
- Developing ideas of grouping, sequences, cause and effect

Working with ideas (critical thinking)
- Planning, making decisions about how to approach a task, solve a problem and reach a goal
- Checking how well their activities are going
- Changing strategy as needed
- Reviewing how well the approach worked

Adapted from *Birth to 5 Matters* (2021) pp. 52–4.

It can be seen that the three characteristics interact with each other and overlap in practice. In play and exploring, for instance, a child will be actively involved and motivated as well as thinking creatively and critically.

Children are born playful and curious and need time and space to develop and learn through their natural desires to engage with other people and the environment in which they live.

This process is represented in *Birth to 5 Matters* (Early Education 2021) as a simple sum.

Figure 1.1 A child learning

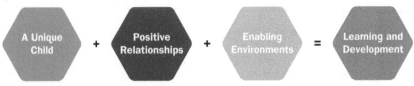

Source: Early Education (2021)

A Unique Child, Positive Relationships, Enabling Environments and Learning and Development are the four themes of the EYFS and are inter-related:

A Unique Child actively drives their own learning, reaching out and making sense of their experiences with people and world around them. Within warm and loving **Positive Relationships** the child experiences emotional safety which is the bedrock to learning about how to be a person, and joins the world of learning with and from others. **Enabling Environments** provide the stimulating outdoor and indoor experiences – in settings and at home – which challenge children, respond to their interests and meet their needs. The result of these three elements interacting together is the child's **Learning and Development.** (Moylett and Stewart 2012:6)

Self-regulation

In the UK, today's practitioners are the inheritors of a long tradition of good early years practice based on play and hands-on experiences for young children where practitioners aim to increase children's independence, choice and control over their own learning. Children move from being 'others regulated' to what we now know as being self-regulated. An acknowledgement of the importance of self-regulation lies at the heart of the characteristics. As well as managing feelings and behaviour, self-regulation involves attitudes and dispositions for learning and an ability to be aware of one's own thinking. Moreover, many practitioners have been struck by how much they themselves still use the same learning strategies as adults. We could easily drop the 'early' from the title and they could be the characteristics of effective lifelong learning. We refine and develop our ways of learning as we get older, but essentially we use the same strategies as babies.

Recent research in brain development and psychology provides evidence of the remarkable learning abilities of babies. They may be vulnerable and need care and protection, but they have strong drives to be competent, to engage with others and make meaning. They show curiosity, make choices and are persistent. In other words, they are able to use most of the same strategies that will support them as learners all their lives, such as imitating others, noticing patterns and making predictions. These characteristics can be helped or hindered by the experiences and interactions children have.

When they are encouraged and supported to follow their curiosity, to feel the satisfaction of meeting their own challenges, to think for themselves, and to plan and monitor how they will go about their activities, they become self-regulated learners who later outstrip children who may have developed more early subject-based knowledge but are more passive in their learning.

(Moylett and Stewart 2012:10)

Research and practice have confirmed the claims that John Holt was making in the 1960s in books such as *How Children Fail* (Holt 1964) that since we cannot know what knowledge will be most needed in the future, it is senseless to try to fill young children with our current knowledge. Instead, we should be focusing on *how* they learn and help them to love learning so much that they will be able to learn whatever they need in a changing world.

Attachment

Being in love with learning starts with people being in love with us. Every few seconds another human is born into the world. How long each baby survives, and whether they lead happy lives between birth and death, will depend on many factors, the most important being whether they are loved and cared for in their early years. The fact that well-being underpins learning has been known about for many years, and developments in neuroscience have confirmed that early attachment relationships are crucial for brain development (Gerhardt 2004). Warm, positive interactions and exploring the world with the senses build a brain that can trust and care for others, manage emotions, and learn effectively. When babies work out that they can depend on and trust a caregiver (usually, but not always, their mother) who is consistently responsive and sensitive to their physical and emotional needs they have what is called a 'secure attachment'. Babies can also form close bonds with a small group of other people who know them well. These relationships are vital to their learning and development and explain why the key person role in settings is so important.

As babies we all need and seek constant repetition of acts of being loved, trusted and given control to begin to understand ourselves and others. The most fundamental task of a baby is to learn how to meet her needs. When her signals are recognised and she receives what is often referred to as a 'contingent' response based on what she actually needs, rather than on what the carer thinks she might or should need, she will calm, feel secure and begin to be able to regulate her own behaviour.

Secure attachment supports us to be effective learners as well as happier, healthier people and this has been recognised in various government and public body commissioned reports (Marmot 2010 and 2020; Children's Commissioner 2020; Ipsos Mori 2020; Field 2010 for example,) which argue for more investment in early years. The sub-title of this book 'helping young children become effective learners for life' underlines the importance of that investment. Although clearly the early years sector needs more financial investment, in the context of this book we are talking about what adults invest in terms of time, knowledge and skills when they work with children. If we want a return on that investment that means more children becoming lifelong learners, then we have to think seriously about whether we are really focused on long-term gains or short-term quick fixes.

High Scope

The dangers of concentrating on short-term fixes at the expense of deep level learning have been amply demonstrated by one of the strongest sources of evidence we have about the long-lasting effects of how we are encouraged to learn when we are young – the High Scope Perry Pre-School evaluations (Schweinhart and Weikart 1997). The heart of the High Scope approach is supporting children to plan, carry out and review their own learning, motivated by their own ideas and interests, and supported by skilled practitioners as appropriate. The original High Scope project was the subject of a rigorous longitudinal study following children who took part in the programme until they were over 40 years old. One strand of the research compared children who had been in the project with those who attended 'direct instruction' (behaviourist/formal, practitioner-led) pre-schools.

Children who had attended direct instruction settings showed early achievement gains in English and Maths but, as the children got older, that advantage disappeared and the balance shifted. By the age of 15, children from the direct instruction group were half as likely to read books, twice as likely to have committed 'delinquent acts' and were far more likely to be socially and emotionally troubled than children from High Scope and traditional nursery schools. By the age of 23, the direct instruction group were almost four times more likely to have been arrested and had almost eight times the rate of emotional impairments. They were about half as likely to have graduated from college.

When, at age 40, the High Scope group were compared with children who did not go to any pre-school provision it was found that they exhibited less anti-social and criminal behaviour and were less likely to be drug users. They were far more likely to be doing voluntary work in the community, have stable marriages and higher earnings. It is significant that these High Scope children were all born in poverty and had been identified as at risk of academic failure. In other words, social disadvantage does not have to be a life sentence – good quality early years settings can make a difference.

Persistence

Both High Scope in the US and the Effective Provision of Pre-School Education (EPPSE) in the UK (Sylva et al. 2012) focused on children in provision aged 3 to 4 years old. Other studies have linked babies' persistence at various ages with parenting style and toddler outcomes. For example, one study compared babies' persistence at 6 and 14 months with their mothers' 'teaching style'. They found that mothers who provide access to stimulating objects, are sensitive and responsive to children's emotions and support children's behaviours just above their current level may foster both persistent behaviour and advanced cognitive development in the future. They suggest that practitioners should work with at risk children and families to develop strategies that support the development of persistence (active learning: keeping on trying) as early as possible (Banerjee and Tamis-LeMonda 2007).

These findings are supported by more recent research (McClelland et al. 2012) which interestingly compares the long-term effects of early persistence with the long-term effects of reading and maths ability. The study followed 430 children from pre-school age to adulthood. Contrary to researchers' expectations, they found that maths and reading ability did not have a significant effect on whether or not students gained a university degree. But those who could concentrate and persist at the age of 4 were almost 50 per cent more likely to have completed a degree course by the age of 25.

The overarching message from all this research, and indeed from every chapter of this book, is that what practitioners do in the early years matters for life. As individuals we cannot stop children being born into poverty and disadvantage, but our practice can improve their long-term outcomes and help prevent poor children becoming poor adults. The formal behaviourist view that all learning is shaped by the teacher (as in the direct instruction pre-schools of the High Scope evaluation) does not have long-term impact on aspects of life which help us sustain our learning, loving and earning power. Concentrating in the early years on *how* children learn, by supporting their well-being and learning strategies, enables them to be more self-reliant active learners who can exercise control over their own lives. If we concentrate on what, rather than how children learn, any short-term gain soon wears off and these children are then left with insufficient emotional and cognitive self-regulation resources to manage their lives successfully. It was the focus on how we learn that ensured the High Scope children were more likely to go to college, rather than filling them up with knowledge that is soon forgotten.

Positive relationships

A theme of this book that can be seen in every chapter is the importance of relationships and well-being underpinning learning. As *Every Day's a Learning Day* so eloquently puts it 'Health and Wellbeing ... is about learning how to lead healthy and active lives, becoming confident, happy and forming friendships and relationships with others that are based on respect. *It is also about managing feelings and having the skills to meet challenges, make good choices and manage change*' [my italics] (Education Scotland 2012a,b:4).

The diagram below attempts to represent the way in which to see the whole picture of self-regulating learners. We cannot think and learn effectively if we do not feel safe, cared for and well. If there is not emotional safety, we cannot take risks and push our boundaries. And we learn within relationships – with both adults and peers.

In New Zealand, children's dispositions for learning are the main focus of assessment, and are described as stages of 'ready, willing, able' (Carr 2001). This terminology is a good fit with the characteristics of effective learning.

- Playing and exploring (engagement) – Children seek out and engage in first-hand and imaginative experiences, gathering the material to feed their learning and being prepared to take a risk in new experiences – they are **ready** to learn.
- Active learning (motivation) – Children invest concentration and energy in following their interests, seek the satisfaction of meeting their goals and show perseverance in the face of difficulty – they are **willing** to learn.

- Thinking creatively and critically (thinking) – Children have their own ideas of how to do things, they make sense of their experiences by linking ideas, and they choose how to do things including thinking about their goals and strategies and monitoring their success – they are **able** to learn.
- Alternatively, they have the **skill** in playing and exploring, the **will** and the **thrill** of doing and thinking – recognising their own power as learners, as illustrated in Figure 1.2 by the questions in the speech bubbles.

Figure 1.2 Emotional and cognitive self-regulation

Emotional self-regulation	Cognitive self-regulation positive dispositions to learning plus awareness and control of one's own thinking		
Personal, social and emotional development / Well-being	Playing and exploring *Engagement*	Ready	Skill	What shall I do?
	Active learning *Motivation*	Willing	Will	Do I want to?
	Thinking creatively and critically *Thinking*	Able	Thrill	How shall I do it?

This is a book which recognises both the powerful learning capacities of young children and the need for practitioners to see themselves as learners too, who work hard on forming positive relationships and providing enabling environments for children – in order to be like the inspiring practitioners that Tina Bruce (1999:36) praises and thanks for her own lifelong interest in learning. 'These were not quick fix, get there early, get good outcomes, good SATS results, League Table teachers. These were help-you-to-be-long-term-forever-learner kinds of teacher.'

Although there are lots of examples from practice here, this is not a 'top tips' book; nor a textbook where every chapter follows exactly the same format; nor does it pretend to cover every aspect of early years. Respecting, valuing and listening to the voices of all children is a theme almost woven into the paper of the book but there are inevitably areas of the early years holistic curriculum missing. Despite these limitations, this volume shares some of the main ideas we believe to be important about how children learn, while recognising that children and adults are all different and everyone's practice is rooted in their values, beliefs and knowledge and supported by theory and experience as well as the social and cultural context in which they work. Therefore, every writer has a different 'voice' and every reader will 'hear' those voices differently. As editor, my wish is that all readers find much on which to reflect as well as support to be advocates for early childhood learning as important in its own right and as the foundations of the future.

Chapter order

The chapters are placed in what seems a logical order – starting with this general overview and then moving from self-regulation, the underpinning rationale for all three characteristics, through each of the characteristics, then on to observing, assessing and planning for how children learn, followed by two chapters which are new for this edition on the importance of both conversational interaction and affirmative parenting for children's thinking and learning These new chapters are followed by how adults set up and maintain settings as learning communities and the final chapter explores taking the early years focus on how children learn into Key Stage 1. There are overlaps between chapters, and themes which are common, however each chapter also stands alone and readers can dip in and out in any order without losing the main plot – the importance of children learning how to learn and adults supporting and extending that learning.

In Chapter 2 David Whitebread presents a comprehensive overview of research on self-regulation – a concept at the heart of this book. He explains how practitioners can most effectively support the development of children's metacognitive skills and positive emotional/motivational dispositions towards themselves as learners. He draws on his involvement with the Cambridgeshire Independent Learning Project to examine the possibilities for a pedagogy for self-regulation in early childhood education where children initiate activities, making the decisions about what to play, where and with whom; setting their own goals and challenges; self-directing the learning and resolving problems. In order for this to work, four principles have to be recognised. The first is the need for emotional warmth and security. Closely related to this are emotional and intellectual control, alongside cognitive challenge and opportunities for children to articulate their learning. The importance of these evidence-based principles is demonstrated throughout the subsequent chapters, both in discussions of other research and in examples of effective practice.

Chapter 3, by Sue Rogers and Shabana Roscoe, considers the ways in which play and exploratory behaviours change and develop in children from birth to 6 and suggests ways in which adults might engage with and support children's understanding of the world around them during this critical period, both indoors and outdoors. The importance of relationships is highlighted throughout with reference to attachment and attunement in the earliest forms of play, sensori-motor activities, the growth of imagination and theory of mind, and the development of highly complex social play. Sue and Shabana point out that, although play provision needs to be planned carefully to ensure that children have access to a wide range of possibilities and opportunities, if the purpose is more important than the act of play then it probably isn't play! They argue that young children need to take risks, to explore a wide range of materials, environments and social situations in order to approach learning with confidence. They are clear about the benefits of this approach as children make the transition into Key Stage 1 – a theme which is picked up again by Elaine Bennett and Kim Porter in Chapter 10.

In Chapter 4 Nancy Stewart explores active learning which is all about motivation. She underlines the importance of children's commitment, energy and perseverance toward achieving a goal. She refers to social psychology theories about the impact of developing orientations toward either performance or mastery goals, and of intrinsic versus extrinsic motivation. The strand of 'being involved and concentrating' is related to Ferre Laevers' involvement signals and the concept of flow, as children follow their own fascinations to satisfy their curiosity and their own purposes. Perseverance, described in the EYFS as keeping on trying, is linked to self-efficacy and autonomy. The third strand of 'enjoying achieving what they set out to do' refers to the importance of intrinsic motivation, linked to a mastery orientation and the satisfaction of the drive for competence. Nancy explores Carol Dweck's work on mindset and the need to encourage a growth mindset by praising and recognising children's efforts and power to evaluate their own learning (mastery), rather than focusing solely on their achievements. Implications for early years practice are identified in relation to each strand of active learning.

Di Chilvers in Chapter 5 picks up the thread of the drive for competence and the ways in which playing and exploring create the ideal context for thinking creatively and critically. She focuses on how we recognise and understand this thinking in babies, toddlers and young children and how this supports their development as thinkers and learners. The careful and sensitive observation of children is a key theme. Two conversations – between Corey and Alfie (6 years) and Amy (adult) and between William (4 years) and Iva (adult) – are an interlinking thread which illustrate the language of thinking and the many elements that are combined together in holistic patterns of learning. Examples of this include children developing their own ideas and possibilities, setting and solving problems, making connections between ideas, playing with ideas and using conversational language to interpret their thinking, ask questions and try things out. The development of the imagination is stressed and links made to Anna Craft's work on 'small c' creativity and possibility thinking. Play and active learning are discussed as contexts for creative and critical thinking. Di also stresses the importance of the observation, assessment and planning cycle in supporting practice.

This is the theme that is developed in more depth by Judith Stevens and myself in Chapter 6. The chapter focuses on the inclusion of the characteristics of effective learning in assessment and the need to focus observation, assessment and planning on *how* as well as *what* children are learning. Flexibility in planning and tuning into young children's current enthusiasms and fascinations is seen as key. We point to the danger of getting so focused on 'learning intentions', that practitioners may miss the key, significant learning that is going on all around them. One example is being so busy 'observing' how children are ordering numbers from zero to ten, as they peg number cards they have made onto a washing line, that other more significant behaviours are missed. Many other illustrations from practice show how practitioners can tune into the children and their learning and work closely with parents, valuing their contributions to the observation, assessment and planning cycle. This respect for how parents contribute to their children's learning is picked up in more detail by Chris Pascal and Tony Bertram in Chapter 8.

In Chapter 7 Nancy Stewart and I explore in depth one of the themes that is a feature of all the other chapters. The importance of communication and language – particularly talk, for supporting thinking and learning. We are firm believers in positive interactions with skilful adults being the place where young children learn most about language and about how their own experiences and culture are valued. A setting can have the most beautiful environment, full of lovely resources and well-planned, adult-led language activities, but they will not be of much benefit to children if the practitioners lack the knowledge and skills to use everyday interactions and conversations about children's interests as a powerful teaching tool. We discuss practical ways that adults can be sensitive, supportive and stimulating communication partners with young, motivated learners who are playing and exploring and thinking creatively and critically about the people, environments and concepts they encounter.

The theme of everyday interactions is picked up again in Chapter 8 where Chris Pascal and Tony Bertram explore some of the lessons from the High Achieving White Working Class Boys (HAWWC) research project. Poverty and low income affect increasing numbers of families alongside other injustices, including racist discrimination against Gypsy, Roma and Traveller, black and many other minority communities. Far too many children underachieve in the education system. This chapter is based on research which highlights the central role of the characteristics of effective learning in the parenting and home learning experiences that have been a central feature of the lives of white working-class boys who have succeeded 'against the odds'. Chris and Tony explore and value the 'parenting resilience' which has led to the 'academic resilience' of these children. They found that the parents tended to be playful and follow their son's interests, bearing out some of the research cited by David Whitebread in Chapter 2 which demonstrated that children who, in their home life, spent more time playing had higher levels of self-regulation than the children who spent more time in structured activities, even after controlling for age, verbal ability and household income. This chapter challenges the deficit models of poor families and children, which tend to define policy discourse and decision making, and provides powerful messages about appropriate practice with other underachieving groups.

The previous chapters all reflect on the crucial role of the adults who work and live with children in supporting and extending children's abilities as learners. While sharing some of this approach, Clare Crowther in Chapter 9 explores in more detail the ways in which adults have to be learners themselves in order to establish a setting as a true community of learners where children, staff and parents learn together in a supportive environment and understand how the characteristics of effective learning apply both to the children and themselves. As Clare explains, her setting vision includes the aspiration that just like the children 'we want our staff to hold the "skill, the will and the thrill" to learn more'. Using examples from her own and two other settings, Clare unpacks the joys and challenges involved in successfully leading learning communities which value children and adults as active, playful, creative learners and thinkers. Leadership and management at any level are about learning and development. Settings, and the adults working in them, grow and develop in response to positive relationships and enabling environments – just like the children. Clare talks about all three settings striving to be 'places of trust' where 'uncertainty and mistakes are viewed by everyone as an opportunity for learning and development; where positive errors can be made and reflections and processes shared'.

Clare and her colleagues have faced challenges in becoming the sort of leaders and staff teams they want to be, but they illustrate the principle that if you are motivated enough, and prepared to collaborate and sometimes compromise, there is always a way. Chapter 10 is also about finding ways. It is the final chapter in the book and Elaine Bennett and Kim Porter deal with one of the hardest issues for Nursery and Reception practitioners who see children who are accustomed to being independent, competent learners, excited by their own learning, move on to the next phase of their education in Year 1 and become swiftly and sadly disempowered. Elaine and Kim explore ways to provide the best for children as they make the transition into Year 1. Elaine shares her own experience of making that transition herself as a teacher and the ways in which she worked with colleagues to change the existing practice using early years principles. Suggestions are also provided for ways to improve practice and face challenges for practitioners who may not be able to do everything Elaine did but who want to move forward in this way.

As Elaine and Kim emphasise, globally the focus in education has moved away from giving information and towards supporting learning skills – what Guy Claxton has called 'building learning power'. Learning to learn has been identified as crucial for personal success and participation as citizens in an inclusive society and projects all over the world are focusing on the learner as a whole person. Yet, despite all this ongoing interest and activity, we have too many children whose capacities to be citizens of the twenty-first century are being wasted by an accountability driven school system. As long ago as 2004, Claxton shared this concern of Emily's, a 15-year-old GCSE student. 'I guess I could call myself smart. I mean I can usually get good grades. Sometimes I worry though that I'm not equipped to achieve what I want, ... I worry that once I'm out of school and people don't keep handing me information with questions ... I'll be lost' (Claxton 2004:1). As Claxton puts it, 'Emily sees herself as ready for a life of tests, but not the tests of life' Emily appears to have no sense of agency as a learner and to be sadly aware of her learned helplessness – to have what Carol Dweck (2006) calls a 'fixed mindset'. Elaine and Kim are passionate in their commitment to a focus on how children learn, so that children make the most of their primary school experience and are not just prepared for tests like Emily.

It is sad that these suggestions for placing the 5- and 6-year old children in Year 1 at the centre are still necessary, 54 years since the Plowden report (commissioned by the English government) so memorably declared: 'At the heart of the educational process lies the child' (Plowden 1967:7). In many countries children do not start formal education until they are seven. England and its new statutory framework is out of step with not only most of the rest of the world, but also with the rest of the UK. In Northern Ireland and Wales, the foundation phase lasts until children are six and seven respectively. In Scotland the early years are defined as pre-birth to eight and the framework talks about the Scottish government's vision for a good childhood and sound education based on children's rights and the need for transformational change to deal with inequality and poverty. It also states: 'transition will likely be smoother for the child if play remains and continues as the main vehicle for their early learning in Primary 1 and beyond' (Education Scotland 2020).

I hope that this book will support readers, wherever they are, to continue gaining confidence in children's abilities as learners and adults' capacities to support and extend their learning. We have to resist the pressure to make early years more like primary education because it is harmful for children and is advocated by those who do not understand child development. Early childhood is an important stage in its own right, where children learn more than they ever will again. It is far more than a waiting room where children are made 'school-ready'. We need to think carefully about what we mean by 'school-readiness' and how to look at this concept holistically (Grimmer 2018). Like Elaine and Kim in Chapter 10, many are looking for and finding ways to make primary more continuous with early years and more like successful early years provision elsewhere, such as in the Nordic countries where the importance of the foundations we are laying for lifelong learning are recognised. Elaine and Kim cite Julie Fisher's (2020) important work on transition and the many examples she provides from her research into the practice of UK schools where early years approaches continue with the child.

Conclusions

This book is designed to help readers reflect on how children learn and how adults use their attuned understanding and experience to support, challenge and extend that learning. Pleas to re-think the way in which we test children in schools and let summative assessment shape the curriculum are becoming common. The *Times Educational Supplement* recently published a special report entitled 'Re-imagining Schools'; this and 'More Than a Score' has a lot of support from parents as well as practitioners for their campaigns to ban SATs and Reception baseline testing (Times Educational Supplement 2021). The Children at the Heart Campaign, supported by over 140 organisations, has urged the government to put the voices of children, young people and families at the centre of the rebuild and recovery process and commit to more support for early years services, saying 'it is now time for the nation to put children at the heart of its plans for the future' (Children at the Heart Campaign 2021).

This widespread support for rethinking education challenges current government policy. We should not deny children a recovery curriculum (see, for example, Carpenter 2020) or their right to learn in a way that supports their natural creativity. We are in danger of perpetuating a deficit model which sees children (particularly poor children, those from black and minority ethnic (BAME) backgrounds, those with special educational needs and disabilities and summer-born children) as somehow lacking or deficient. It is way past time to stop accepting these messages and start asking the fundamental question of every initiative 'Does this promote a pedagogy of equality and inclusion?' (Moylett 2020).

Harris (2020) maintains that we cannot go on with 'deep inequalities of race and class constantly exploding before our eyes, the need for food banks extending into the distance and voices at the top willing us back towards the very social and political dead end that ensured the virus has had such a disastrous impact.' He asserts that there are the seeds of improvement in the spontaneous way in which people acted collectively during the pandemic.

We can grow those seeds in early years and take collective action. All young children have the right to quality early education and care based on sound principles. The principles on which the Early Years Foundation Stage and other UK and international early years frameworks are based are not new. They are the result of much practice, research and theory going back centuries.

Many famous educators and learning theorists cited in this book, such as Froebel, Dewey, the MacMillans, Susan Isaacs, Montessori, Piaget and Vygotsky, talked about the need for children to be active learners, playing, exploring and finding out for themselves as well as interacting with adults. Their theories have become mainstream and are widely taught on early years training courses. They, and others such as Freud and Bowlby, recognised the fundamental influence of our early relationships and experiences on our lifelong social and academic well-being and achievement.

In this history we have a rich cultural resource which deserves to be cited and called on when we are up against those who think that making young children engage in formal learning earlier and earlier will somehow make them better learners rather than disenfranchise them from the world of ideas and creativity. Now, more than ever, our society needs people who have developed lifelong learning skills. These are most effectively learnt in early childhood.

This requires radical educators – adults who are not afraid to defend early childhood from those who would trespass upon it and steal time from children's well-being, play, active learning and creative and critical thinking before they are confident strong learners who have the power to learn anything and the confidence to 'know what to do when they don't know what to do'.

We have to let children guide us if we are to help them become lifelong learners and we have to be learners with them – all of them, not just those who arrive in our settings and schools able to immediately show us how ready, willing and able they are but also those who need more nurturing and care to relax and flourish. We have to understand and value the cultural capital and funds of knowledge (Chesworth 2016; Hill and Wood 2019) that all children and families bring to us and learn from them. This investment of our time, care and attention will pay dividends for the children and also the adults for, as Vivian Gussin Paley (2004:8) said, 'It is in the development of their themes and characters and plots that children explain their thinking and enable us to wonder who we might become as their teachers.'

References

Banerjee, P.N. and Tamis-LeMonda, C.S. (2007) Infants' persistence and mothers' teaching as predictors of toddlers' cognitive development, *Infant Behavior & Development* 30: 479–491.

Bruce, T. (1999) In praise of inspired and inspiring teachers, in L. Abbott and H. Moylett (eds) *Early Education Transformed*. London: Falmer.

Carpenter, B. (2020) *Recovery Curriculum*. Available at: https://barrycarpentereducation. com/2020/04/23/the-recovery-curriculum/ (accessed 21 March 2021).

Carr, M. (2001) *Assessment in Early Childhood Settings*. London: Sage.

Chesworth, L. (2016) A funds of knowledge approach to examining play interests: listening to children's and parents' perspectives, *International Journal of Early Years Education*, 24(3): 294–308.

Children At the Heart Campaign (2021) Available at: www.ncb.org.uk/what-we-do/ influencing-policy/policy-campaigns/children-heart (accessed 20 March 2021).

Children's Commissioner (2020) *Best beginnings in the early years*. Available at: www. childrenscommissioner.gov.uk/wp-content/uploads/2020/07/cco-bestbeginnings-in-the-early-years.pdf (accessed 20 March 2021).

Claxton, G. (2004) *Learning to Learn: A Key Goal in a 21st Century Curriculum*. A discussion paper for the Qualifications and Curriculum Authority, November 2004. Available at: http://escalate.ac.uk/downloads/2990.pdf (accessed 11 November 2021).

DfE (2021) *Statutory Framework for the Early Years Foundation Stage: Setting the standards for learning, development and care for children from birth to five*. Available at: https://assets.publishing.service.gov.uk/government/uploads/system/uploads/ attachment_data/file/974907/EYFS_framework_-_March_2021.pdf (accessed 13 April 2021).

Dweck, C. (2006) *Mindset: The New Psychology of Success*. New York: Ballantine Books.

Early Education (2012) *Development Matters in the Early Years Foundation Stage*. London: Early Education, Crown copyright. Available at: https://early-education.org. uk/development-matters (accessed 3 March 2021).

Early Education (2021) *Birth to 5 Matters: non-statutory guidance for the EYFS*. London: Early Education. Available at: https://www.birthto5matters.org.uk/wp-content/uploads/2021/04/Birthto5Matters-download.pdf (accessed 10 April 2021).

Education Scotland (2012a) *Every Day's a Learning Day: Birth to 3 years*. Glasgow: Education Scotland. Available at: https://education.gov.scot/parentzone/Documents/EveryDaysaLearningDay0to3.pdf (accessed 3 March 2021).

Education Scotland (2012b) *Every Day's a Learning Day: 3 to 6 years*. Glasgow: Education Scotland. Available at: https://education.gov.scot/parentzone/Documents/EveryDaysaLearningDay3to6.pdf (accessed 3 March 2021).

Education Scotland (2020) *Realising the ambition: Being Me*. Glasgow: Education Scotland. Available at: https://education.gov.scot/improvement/learning-resources/realising-the-ambition/ (accessed 12 November 2021).

Field, F. (2010) *The Foundation Years: Preventing poor children becoming poor adults*. The report of the Independent Review on Poverty and Life Chances. London: Cabinet Office, Crown copyright.

Fisher, J. (2020) *Moving on to Key Stage 1: Improving Transition into Primary School*. Maidenhead: Open University Press.

Gerhardt, S. (2004) *Why Love Matters: How Affection Shapes a Baby's Brain*. London: Routledge.

Grimmer, T. (2018) *School Readiness and the Characteristics of Effective Learning: The Essential Guide for Early Years Practitioners*. London: Jessica Kingsley Publishers.

Grimmer, T. (2021) *Developing a Loving Pedagogy in the Early Years: How Love Fits with Professional Practice*. London: Routledge.

Gussin Paley, V. (2004) *A Child's Work*. Chicago: University of Chicago Press.

Harris, J. (2020) We can't hide behind the bunting – let's face up to what's happened to Britain. *The Guardian, 11.05.20*, available at: www.theguardian.com/commentisfree/2020/may/11/bunting-britain-covid-19-crisis-nationalist (accessed 21 April 2021).

Henry-Allain, L. and Lloyd-Rose, M. (2021) *The tiney guide to becoming an inclusive, anti-racist educator* tiney.co. Available at: https://drive.google.com/file/d/16dX9uYy3i-4U8VJShBUrWyESgkznqoUp/view (accessed 20 May 2021).

Hill, M. and Wood, E. (2019) 'Dead Forever': An ethnographic study of young children's interests, funds of knowledge and working theories in free play, *Learning Culture and Social Interaction* 23 100292. Available at: https://doi.org/10.1016/j.lcsi.2019.02.017

Holt, J. (1964) *How Children Fail*. London: Penguin.

Ipsos Mori for The Royal Foundation (2020) *State of the Nation: Understanding Public Attitudes to the Early Years*. Available at: https://www.ipsos.com/sites/ default/files/ct/news/documents/2020-11/ipsos_mori_son_report_final.pdf (accessed 2 April 2021).

Marmot, M. (2010) *Fair society, healthy lives: equity from the start*. London: UCL Institute of Health Equity.

Marmot, M., Allen, J., Boyce, T., Goldblatt, P. and Morrison, J. (2020) *Health Equity in England: The Marmot Review Ten Years On*. London: UCL Institute of Health Equity.

McClelland, M., Acock, C., Piccinin, A., Rhea, S.A. and Stallings, M. (2012) Relations between preschool attention span-persistence and age 25 educational outcomes, *Early Childhood Research Quarterly, 28*.

Moylett, H. (2020) *Time to Say NO!* Available at: https://earlyyearsreviews.co.uk/helen-moylett-time-to-say-no/ (accessed 20 April 2021).

Moylett, H. and Stewart, N. (2012) *Understanding the Revised Early Years Foundation Stage*. London: Early Education.

Plowden Report (1967) *Children and their Primary Schools: A Report of the Central Advisory Council for Education (England)*. London: Her Majesty's Stationery Office

1967. Available at: www.educationengland.org.uk/documents/plowden/plowden1967-1.html (accessed 10 March 2021).

Schweinhart, L.J. and Weikart, D.P. (1997) *Lasting differences: The HighScope Preschool Curriculum Comparison study through age 23* (Monographs of the HighScope Educational Research Foundation, 12). Ypsilanti, MI: HighScope Press.

Solly, K. (2020) *A once in a lifetime opportunity.* Available at: https://early-education.org.uk/news/guest-blog-once-lifetime-opportunity-kathryn-solly (accessed June 2020).

Sylva, K., Melhuish, E., Sammons, P., Siraj-Blatchford, I. and Taggart. B. (2012) *Effective Pre-school, Primary and Secondary Education 3-14 Project (EPPSE 3-14) - Final Report from the Key Stage 3 Phase: Influences on Students' Development from Age 11–14.* Department for Education.

Times Educational Supplement (2021) Re-imagining Schools, 1 March. Available at: www.tes.com/magazine/article/tes-special-report-reimagining-schools (accessed 20 April 2021).

Yates, D. (2020) *Sharing home learning at a distance – loving home learning in lockdown.* Available at: https://early-education.org.uk/news/guest-blog-sharing-home-learning-distance-%E2%80%93-loving-home-learning-lockdown-david-yates (accessed 29 October 2021).

2 The importance of self-regulation for learning from birth

David Whitebread

Chapter summary

The most significant determinant of children's success as learners is their development of what are termed 'metacognitive skills' (i.e. their awareness, knowledge and control of their own mental processes) and positive emotional and motivational dispositions towards themselves as learners. These elements combined have come to be referred to as the development of 'self-regulation'.

This chapter reviews important research and is organised into four sections, dealing with the following topics:

- the nature and characteristics of self-regulation;
- the early emergence of self-regulation in young children, including cognitive, emotional, social and motivational elements;
- the importance of developing self-regulation for children's success as learners and for their emotional well-being;
- environmental and social interaction factors which support children in developing self-regulation and implications for practice in early childhood education settings.

Introduction

While these abilities were once thought to be late developing, emerging in children only towards the end of their primary schooling, early indications of abilities which underpin self-regulation have now been detected in children when they are only a few months old. As I want to argue in this chapter, there is therefore now good evidence to suggest that it is self-regulatory abilities which lie at the core of children's development as effective, powerful learners, from birth.

Combined with this evidence of the fundamental importance of self-regulation for learning, what makes this research particularly exciting for those of us involved in early childhood education is the further evidence that there are large individual differences in the development of these abilities, but that they are very heavily influenced by young children's early experience. In other words, early years educators are in a unique position to have a major beneficial influence on children's development, their realisation of their full potential as learners and a whole range of positive life outcomes.

The nature and characteristics of self-regulation

Three theoretical and research traditions have contributed to the development of our understanding concerning the nature of self-regulation abilities and dispositions. These arise from: the cognitive psychology tradition, originally inspired by the Swiss developmentalist, Jean Piaget, which has developed the notion of 'metacognition'; the socio-cultural tradition, within which the theoretical ideas of the Russian, Lev Vygotsky, have been pre-eminent; and the social cognitive theories of motivation, inspired by the ideas and research of the influential American, Albert Bandura.

Perhaps the simplest way to convey what is meant by 'self-regulation', and the contribution of each of these traditions to this phenomenon, is to ask you to undertake a short task. You are asked to carry out the following subtraction sums in your head (i.e. without writing anything down), but then write down what you did in your head to work out the answer:

A. 58 – 23
B. 72 – 37
C. 104 – 97

The first thing to note is that, as an adult, you were able to select a way (or 'strategy') for doing these subtractions. In other words, you have *knowledge*, in your long-term memory, of how to do this type of sum, and this is something you could not do when you were a very young child but have learnt or developed over the years.

Second, you probably have more than one strategy for doing subtractions, and you may have used more than one of these in undertaking these three sums. For example, many people would do sum A by taking 3 from 8 (the units) and then 2 from 5 (the tens). However, in sum B, because 7 is greater than 2, many people change their strategy, so they might, for example, count on from 37 to 40, then from 40 to 70, and then from 70 to 72, and add up the three amounts to get the answer. In sum C, again, as the numbers are close together, and as they fall either side of 100, many people will just count on in ones from 97 to 104, or visualise the two numbers on a number line with 100 in the middle, and see that they need to add 3 (because 97 is 3 below 100) to 4 (because 104 is 4 above 100). There are, of course, many other strategies you could have used which would work perfectly well, and which you have devised and developed over the years. In other words, as an adult, you have a repertoire of strategies, and you are able to select which one to use, for any particular task, based on your knowledge of such tasks, and on what works for you, i.e. you exercise *control* over your own mental processing.

And finally, not only can you do these subtractions in your head but, simultaneously, you are able to *monitor* what you are doing and can report it afterwards. In other words, you are aware of your own mental processes. In addition to allowing you to articulate what you have done, this monitoring process is vitally important, as it allows you to keep track of where you are in the task, to detect errors, to be aware of how easy or difficult you are finding the task and whether you need to change your approach or strategy. In turn, the information derived from monitoring can then be used to exercise various control functions including correcting errors, going back to an earlier stage of the task, changing or modifying strategies and increasing concentration.

The dominant model used to represent the interactions of metacognitive knowledge, control and monitoring is that developed by Nelson and Narens (1990). Here these internal mental processes are represented as a feedback loop between two spheres of activity, which occur simultaneously within the brain, which they refer to as the **meta** level (in which metacognitive knowledge of relevant strategies is stored and referred to) and the **object** level (in which the actual task, in this case the subtraction sum, is undertaken). The Monitoring function consists of information about where you are up to in the task, how well it is going, and so on, flowing from the **object** level to the **meta** level; and the Control function consists of instructions from the **meta** level to the **object** level either to continue with the procedures as planned, or to change strategy in some way if a difficulty or an error has been detected (see Figure 2.1).

Figure 2.1 Nelson and Narens' model of metacognition

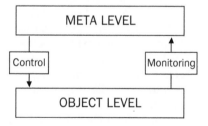

Metacognition

According to the theoretical models of the self-regulated learner developed within the three research traditions mentioned above, you have learnt how to become an able learner, thinker and social being in the world because you have developed the 'metacognitive' knowledge, monitoring and control you used when doing the subtraction sums, and apply these whenever you undertake any kind of mental task, or solve any type of problem, or exercise your creativity, or manage and negotiate a social situation, or manage and control your own emotions and motivations. The purely 'metacognitive' research has been concerned with exploring the internal mental processes involved in these achievements; the socio-cultural, Vygotskian research has explored the social and educational processes which support the development of these abilities; and the motivational research has explored the processes which provide the mental energy or effort to undertake this metacognitive learning.

Within the cognitivist tradition, the term 'metacognition' was originally coined by Flavell (1979) to describe a phenomenon he observed in a series of investigations concerning the development of children's memory abilities, and the strategies they used to help them remember (Flavell et al. 1966). In these experiments, he presented children in the age range 5 to 10 years with a set of objects, and then pointed to some of the objects in a set order. After a delay of 20 seconds or so, during which he observed the behaviour of the children, he then asked the children to indicate the objects he had pointed to, and in the correct order. Not surprisingly, the older children were more likely to be observed using an appropriate strategy (in this case, 'verbal rehearsal', involving saying or whispering the names of the objects, in order, to themselves) and were much more successful than the younger children at the memory task.

The gradual emergence of a wide range of such cognitive strategies, related to many different areas of learning, had been documented in children by this time, and it was generally considered that strategies were adopted by children when they became able to use them. However, Flavell realised that it might not be that simple. It could be that the younger, 5-year old children were capable of using the verbal rehearsal strategy but were just not aware of it. So, he taught it to them and showed that they were capable of verbally rehearsing and, when they did so, they performed as well on the memory task as the 10-year-old children. However, when given a similar task a few days later, many of the 5-year-olds failed to use verbal rehearsal and again failed the task. Flavell termed this a 'production deficit', i.e. the children could use verbal rehearsal but failed to produce it spontaneously in relation to an appropriate task.

Those of us who have experience of working regularly with young children will recognise this phenomenon. Young children can often do something one day but, when it is presented to them subsequently in a slightly different form, the connection is not made with the earlier experience and they are not able to apply what they have learnt to the new situation. In these landmark studies, Flavell demonstrated that this behaviour is not a consequence of children's inabilities to use particular strategies before a certain age. The children in his studies did not lack the basic cognitive resources to verbally rehearse. Rather, he argued, their difficulties should be conceptualised as a 'metacognitve' problem: they could learn *how* to verbally rehearse, but did not have sufficient experience to know *when* to do so. In relation to Nelson and Narens' model, represented in Figure 2.1, the limits on what the children could do were located in the monitoring and control processes, and at the **meta** level, rather than at the simply cognitive **object** level.

This early work, and subsequent research establishing the fundamental significance of metacognitive abilities for learning, has led to an explosion of research concerned with the development of metacognition in children, teenagers, students and adults of all ages. This has included, in recent years, some initial studies in the development of metacognitive abilities in young and very young children, to which we will return in the next section.

Social processes

Paralleling this work concerned with the internal mental processes of metacognition, has been a body of research inspired by the theoretical work of Vygotsky (1978, 1986) concerned with the social processes through which children learn, and learn to self-regulate. The fundamental idea here is that, at any point in time, and in relation to any area of understanding or skill, the developing child has two levels of capability. The first, developmentally lower level consists of what the child is currently able to do on his or her own. The second, higher level, is what they are able to do with some help or guidance from an adult or more experienced peer. The ideas, understanding and skills or abilities which need to be mastered to move from the lower to higher level are referred to by Vygotsky as the 'zone of proximal development' (see Figure 2.2).

Figure 2.2: Vygotsky's Zone of Proximal Development (ZPD)

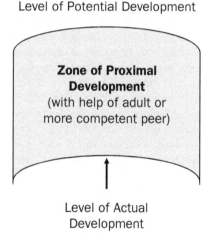

Level of Potential Development

Zone of Proximal
Development
(with help of adult or
more competent peer)

Level of Actual
Development

Think, for example, of a young child attempting a jigsaw which is slightly too difficult for them. On their own they will fail and give up. However, an adult working with them can model useful ways of proceeding (e.g. collecting and joining up the edge pieces, looking at the picture and then looking for pieces that match items seen in it), can make suggestions and give prompts (can you find the corner pieces, shall we find all the blue bits for the sky?), can ask strategic, 'metacognitive' questions which direct the child to think through the task (would it help to sort the pieces in some way? Which part of the jigsaw should we start with? Does some of it look easier and some harder?) and so on.

This type of supportive interaction, referred to in the research literature as 'scaffolding', has been shown to be consistently beneficial to children's learning. One key element, here, however, has been shown to be the sensitivity with which the adult hands over the regulatory role to the child, as the child gradually acquires the skills and understandings they need to be able to do the task on their own. The contingency with which the adult withdraws, just doing enough at all times to enable the child to proceed with the task, and consequently supports the child's autonomous action in relation to the task, has been consistently shown to be crucial in this regard (Wood et al. 1976). Where this is done skilfully, the child is supported in making the transition from being 'other-regulated' by the adult, to being 'self-regulated' by themselves in relation to that area of learning. This area of research, which demonstrates and explores one of the key elements in the processes by which children can be supported to develop their self-regulation abilities, has led to significant findings in relation to supportive styles of interaction, and the role of language in the development of self-regulation. These are issues to which we will return in the final section of this chapter.

Motivation

The final element which has recently been integrated in models of self-regulation relates to theory and research concerned with motivation. It has been increasingly recognised that the exercise of metacognitive skills and self-regulation requires mental effort. Work in this area was originally inspired by Bandura's (1997) theory and research related to the notion of self-efficacy, which refers to the human need to feel competent, the positive feelings which we experience when we achieve something new, and the consequences for our approach to new tasks when we have an underlying belief in our own competence to tackle new challenges. A further significant contribution in this area is that made by Dweck's work concerned with what is termed 'attribution' theory (Dweck and Master 2008). This concerns to what we attribute our successes and failures. Put simply, she has demonstrated that some individuals attribute their successes and failures on tasks to factors outside their control, such as fixed ability, luck and so on. Failure on a task, resulting in this type of attribution, leads to a range of negative consequences, including avoiding such tasks in future and quickly giving up when any difficulty is encountered. In contrast, other individuals attribute their level of performance to the amount of effort they put into a task or activity. For these people, failure on a task leads to renewed effort, increased concentration and perseverance. A considerable body of research has now shown the very strong links between self-efficacy, attributional beliefs and other related aspects of motivation to children's developing self-regulation. Positively motivated children have been consistently shown to control their attention more effectively, to persist when facing difficulties and to enjoy tackling new problems, among a number of other key features of the self-regulated learner (Schunk and Zimmerman 2008).

Theory and research, which was initially quite separate from these cognitively focused motivational theories but is now increasingly recognised as a crucial element in motivational aspects of self-regulation, concerns children's developing abilities to regulate their emotions. Research in this area, for example, has built on early work showing that securely attached children are more playful, more positively curious about new objects and experiences, more able to cope with change and happy to take risks and make mistakes. Extensive research on the relationships between attachment and emotional self-regulation has been reviewed by Calkins and Leerkes (2011). In other related work with pre-school children, Eisenberg et al. (2011) reviewed work related to the relations between effortful control (an early element of self-regulation, as we will review in the following section) and the development of emotion regulation and well-being. In a review of five qualitative studies with older students, Pekrun et al. (2002) found that positive emotions were consistently related to effort, interest, use of elaboration strategies (i.e. searching our memories for similar tasks or problems) and self-regulation, and negatively related to irrelevant thinking. Negative emotions showed the opposite pattern, being negatively related to interest, effort, elaboration strategies and self-regulation and positively related to irrelevant thinking and the need for external, or 'other' regulation.

The gradual integration of theories and research related to emotional development, motivation and cognitive aspects of self-regulation has recently been accomplished through the development of a new and widely accepted, over-arching model of human motivation, originally developed by Deci and Ryan (2008) which is termed 'self-determination theory'. This proposes three basic human needs for feelings of autonomy, competence and relatedness. The first two needs clearly relate to feelings of control and self-efficacy, and relatedness (a feeling of being valued and loved by significant others) clearly relates to the work on attachment and emotion. Within this model, the majority of the latest research has focused on the notion of autonomy, or the child's sense of 'agency', 'empowerment' or control. Reeve et al. (2008) provided a review of the extensive work showing the strong links between feelings of autonomy and self-regulation development. This clearly relates to the early work of Wood et al. (1976) and much more recent work, which is discussed in the final section of this chapter, concerned with autonomy-promoting practices in interactions between adults and children. There are highly significant insights emerging from this work which provide strong guidance for early childhood educators keen to promote children's self-regulation. In summary, the established view of self-regulation which is currently widely adopted within the research community is that expressed by two of its leading members. The modern, integrated view of self-regulation is that it consists of:

> *The process whereby students activate and sustain cognitions, behaviours, and **affects**, which are systematically oriented toward attainment of their goals.*
>
> (Schunk and Zimmerman, 1994, p. 309).

This leads me onto one final point concerning what is meant by self-regulation and, particularly, what is *not* meant. In some of the literature, and certainly in some commentaries written upon it for the educational profession, there is an unfortunate confusion between self-regulation and compliance. Within Schunk and Zimmerman's definition, however, it is important to notice that we are talking about children's ability to organise themselves mentally in relation to the achievement of *their* goals. Of course, many young children will share or happily adopt their teacher's goals as their own. However, some will not, for various reasons which are beyond the remit of this chapter. Being self-regulated, however, is not the same as being compliant or conventionally a well-behaved 'good' pupil. This is a vitally important point as this confusion does a disservice to children who are non-compliant, but have well developed self-regulation abilities, and to children who are compliant, but who are disposed to be dependent on adults, and have not developed good self-regulation abilities.

The early emergence of self-regulation in young children

In early theory and research on metacognition and self-regulation, the view was originally taken that these skills are sophisticated and advanced and do not emerge in children until they are towards the end of the primary school. However, extensive, more recent research has established that this is a misguided view and that, if children are observed undertaking tasks which are age-appropriate and meaningful to them, the early building blocks of metacognitive and self-regulatory abilities can be discerned in very young children. At the turn of the new millennium, Bronson (2000) provided a comprehensive review of research up to that date on self-regulation in children from birth to the end of the primary school phase, covering cognitive, emotional, motivational and social areas of development and, in a more recent paper, myself and a colleague reviewed progress in this research over the following decade (Whitebread and Basilio 2012). Table 2.1 provides a summary of the key findings available at that time, related to Bronson's review, in relation to early cognitive aspects of self-regulation.

In the period of 20 years since Bronson's review, work on the early emergence of cognitive self-regulation has been considerably developed and now focuses predominantly on three areas of early cognitive control, or 'executive functioning', which have been established as fundamental processes through which the human brain operates and learns. In an influential review, Garon et al. (2008) identified these processes as 'working memory' (the ability to hold

Table 2.1 Early development of cognitive self-regulation (adapted from Bronson, 2000)

From 0 to 12 months old	Focuses attention on specific others, objects, and own activities (reaching, grasping, manipulating objects)
	Notices regularities and novelties in the social and physical environment
	Begins to participate and predict sequences
	Begins to initiate behaviour sequences with people and objects
	Notices effects of own actions
From 12 to 36 months old	Wants predictable routines and resists change
	Can choose among a limited number of alternatives
	Goal directed behaviour
	Begins to notice and correct errors in goal directed activities
	Uses an increasing number of strategies to reach goals
	Shows cognitive organization by matching, sorting, and classifying
From 3 to 6 years old	Can engage in a wider range of cognitive activities
	More able to carry out multi-step activities
	More able to control attention and resist distraction
	Can learn to use more advanced problem-solving strategies
	More able to choose tasks appropriate for own level of skill

information in mind while operating on it), 'inhibitory or effortful control' (the ability to stop an initial, prepotent, automatic or perceptually driven response and replace it with a response related to an internal goal or thought) and 'cognitive or attentional flexibility and focus' (the ability to control attention, to focus on key elements of a task, and to switch attention when required). Evidence of each of these abilities has been reported during the first year of life, when they are strongly dependent, of course, on environmental factors such as novelty. From the second year onwards, however, progress has been documented in each of these abilities as the child becomes able to handle more information for longer periods of time, and their attention and behaviour is increasingly under control and independent of context.

Hofmann et al. (2012), for example, produced one of a number of papers demonstrating ways in which these early executive functions form the building blocks for the beginnings of cognitive self-regulation. A range of studies have demonstrated, for example, very early examples of children's emerging abilities, at 10 months, to use something learnt in one context and apply it to another (analogical learning), to request help appropriately, at 14 months, based on recognition of the limits of their own abilities, and to recognise and correct errors (at 18 months) in manipulative play.

In the last few years, a number of these findings from behavioural observations have been supported through the emergence of developmental neuroscience techniques. Goupil and Kouider (2019), for example, have recently reported developmental neuroscience data to support the position, derived from behavioural observational data, that basic forms of metacognition, such as the ability to monitor errors, are present even in preverbal infants. A recent special issue of *Developmental Neuropsychology* (Espy 2020), also, has brought together a number of papers concerning developmental, cognitive and neuroscience approaches to explore the development of executive control in young children.

In a paper reporting a study carried out in the early 1970s, concerned with 3- to 6-year-old children's memory abilities in meaningful tasks, a Russian psychologist, Z.M. Istomina (1975), included a number of transcripts of the children's performance which illustrate beautifully the early emergence of cognitive self-regulation. The task required the child to remember a list of five food items which were needed for a pretend lunch party (set out in one corner of a large room) so that she could ask the shopkeeper (at a pretend shop in the far corner of the room) for the correct items. Here is Istomina's record of the performance of a 5-year-old girl called Alochka on this task:

Alochka (five years, two months) was busily engaged in preparing lunch, and several times reminded the experimenter that she needed salt.
When it was her turn to go to the store, she asked, with a busy expression on her face:
'Z. M., what should I buy? Salt?'
The experimenter explained to her that this was not all and named four more items that were needed. Alochka listened attentively, nodding her head. She took the basket, the permission slip and money and went off, but soon came back.
'Z. M., I have to buy salt, milk, and what else?' she asked. 'I forgot'
The experimenter repeated the items. This time Alochka repeated each word after the experimenter in a whisper and, after saying confidently, 'Now I know what I had forgotten', went off.
In the store, she went up to the manager and, with a serious expression, correctly named four items, with slight pauses between each.
'There is something else, but I forgot' she said.
(Istomina, 1975, pp. 25–26)

We can clearly see here evidence of emerging metacognitive awareness and cognitive self-regulation in Alochka. Throughout she is aware of what she has remembered and what she has forgotten. To begin with she tries the simple strategy of 'nodding her head' for each item on the list, but quickly realises this hasn't worked. So, the second time, she uses a different strategy, 'repeat(ing) each word after the experimenter in a whisper', and this is much more successful. Aloshka is clearly an able 5-year-old, but already, at this very young age, she is showing some important elements in the process of developing into a very successful self-regulated learner.

Table 2.2   Early development of social-emotional regulation (adapted from Bronson 2000 and Kopp 1982)

From 0 to 12 months old	Regulation of arousal and sleep/wake cycles Responsive interaction with others Attempts to influence others Begins to anticipate and participate in simple routines Responsiveness to emotional expressions of others
From 12 to 36 months old	Increasing voluntary control and voluntary self-regulation Growing ability to comply with external requests and awareness of situational demands Increasing assertiveness and desire for independent action Increasing awareness of others and the feeling of others (empathy) Some spontaneous helping, sharing and comforting behaviours Increasing awareness of social rules and sanctions Increasing ability to inhibit prohibited activities and delay upon request
From 3 to 6 years old	More capable of controlling emotions, abiding by rules and refraining from forbidden behaviours More capable of using language to regulate own behaviour and influence others More interest in peers and peer acceptance, so more apt to regulate self in relation to peers Can learn more effective interaction strategies Can engage in dramatic play with roles and rules Begins to talk about mental states of self and others Better understanding how others may feel Can engage deliberate helping, sharing and comforting behaviours Internalising standards of behaviour Developing more stable prosocial (or antisocial) attitudes and behaviours

Similar advances have taken place in our understandings about the achievements of young children in the emotional, social and motivational (affective) domains, and these are similarly reported in detail in Whitebread and Basilio (2012). Once again, this later review builds on the earlier work of Bronson (2000). Table 2.2 provides a summary of the key findings available at that time, related to Bronson's review, in relation to early affective self-regulation.

Over the last 20 years research in this area has focused on the development of two key phenomena. First, we now have good evidence that young children develop what is commonly referred to as a 'theory of mind', or an understanding that other individuals have a mind like their own, and their own perspectives, much younger than was previously thought. This understanding is of vital importance to the developing child's emotional well-being, forming the basis for effective social interaction and sensitivity, empathy, the development of friendships and positive relationships with adults.

Following Piaget's early work suggesting young children are 'egocentric' (i.e. not able to take on the perspectives of others), and early research using language-based laboratory tasks, children were not thought to develop these understandings until around 5 years of age. However, recent work focusing on where younger children look rather than what they say, and using non-verbal tasks, have demonstrated that children as young as 15 months appeal to mental states, such as beliefs, to explain the behaviour of others. In imitation tasks, children of a similar age have also been shown to imitate precisely the actions of a machine or robot, but to do what a human model appeared to intend to do (e.g. place a toy on the edge of a table), rather than what they actually did (e.g. apparently accidentally drop the toy on the floor) (Meltzoff 2011). Recent research has also focused on the social processes responsible for early individual differences in children's abilities to 'read' others' minds (Hughes and Devine 2019).

The second main focus of research in the area of affective self-regulation has concerned children's developing inhibitory and effortful control abilities. This work has used 'Do's and Don'ts' and 'Go/NoGo' tasks (where the child has to perform an action, or not, depending on a rule) and delay of gratification tasks, such as the famous marshmallow task, where the child has to resist touching or eating an attractive toy or sweet. As in all areas of self-regulation development, considerable progress has been found in children within the first few years of life in their performance on these tasks (Holmboe et al. 2018). Once again, significant individual differences have also been found, however, a number of studies have shown that early secure attachments are strongly associated with these affective self-regulation abilities. We will return to the issue of environmental and social factors which seem to support the early development of children's self-regulation in the final section.

Once children enter educational institutions, of course, the demands on their cognitive and affective self-regulatory abilities are considerable. There is strong evidence, as we shall see in the next section, that well-developed self-regulatory abilities help children to make a smooth transition into pre-school and early schooling. At the same time, however, the more challenging opportunities that a high-quality early childhood educational setting can offer can also significantly enhance all young children's early self-regulatory abilities. This will be the topic of the final section of this chapter.

In my own research, within the Cambridgeshire Independent Learning (CIndLe) Project (Whitebread et al. 2005, 2007, 2009), I have particularly explored the development of 3- to 5-year-olds' self-regulatory abilities. In this study we worked with 32 nursery and reception class teachers, and the children in their classes (just under 1,500 children altogether) and we video-recorded around 700 self-regulatory 'events' in these settings. One outcome of this study was the production of an observational instrument, the Checklist of Independent Learning Development (CHILD 3–5), which includes 22 statements, in the areas of cognitive, emotional, pro-social and motivational self-regulation (see Table 2.3). These statements were selected from a longer list, derived from the

Table 2.3 Checklist of Independent Learning Development (CHILD) 3–5

Name of child: _____ Teacher: _____ Date: _____
School/setting: _____

	Always	Usually	Sometimes	Never	Comment
Emotional Can speak about own and others' behaviour and consequences Tackles new tasks confidently Can control attention and resist distraction Monitors progress and seeks help appropriately Persists in the face of difficulties					
Pro-social Negotiates when and how to carry out tasks Can resolve social problems with peers Shares and takes turns independently Engages in independent cooperative activities with peers Is aware of feelings of others and helps and comforts					
Cognitive Is aware of own strengths and weaknesses Can speak about how they have done something or what they have learnt Can speak about future planned activities					

(Continued)

Table 2.3 (Continued)

	Always	Usually	Sometimes	Never	Comment
Can make reasoned choices and decisions Asks questions and suggests answers Uses previously taught strategies Adopts previously heard language for own purposes					
Motivational Finds own resources without adult help Develops own ways of carrying out tasks Initiates activities Plans own tasks, targets and goals Enjoys solving problems					
Other comments:					

research literature, of children's self-regulatory achievements in this age range, and indicate the abilities which distinguish high from low, or well from poorly, self-regulated children at this stage of their development. This instrument has subsequently been translated into a number of languages, and has been extensively used in research, and by practising early childhood educators, both within the UK and internationally. As well as providing a valuable and teacher-friendly assessment tool related to individual children's development, it has also been effectively used as a basis for discussions about children's development with parents, and as an audit of practice supporting self-regulation development within classes and settings.

The importance of developing self-regulation

I have devoted a good part of this chapter to describing the nature of metacognition and self-regulation, and their development in young children, because it is vitally important that early childhood educators have a deep understanding in this area. This arises from two now widely accepted findings from a considerable body of research. First, that metacognitive and self-regulatory abilities are the single most powerful determinants of children's academic success and a range of positive life outcomes; and, second, that these abilities are significantly affected by environmental and social interaction factors in children's early experience. Early childhood educators are, as a consequence, in a position to make a very positive difference to children's developmental outcomes. This section addresses the findings regarding the significance of developments in this area, and what we can do about it is addressed in the final section.

Outcomes of early childhood education provision

There are essentially three types of evidence that have convinced the research community, and early childhood policy decision-makers, internationally, about the importance of this area. First, there have been a number of longitudinal studies looking at the short-term and long-term outcomes of different types of pre-school and early childhood education provision. Sylva and Wiltshire (1993) provided a very useful review of this evidence. One particular study was that carried out in relation to the Perry Pre-school Project in Ypsilanti, Michigan, directed by David Weikart, as part of the Head Start initiative in the USA to provide good quality pre-school provision for children from disadvantaged neighbourhoods. This later developed into what is now known as the High/Scope programme. Weikart conducted a follow up study with a cohort of 65 children who had attended this half-day educational programme over two years during the mid-1960s. Their outcomes at age 27 were compared to a control group of children from the same neighbourhood who had not attended the pre-school programme. What appears is that, as well as achieving significantly better high school grades, the children who had attended the pre-school programme had been arrested on significantly fewer occasions, had higher earnings, had needed to receive less support from social services, and were much more likely to own their own house.

This research established that, as a result of these outcomes, 7 dollars of Federal funding was saved for each dollar spent on the project. As a consequence, it had a not surprisingly dramatic impact on governments internationally and education policy makers. It also led to renewed research to attempt to identify which features of such a high-quality early education programme contributed to these outcomes. In the UK, the Effective Provision of Pre-School Education (EPPE) project (Sylva et al. 2004), for example, was set up to address this question and has provided important complementary evidence.

What emerges as significant about effective early educational environments are features which crucially support young children's developing self-regulation. These environments offer real intellectual challenge with emotional support and put the child very much in control of their own learning. In the High/Scope regime, for example, the central model of learning is the 'plan, do and review' cycle. Each child plans their activities for the session or the day in a small group with an adult educator, often referred to as a 'key-worker'.

The children then move off to carry out their planned activities, and later return to review progress again with their small group, again supported by their key-worker.

This pattern of working also builds in purposeful adult–child and child–child conversations, which oblige and offer children the opportunity to reflect upon and talk about their learning. Sylva et al. (2004) particularly identified, within the highest quality settings, the occurrence of episodes of 'sustained shared thinking' between adults and children, where adults supported children's ideas and helped the children to extend and develop them. As we shall see, providing opportunities for children to talk authentically about their learning is an important component in helping them to develop as self-regulating learners. This is also not just a matter of cognitive activity but has important emotional and motivational elements. What all the high-quality early years programmes identified by Sylva and Wiltshire (1993) did was to help children develop what they term a 'mastery' orientation to learning and to themselves. Children in high-quality early years environments developed feelings of high self-esteem, with high aspirations and secure feelings of self-efficacy. Such children grew to believe that, through effort, they could solve problems, understand new ideas, develop skills and so on. They felt in control of their environments and confident in their abilities.

Cognitive and affective areas of development

The second, very considerable, body of evidence that has established the importance of early metacognitive and self-regulation abilities, consists of a huge range of studies that have looked at the role of these abilities in a wide range of cognitive and affective areas of development. Studies have shown that in cognitive areas such as maths, reading, writing, thinking skills and problem solving, and in affective areas such as social relationships, tolerance, co-operation, impulsiveness, addiction and eating disorders, self-regulation skills are of vital significance. Some studies have looked specifically at the immediate short-term outcomes of children's individual differences in this area. Essentially, these studies are often focused on the consequences for young children's transition into their early years of pre-school and schooling. So, for example, in the area of cognitive self-regulation, Blair and Razza (2007) found that, out of a range of possible factors, including a measure of their general intelligence, the level of inhibitory control shown by 3- to 5-year-olds from low-income families most clearly predicted their reading and maths abilities a year later. In relation to affective areas, Denham and Burton (2003) showed that emotion regulation in pre-school children predicted their peer status, friendship, academic competence, self-image and emotional well-being.

Other studies have used sophisticated statistical techniques to determine which elements within young children's early development most powerfully predict long-term achievements. McClelland et al. (2013), for example, examined the factors in 430 children's early development that most strongly predicted their academic achievements by the time they were young adults. They found that children's attention span persistence at age 4 years (a key early indicator of self-regulation skills, related to inhibitory control and emotion regulation) significantly predicted maths and reading achievement at age 21 after controlling for achievement levels at age 7, child vocabulary skills, gender, and maternal education level. In a similar study, focused on long-term health and well-being outcomes, Anzman-Frasca et al. (2015) explored the relations between 192 girls' inhibitory control at age 7 and their psychosocial (self-reported depressive symptoms and perceived self-competence) and weight outcomes at ages 9, 11, 13 and 15. Their results showed that greater inhibitory control was independently associated with beneficial emotional, mental health and physical health outcomes.

Meta-analyses of educational interventions

Finally, there have been a number of meta-analyses conducted of studies devoted to establishing the effectiveness of all kinds of educational interventions. Hattie (2008) is pre-eminent in this area, having reported the results of 800 such meta-analyses related to a huge range of educational interventions conducted all over the world. His conclusion from this vast analysis is that a range of approaches which teach children metacognitive strategies, or which support children's metacognitive awareness by encouraging them to talk about their learning, such as reciprocal teaching or peer tutoring, are among the most effective in relation to academic outcomes. Within the UK, Higgins et al. (2011) carried out a similar exercise, but just looking at around 50 meta-analyses within the UK, particularly focusing on interventions directed towards children from disadvantaged backgrounds who would qualify for the Pupil Premium. The conclusions were very similar to Hattie's (2008). The most successful interventions focused on supporting children to monitor their own learning or to work collaboratively with peers in ways which required them to articulate what they understood or had learnt.

Supporting children's self-regulation in early childhood education

I have written elsewhere setting out some of the basic characteristics of early childhood education settings which appear to most effectively support young children's developing self-regulation (see Whitebread 2012; Whitebread and Coltman 2017). The main four elements I have stressed involve establishing an emotionally warm, secure and encouraging classroom climate, providing tasks which are appropriately challenging, giving children a real sense of control or autonomy in relation to their activities and their learning, and making the processes of learning 'visible' by encouraging children to talk about their learning. I hope at least some of the underlying rationale for each of these points has emerged from the foregoing review of aspects of the research in this area.

In this final section I want to review some of the key pieces of research which support these general conclusions, and hopefully to deepen and extend them a little by reference to some of the very interesting specific findings which have emerged. Two bodies of research have made particular contributions in this regard: research looking at classroom practices which support self-regulation, and studies of interactions with much younger children with their parents (usually their mothers). Research in classrooms has examined the characteristics of effective interventions and the consequences of naturally occurring differences between teaching practices. This research has mostly been undertaken with slightly older primary classes, but there are key features of effective practice which emerge that can equally well be applied to working within early childhood settings. These relate to the emotional and motivational context of the classroom and the significance of social processes in self-regulation development.

As regards the first point, Perry (1998), for example, observed second and third grade classrooms doing literacy activities over a period of six months and, through observations and interviews with the children, she explored the impact of types of tasks, forms of assessment and authority structures on the students' self-regulation during writing tasks. Based on her observations she concluded that classrooms supporting self-regulation were characterised by challenging and open-ended writing activities, opportunities for children to control the level of challenge and opportunities for them to engage in self-assessment, autonomy support (through being taught strategies to undertake certain types of task), encouragement of positive feelings towards challenge, an emphasis on personal progress and seeing mistakes as opportunities for learning. In contrast, in classrooms which did not effectively support children's self-regulation, children were more likely to be engaged in restricted types of activities with limited choices, assessment procedures were mainly controlled by the adult, with an emphasis on performance and social comparison between children. It is very clear from Perry's descriptions of these classrooms that the emotional and motivational climates arising from these different practices were key to fostering children's developing self-regulation.

The work on social processes in classrooms has mostly focused on the production of 'metacognitive talk' by teachers and on pedagogical practices which support children's talk about their learning. Typically, effective self-regulation interventions have involved the teacher making metacognitive and learning strategies explicit and encouraging children to reflect upon and talk about their learning. The value of the first of these arises from the established finding, first identified experimentally by Flavell in the early studies we reviewed in the first section of this chapter, that young children often fail to produce an appropriate strategy in relation to a task, even though they have previously shown themselves to be capable of performing it. Subsequent research demonstrated one reason why this might occur. Fabricius and Hagen (1984), for example, explored the use of an organisational strategy with 6- and 7-year-olds. Following improved performance some of the children attributed this to the use of the strategy, but others thought they had recalled more because they had looked longer, used their brains more, or slowed down. While only 32 per cent of the children in the latter group transferred the use of the strategy to a second recall task, 99 per cent of those who explicitly recognised the impact of the organisational strategy they had been taught did so. In other words, it is clear that, in the early stages of self-regulation development, we need to do some of the metacognitive work for the children. For example, when introducing a new way of doing something, which helps the children perform at a higher level, we need to explicitly discuss why this worked. And, when introducing a new task, we need to explicitly remind the children of when they faced something similar before, and what worked then.

Ornstein et al. (2010) have supported this view in a study in which they monitored the amount of 'metacognitive talk' among first grade teachers in mathematics lessons. Such talk included teachers making suggestions of memory strategies the children could use, asking metacognitive questions aimed at eliciting strategy knowledge from the children, such as 'how could you help yourself to remember this?', and so on. A natural variation in this kind of 'memory relevant' talk was recorded among the teachers, ranging from zero to 12 per cent of their talk during the lessons. Also recorded was the co-occurrence of memory talk and memory demands, i.e. the percentage of times that the metacognitive talk occurred when the children were required to remember something. A highly statistically significant difference was reported between children in classes with high and low occurrences of this kind of metacognitive talk, particularly where it was related to memory demands. Most impressively, they found that children's improved strategy use and ability to remember relevant mathematical facts related to these differences at the end of the first grade, and were still present at statistically significant levels 3 years later, at the end of the fourth grade.

A wide range of self-regulation interventions have essentially developed types of activity which are likely to encourage children to talk about and reflect upon their learning. These include co-operative groupwork (where children work in pairs or small groups to undertake a task, or produce something together), peer-tutoring (where one child is asked to teach something they know or can do to another child), 'self-explanations' (where children are asked to explain their reasoning, or that of another) self-assessment (where children say what they are pleased about in something they have done or select an example to include in a display or portfolio), and debriefing (where an activity is reviewed, perhaps supported by photographs or video). The move towards developing these practices is, in itself, part of a broader recognition of the value of a 'dialogic' approach to teaching in the early years, supporting young children's language and communication skills and their self-regulation development (Grau and Whitebread 2018).

In early childhood settings, a natural context, of course, which stimulates a considerable amount of metacognitive talk is play. In my C.Ind.Le study, reported earlier, a key finding was the frequent occurrence of children in the 3–5 age range demonstrating metacognitive and self-regulatory abilities during playful activities, particularly in constructional and pretence play (Whitebread et al., 2007). The self-regulatory activities and talk during construction play tends to relate to cognitive problem solving. In this context we often observe what is referred to as 'private speech', where children commentate to themselves on their activities. This seems to be a kind of bridge between the speech they experience in situations of adult scaffolding and their use of inner speech, or thought, in order to guide and regulate their activity. Berk et al. (2006), among others, have provided rich examples of children demonstrating and practising self-regulatory abilities during pretence play. In a study of complex social pretend play, myself and a colleague reviewed the now extensive evidence of the self-regulatory opportunities within this kind of play, as children guide the play narrative forward either in character ('Oh dear, the baby's crying!') or by stepping momentarily out of character ('OK, you pretend you're the baby and you're crying because you're upset') (Whitebread and O'Sullivan 2012). This is perhaps the most sophisticated type of play in which young children engage, and one that many children struggle to perform well. As such, it is a prime example of where a skillful adult can participate, taking on some of the regulatory role, and, if they are able to sensitively withdraw as the children become more competent, it can be an excellent vehicle to support a range of linguistic and self-regulation abilities.

Two more recent studies, using very different methodologies, have further evidenced the role of autonomy and of pretence, afforded through play activities, in supporting young children's self-regulation. The first of these surveyed 6- to 7-year-olds' out-of-school activities and noted the prevalence of 'structured' (e.g.: homework, adult-led lessons and practices) as compared to 'less-structured' (e.g.: play, spontaneous practice, reading, visits to a museum or zoo). These were then correlated with the children's scores on measures of self-regulation. What emerged was that children who, in their home life, spent more time on the less-structured activities had higher levels of self-regulation than the children who spent more time in structured activities, even after controlling for age, verbal ability, and household income. This clearly evidences the importance of supporting children's autonomy for developing self-regulation (Barker et al. 2014). The second, laboratory study required 4- and 6-year-olds to undertake a 10-minute vigilance task, pressing a button each time a piece of cheese appeared on a computer screen, while they were being distracted, on a second screen, by a funny cartoon. They were asked to do this in a non-play condition, as themselves, and while pretending to be the superhero Batman. This effect of the of the pretence play condition on their control of their attention was so marked that, when pretending to be Batman, the 4-year-olds performed at the same level as the 6-year-olds in the non-play condition: i.e., their performance was enhanced by 2 years (White et al. 2017).

I want to end by reviewing evidence concerning children's language development and self-regulation. In a way, we might characterise these as the two twin pillars on which children's development as learners is founded. A number of studies have shown that they are intimately related in early childhood. An American study of 120 toddlers in New England, for example, showed strong relationships between vocabulary size at 14, 24 and 36 months and a range of observed self-regulatory behaviours (e.g. the ability to maintain attention on tasks; the ability to adapt to changes in tasks and procedures) (Vallotton and Ayoub 2011).

Many of the studies contributing to this area of research have investigated early interactions between children and their mothers, often in the context of what have been termed 'joint attention episodes', where mother and child are jointly focused on a particular object or event, and communicate pre-verbally, or non-verbally, or talk about it together. Brinck and Liljenfors (2013), for example, reported evidence that metacognitive and self-regulatory abilities can be identified between two and four months of age in episodes of dyadic interaction between mothers and their infants. In such episodes, they argued, the adult is both a model for the child, and a source of feedback guiding their early attempts at cognitive control. We know from a range of research that the amount of time children spend in episodes of joint attention is directly related to their language development and, thus, to their self-regulation development also. Schaffer (2004) gives a very clear example of such an episode and its key features. She describes a mother and her 2-year-old child playing with some toys. The child chooses one of them and starts to play with it:

> the mother thereupon starts talking about that toy; she may name it, point out its uses and features, comment on the child's previous encounters with it or similar toys, and in this way verbally enlarges on the specific topic that the child is attending to at that moment.
>
> Schaffer (2004: 299)

In addition to differences in the time young children spend in such episodes with their parents, there are also significant differences in the sensitivity, or responsiveness, of parents or caregivers to their children, and this also impacts upon language development. Some adults are much more aware of the child's pointing gestures or gaze as indicators of their focus of attention. Furthermore, while many adults behave as described by Schaffer, following and responding to the focus of the attention of the child, others tend to attempt to switch the child's attention to their own focus of interest. Not surprisingly, the former 'attention-following' strategy, building on the child's current interest and attention, has been found to support language development much more effectively than the 'attention-shifting' approach, with consequent outcomes also for the child's self-regulation development.

Other research has also investigated the style and content of mother's speech during joint activities with their young children. Bibok et al. (2009), for example, reviewed a range of evidence concerning the relative frequencies of 'directive' and 'elaborative' utterances in mother's talk in joint attention episodes. Directive utterances are those which directly request a specific action or behaviour, while elaborative utterances provide contextual information of the type listed above by Schaffer, or give reasons for actions, or in other ways encourage the child to think beyond the immediate context of the task at hand. The more frequent use by mothers of elaborative styles of speech was found to be related to young children's executive function development which, as we discussed earlier, is a key building block in the early emergence of self-regulation. In a more recent study with 12- to 24-month-old infants, Neale and Whitebread (2019) showed that the sensitivity and contingency of mothers' talk supporting children's play with toys at 12 months predicted children's inhibitory and effortful control at 24 months. This suggested that maternal talk during play could lay the foundations for young children's strategic regulation of their cognition and behaviour.

Conclusion

It is still very early days in our investigations of the fascinating and complex processes of metacognition and self-regulation, their very early emergence in young children, right from birth, and their exciting and rapid development throughout early childhood. As I hope I have shown in this chapter, however, while we have much to discover, the research so far in this area has revealed illuminating and important insights into the early cognitive and affective aspects of self-regulation development and some of the environmental factors which impact upon it. Its importance in determining developmental outcomes for young children, both in the short and long terms, cannot be over-estimated. At the same time, it is clear that the quality of the environments and experiences we provide for young children within early childhood educational contexts can have a profound effect on these developments. In particular, we need to pay attention to the emotional climate of our settings, so that the young children in our care feel secure and valued, to the extent to which we support children's feelings of autonomy and competence, and to the quality of the talk we provide when we interact with them in playful and conversational episodes.

Key messages

- Metacognitive and self-regulatory abilities are the single most powerful determinants of children's academic success and a range of positive life outcomes.
- Therefore, an emphasis on the characteristics of effective learning is crucial for children's future social, emotional and academic success.
- A pedagogy which supports children as self-regulating learners provides: emotional warmth; feelings of control and agency; cognitive challenge – including the challenges children set themselves in play, and adults providing and supporting achievable challenges and articulation of learning – using talk, as well as other ways children express themselves, to help children to recognise and clarify the way they think and learn.

References

Anzman-Frasca, S., Francis, L.A. and Birch, L.L. (2015) Inhibitory control is associated with psychosocial, cognitive, and weight outcomes in a longitudinal sample of girls, *Translational Issues in Psychological Science*, 1(3): 203.

Bandura, A. (1997) *Self-Efficacy: The Exercise of Control*. New York: W. H. Freeman.

Barker, J.E., Semenov, A.D., Michaelson, L., Provan, L.S., Snyder, H.R. and Munakata, Y. (2014) Less-structured time in children's daily lives predicts self-directed executive functioning, *Frontiers in Psychology*, 5: 593.

Berk, L.E., Mann, T.D. and Ogan, A.T. (2006) Make-believe play: wellspring for development of self-regulation, in D.G. Singer, R.M. Golinkoff and K. Hirsh-Pasek (eds), *Play=Learning: How Play Motivates and Enhances Children's Cognitive and Social-Emotional Growth*. Oxford: Oxford University Press.

Bibok, M.B., Carpendale, J.I.M. and Muller, U. (2009) Parental scaffolding and the development of executive function, in C. Lewis and J.I.M. Carpendale (eds) Social interaction and the development of executive function, *New Directions in Child and Adolescent Development*, 123: 17–34.

Blair, C. and Razza, R.P. (2007) Relating effortful control, executive function, and false belief understanding to emerging math and literacy abilities in kindergarten, *Child Development*, 78: 647–663.

Brinck, I. and Liljenfors, R. (2013) The developmental origin of metacognition, *Infant and Child Development*, 22: 85–101.

Bronson, M. (2000) *Self-regulation in Early Childhood*. New York: Guilford Press.

Calkins, S.D. and Leerkes, E.M. (2011) Early attachment processes and the development of emotional self-regulation, in K.D. Vohs and R.F. Baumeister (eds). *Handbook of Self-regulation: Research, Theory and applications*, 2nd edn. New York: Guilford Press.

Deci, E.L. and Ryan, R.M. (2008) Self-determination theory: a macro theory of human motivation, development and health, *Canadian Psychology*, 49 (3): 182–185.

Denham, S.A. and Burton, R. (2003) *Social and Emotional Prevention and Intervention Programming for Pre-schoolers*. New York: Plenum.

Dweck, C.S. and Master, A. (2008) Self-theories motivate self-regulated learning, in D.H. Schunk and B.J. Zimmerman (eds) *Motivation and Self-Regulated Learning*. Mahwah, NJ: Lawrence Erlbaum.

Eisenberg, N., Smith, C.L. and Spinrad, T.L. (2011) Effortful control: relations with emotion regulation, adjustment and socialisation in children, in K.D. Vohs and R.F. Baumeister (eds), *Handbook of Self-regulation: Research, Theory and Applications*, 2nd edn. New York: Guilford Press.

Espy, K.A. (ed.) (2020) *Using Developmental, Cognitive, and Neuroscience Approaches to Understand Executive Control in Young Children: A Special Issue of Developmental Neuropsychology*. Hove: Psychology Press.

Fabricius, W.V. and Hagen, J.W. (1984) Use of causal attributions about recall performance to assess metamemory and predict strategic memory behaviour in young children, *Developmental Psychology*, 20: 975–987.

Flavell, J.H. (1979) Metacognition and cognitive monitoring: a new area of cognitive developmental inquiry, *American Psychologist*, 34: 906–11.

Flavell, J.H., Beach, D.R. and Chinsky, J.M. (1966) Spontaneous verbal rehearsal in as memory task as a function of age, *Child Development*, 37: 283–99.

Garon, N., Bryson, S.E. and Smith, I.M. (2008) Executive function in preschoolers: A review using an integrative framework, *Psychological Bulletin*, 134(1): 31–60.

Goupil, L. and Kouider, S. (2019) Developing a reflective mind: From core metacognition to explicit self-reflection, *Current Directions in Psychological* Science, 28(4): 403–408.

Grau, V. and Whitebread, D. (eds) (2018) Relationships between classroom dialogue and support for metacognitive, self-regulatory development in educational contexts, *New Directions for Child and Adolescent Development*, 162: 137–150.

Hattie, J. (2008) *Visible Learning: A Synthesis of 800 Meta-analyses Relating to Achievement*. London: Routledge.

Higgins, S., Kokotsaki, D. and Coe, R (2011) *Pupil Premium Toolkit: Summary for Schools*. London: Sutton Trust. Retrieved from: www.suttontrust.com/research/toolkit-of-strategies-to-improve-learning/

Hofmann,W., Schmiechel, B.J. and Baddeley, A.D. (2012) Executive functions and self-regulation, *Trends in Cognitive Sciences*, 16 (3): 174–180.

Holmboe, K., Bonneville-Roussy, A., Csibra, G. and Johnson, M.H. (2018) Longitudinal development of attention and inhibitory control during the first year of life, *Developmental Science*, 21(6): e12690.

Hughes, C. and Devine, R. (2019) Learning to read minds: A synthesis of social and cognitive perspectives, in D. Whitebread, V. Grau, K. Kumpulainen, M. McClelland, N. Perry and D. Pino-Pasternak (eds) *Sage Handbook of Developmental Psychology and Early Childhood Education*. London: Sage.

Istomina, Z.M. (1975) The development of voluntary memory in preschool-age children. *Soviet Psychology*, 13: 5–64.

Kopp, C.B. (1982) Antecedents of self-regulation: A developmental perspective, *Developmental Psychology*, 18(2): 199–214.

McClelland, M.M., Acock, A.C., Piccinin, A., Rhea, S. A. and Stallings, M.C. (2013) Relations between preschool attention span-persistence and age 25 educational outcomes, *Early Childhood Research Quarterly*, 28(2): 314–324.

Meltzoff, A.N. (2011) Social cognition and the origins of imitation, empathy, and theory of mind, in U. Goswami (ed.) *The Wiley-Blackwell Handbook of Childhood Cognitive Development*, 2nd edn. Malden, MA: Wiley-Blackwell.

Neale, D. and Whitebread, D. (2019) Maternal scaffolding during play with 12- to 24-month-old infants: Stability over time and relations with emerging effortful control, *Metacognition & Learning*, 14: 265–289.

Nelson, T.O. and Narens, L. (1990) Metamemory: a theoretical framework and new findings, in G. Bower (ed.) *The Psychology of Learning and Motivation: Advances in Research and Theory, Vol 26*. New York: Academic Press.

Ornstein, P.A., Grammer, J.K. and Coffman, J.L. (2010) Teachers' 'Mnemonic Style' and the development of skilled memory, in H.S. Waters and W. Schneider (eds) *Metacognition, Strategy Use and Instruction*. New York: The Guilford Press.

Pekrun, R., Goetz, T., Titz, W. and Perry, R. (2002) Academic emotions in students' self-regulated learning and achievement: A program of qualitative and quantitative research, *Educational Psychologist*, 37: 91–105.

Perry, N. (1998) Young children's self-regulated learning and contexts that support it, *Journal of Educational Psychology*, 90 (4): 715–729.

Reeve, J., Ryan, R., Deci, E.L. and Jang, H. (2008) Understanding and promoting autonomous self-regulation: A self-determination theory perspective, in D.H. Schunk and B.J. Zimmerman (eds) *Motivation and Self-Regulated Learning*. Mahwah, NJ: Lawrence Erlbaum.

Schaffer, H.R. (2004) *Introducing Child Psychology*. Oxford: Blackwell.

Schunk, D.H. and Zimmerman, B.J. (eds) (1994) *Self-regulation of Learning and Performance: Issues and Educational Applications*. Hillsdale, NJ: Lawrence Erlbaum.

Schunk, D.H. and Zimmerman, B.J. (eds) (2008) *Motivation and Self-Regulated Learning*. Mahwah, NJ: Lawrence Erlbaum.

Sylva, K. and Wiltshire, J. (1993) The impact of early learning on children's later development: A review prepared for the RSA inquiry 'Start Right', *European Early Childhood Education Research Journal*, 1: 17–40.

Sylva, K., Melhuish, E.C., Sammons, P., Siraj-Blatchford, I. and Taggart, B. (2004) *The Effective Provision of Pre-School Education (EPPE) Project: Technical Paper 12 – The Final Report: Effective Pre-School Education*. London: DfES / Institute of Education, University of London.

Vallatton, C. and Ayoub, C. (2011) Use your words: The role of language in the development of toddlers' self-regulation, *Early Childhood Research Quarterly*, 26, 169–181.

Vygotsky, L.S. (1978) *Mind in Society: The Development of Higher Psychological Processes*. Cambridge, MA: Harvard University Press.

Vygotsky, L.S. (1986) *Thought and Language*. Cambridge, MA: MIT Press.

White, R.E., Prager, E.O., Schaefer, C., Kross, E., Duckworth, A.L. and Carlson, S.M. (2017) The 'batman effect': Improving perseverance in young children, *Child Development*, 88(5): 1563–1571.

Whitebread, D. (2012) *Developmental Psychology and Early Childhood Education*. London: Sage.

Whitebread, D. and Basilio, M. (2012) The emergence and early development of self-regulation in young children, *Profesorado: Journal of Curriculum and Teacher Education, Monograph issue: Learn to learn. Teaching and evaluation of self-regulated learning*, 16(1):15–34.

Whitebread, D. and Coltman, P. (2017) Developing young children as self-regulated learners, in J. Moyles, J. Georgeson and J. Payler (eds) *Beginning Teaching: Beginning Learning: In Early Years and Primary Education*, 5th edn. London: Open University Press/McGraw Hill.

Whitebread, D. and O'Sullivan, L. (2012) Preschool children's social pretend play: Supporting the development of metacommunication, metacognition and self-regulation, *International Journal of Play*, 1 (2): 197–213.

Whitebread, D., Bingham, S., Grau, V., Pino Pasternak, D. and Sangster, C. (2007) Development of metacognition and self-regulated learning in young children: The role of collaborative and peer-assisted learning, *Journal of Cognitive Education and Psychology*, 6: 433–55.

Whitebread, D., Anderson, H., Coltman, P., Page, C., Pino Pasternak, D. and Mehta, S (2005) Developing independent learning in the early years, *Education 3–13*, 33: 40–50.

Whitebread, D., Coltman, P., Pino Pasternak, D., Sangster, C., Grau, V., Bingham, S., Almeqdad, Q. and Demetriou, D. (2009) The development of two observational tools for assessing metacognition and self-regulated learning in young children, *Metacognition and Learning*, 4(1): 63–85.

Wood, D. Bruner, J. and Ross, G. (1976) The role of tutoring in problem-solving, *Journal of Child Psychology and Psychiatry*, 17: 89–100.

3 Playing and exploring

Sue Rogers and Shabana Roscoe

Chapter summary

- Adults have much to offer children's play and exploration through the relationships they build with young learners.
- Play provision should be carefully planned but if it is over planned, and the provision matters more than spontaneity and creativity, the result is not play!
- Children need opportunities to take risks and explore a wide range of materials and social situations in order to become confident playful learners

Introduction: setting the scene

> It takes creativity and commitment to get down on the floor and attentively and actively engage a toddler in pretense; such investment fosters developmental advances in children. It appears that children's play is children's work, but [adults] play can repay children some welcome fringe benefits.
>
> (Bornstein et al. 1996, p. 2912)

In a study of mother and toddler play and its impact on cognitive development, Bornstein and his colleagues remind us that adults have much to offer children's play and of the benefits of adopting a playful stance with the children, entering into the game rather than over- or re-directing the play or over-emphasising its realistic and instrumental features. Although conducted some time ago, the research is a timely reminder of the powerful ways in which adults can help to facilitate learning in the context of children's play whether at home or in an early years setting.

The value of play in human development and experience is beyond dispute but *how* precisely play contributes to human development is still open to debate. There is widespread agreement that children play and explore naturally and spontaneously regardless of culture, place or time (Goncu and Gaskins

2006), and that it provides a powerful means through which they come to understand the complexities of the material, conceptual and social world. But while playing and exploring appear to be universal human drivers (Smith 2010), the extent to which such activities are encouraged or limited in children will be determined by specific cultural and social practices, shaped also by experiences of individual children in the home, through early attachments, relationships established with caregivers and the nature of the communicative environment (Roulstone et al. 2011).

Playing and exploring in the EYFS

In England the importance of play and exploration is officially recognised in the Early Years Foundation Stage (EYFS) (DfE 2021), the statutory framework for children from birth to school starting age at 5. But welcome though this may be, increasingly as play has moved into the centre of the official regulatory context, so too have measures for assessment and accountability (Roberts-Holmes 2015), and this has become increasingly evident in the most recent iterations of the EYFS. The value and purpose of play in children's early education and development are related in particular to its contribution to language and literacy learning outcomes. Children's play clearly contributes to language development and can aid the learning of literacy. There is a risk, however, that reducing play to a tick box exercise of learning outcomes will erode enabling pedagogic interactions that underpin and facilitate playful learning interactions between adults and children (Rogers 2010; Wood 2013).

The 2021 EYFS has been criticised for seeming to pay lip service only to play, and certainly not to acknowledge it as important in Year 1 as well as Reception, but rather for it to give way to the teaching of essential skills and knowledge as if this teaching could not be done playfully and through play. It is important, then, that practitioners feel confident in their knowledge and understanding of play and their pedagogical skills in supporting children in playful learning situations. Participating in children's play can be challenging for adults (Anning 2015; Roscoe 2020) and this is especially true in play which contains high levels of fantasy. In this chapter we suggest that play provision needs to be planned carefully to ensure that children have access to a wide range of possibilities and opportunities but, as Brown (2009) suggests, if the purpose is more important than the act of play then it probably isn't play!

Reflecting the importance of play and exploration in early development, 'Playing and exploring' is established as one of three key 'characteristics of effective learning'(CoEL) in the EYFS, and we would argue constitutes the central pedagogical approach to a curriculum for children aged under five. While there may be considerable overlap between the CoEL it is useful, however, to consider each separately as in the chapters of this book, and to consider what is meant by, in this case, playing and exploring and the special ways in which these particular characteristics contribute to and provide the context for children's learning. That said, we should not think only in terms of the characteristics of *effective learning* but also the characteristics of *effective pedagogy* and what these might mean for adults working with young children. We have suggested already that playful interactions with children are one powerful way to engage children. These characteristics are intended to provide the framework for engaging children's interest and emphasise the *process* and *context* rather than the content or outcomes of learning.

A sociocultural approach to play and exploration

This chapter is informed by a sociocultural approach to play and exploration, which acknowledges the way in which learning and development are socially, as well as individually, constructed and where learner agency is central. From this perspective, children are from birth seen as active agents rather than passive recipients in the learning process. As we observe children, so they observe us and learn how to respond to achieve their goals and try to make sense of our words and gestures. Newborn babies actively signal a wide range of feelings such as discomfort, contentment or distress through bodily moves, non-verbal communication and by modifying behaviour according to the responses received. Children very soon learn how to exercise agency and resist adult requests and rules to meet their needs and interests.

> Yelda (aged 5) says she is 'hiding' [in the carpeted role-play corner] with the playdough, (which according to the classroom rules is to be kept on tables), so 'Mrs Tanveer don't see me' (Roscoe, 2020: 131).

We understand 'agency' here to mean a person's capacity to make sense of what they observe and experience – and with this, to respond intentionally in the world (Porpora 2015). There are obvious limits to that agency, where children may not yet have the prerequisite skills to act on their ideas and decisions or where the structural features of early years settings such as rules, routines and regulations constrain what they can do (Klocker 2007: 85; Roscoe 2020). In order for children to exercise agency they require adults who are able to recognise and work with these limits so that they do not come to dominate the child's experiences. This may require early years practitioners to rethink established ways of working and the traditional hierarchical relationship between adults and children, particularly in playful and exploratory situations. It is also possible that if we assume too much for children's agency that we fail to see the times when they need adult guidance, instruction and help in setting boundaries. Moreover, in the play between children, agency is not simply exercised by the individual child, but is mediated by the interactions between children. Play offers children the opportunity to negotiate and contain their desire to act with other children, and thus to self-regulate behaviour and feelings (Roscoe, 2020). Through playing and exploring with adults, children can be encouraged to have an active role in shaping teaching and learning experiences in the early years setting. This might lead us to think of curriculum and pedagogy in the EYFS as co-constructed, a negotiated space, based on a reciprocal relationship between children and adults (Rogers 2010).

Play and exploration: the same or different?

James (3 years, 6 months) is building a 'marble run' with his Dad. Together they connect the pieces that make the tower of winding paths down which the marbles will eventually travel. James releases marbles one by one through the chute, each one following the twists and turns with a clatter and rattle, settling eventually in the container at the bottom. James is clearly fascinated by the movement and the noise and repeats the action many times. Later he takes the box of marbles and releases all of them in quick succession, so that eventually a marble 'jam' is created. When his Dad tries to intervene to unblock the marbles, James is insistent that he wants do this alone, without help and interference. He has deliberately created the marble jam and is fascinated by the long snake-like pattern that the marbles have created in the tube. James plays with the marble run for some 20 minutes before he is called away for supper, somewhat reluctantly. The marble run is packed away in his absence but later James asks for it several times and is clearly still preoccupied by it.

In this fairly typical activity, that we might observe in the home or early years setting, James demonstrates what Laevers (1993) describes as 'involvement':

- recognised by a child's concentration and persistence;
- characterised by motivation, fascination, an openness to stimuli and an intensity of experience both at the physical and cognitive level, and a deep satisfaction with a strong flow of energy;
- determined by the 'exploratory' drive and the child's individual developmental needs.

James clearly derives much pleasure and satisfaction from the activity, evident in the countless repetitions of the action of releasing the marbles. Yet he does not show this pleasure in any overt way, his facial expression remains serious and his gaze fixed on the task at hand. This is a good example of purposeful play/exploration initiated and led by James. His dad played an important role too in helping him to set up the marble run and model what to do with the marbles initially. James's deliberate creation of the marble 'jam' suggests that he is interested in the potential of his actions, the 'what if' question that so often underpins playful and exploratory behaviours. His desire to take control of the activity and to resist the intervention from his dad to conform to the 'correct' use of the marble run is interesting because it reveals also the potential of materials not only to provoke exploratory behaviours, but also the desire in young children to control the course of events and to commit to their ideas even in the face of adult alternatives. James was also exercising agency. When he is called away, he showed displeasure and resistance but eventually complied when his dad insisted.

But is this play or exploration? And what can we learn from this example about the differences between play and exploration? If we think of this example as play, then we can conclude that play is very often serious and involves deep-level engagement and concentration. James was completely absorbed in this solitary activity but it also appeared to include a strong sense of 'what if', a dialogue with the self; what will happen if I release all the marbles at once? Similar questions are suggested in play where children appear to try out and explore new roles: 'what if I pretend to be a monster?' He shows that he is 'willing to have a go' (Early Education 2021) and keen to find out.

The terms play and exploration are often used interchangeably under the broader heading of 'play'. Indeed, the coupling of 'playing and exploring' in the EYFS suggests overlap between them. However, an important distinction is sometimes made between play and exploration. Hutt and colleagues (1989) for example, distinguish two distinct types of behaviour within the activity normally called 'play', observing the ways in which 3- to 5-year-olds responded to an unfamiliar toy, noting striking similarities in children's behaviour patterns. Exploration involved the child in visual inspection, activity investigation and manipulation of the toy. Over a period of 6 days exploratory behaviour decreased and a new set of patterns of behaviour emerged (Hutt et al.1989:4). The child, having acquired information concerning the properties of the novel toy through 'exploration', now utilised that knowledge in what she termed 'play'. Thus: implicit in the behaviours we termed 'exploration' was the question: What does this *object* do? Whilst implicit in the behaviours we termed 'play' was the question: 'What can *I* do with this object? (1989:4, original emphasis). This work suggests that exploration is more likely to occur when the child is faced with the unfamiliar and novel.

On the other hand, Hutt et al. (1989) suggest that play is more likely to occur when the child is faced with a familiar situation, event or object. In play, children may draw on a wide range of prior knowledge, skills and concepts and these can be used in new and novel ways. Vygotsky (1978) wrote that in play 'a stick becomes a horse'. In other words, once the child is familiar with the properties of an object through exploration it can be used by the child in highly imaginative ways. In this example of role play in a Reception class we see children 'playing with what they know' (Early Education 2021) drawing on a wide range of familiar everyday knowledge of objects, places and people in an imaginary context:

Roxanne: You can pretend to take an order but you're not the baby.
                [Runs out of the café and says, 'Can I have a piece of
                paper please to go in the café?']
Roxanne: Right what would you like madam? [pretending to write
                down the order].

Mia pretends to write it down and Roxanne interjects with 'I'm the person that
writes it down and you're in the kitchen and gives it out.' Turning her attention
back to her customer she asks, 'Right what would you like to drink madam?'

Sally: I would like a doughnut.
Mia: A doughnut.
Roxanne: No Mia don't tell her she doesn't know what there is ... I'll
                tell her, there's water. Orange juice and ice-cream. Do you
                want any cereal? She wants an ice-cream' Gives the cus-
                tomer her 'food'.

Roxanne is now using the mobile phone (a brick) and pretends to write down
an order. She says 'who's the mum, who's the mum? I'd like to have an order
for some food but somebody's on the phone, right as soon as we can.'

Roxanne to Mary: 'Somebody's rung up and they want 10 sausages, 10
                  glasses of milk and 10 ice-creams, they want it together,
                  'cos there's 10 of them all together'.

This type of play can be distinguished from the intense and concentrated
observable behaviours typical of learning in a new situation or with a new
material as in the example of James and the marble run. The distinction between
exploration and play is, we think a helpful one, if only because it enables us to
think about the wide range of different behaviours we see in children's activities which we might call play. For babies and toddlers, the emphasis appears to
be on exploration through sensori-motor activity. For children in the 3 to 5
years age group we tend to see a prevalence of pretend play. There may be
good developmental reasons for this, but it does not mean that babies and toddlers do not engage in playful behaviours and that exploration diminishes in
older children. There is also a danger that the research by Hutt might give the
rather misleading and inaccurate impression that exploration is more worthwhile than play since it appears to be linked more directly with the acquisition
of new knowledge. The application of that new knowledge in the context of
play is equally important and powerful and helps children to build their understanding of the world, to try things out in real and imaginary contexts and to
communicate ideas and feelings to others. Drawing on Hutt's distinctions can
help us to think through the range of possibilities available in materials and
spaces made available to children. How often do we offer new and novel

resources to children to stimulate exploratory knowledge-seeking behaviour? Do children have the opportunity to revisit materials so that they can re-use them in the context of their imaginary play once they have explored the physical and sensory properties of them? Do children have opportunities to play with open-ended materials?

It might be more helpful to think in terms of 'exploratory play' (Hughes 1996). Perhaps the most important question to consider is how does naming an activity as play or exploration shape the ways in which adults respond to and support or limit children's experiences?

Exploratory competence and representational competence

Research suggests that to achieve play competence infants need to develop both exploratory and representational competence (Shore 1998; Campbell 2002). Exploratory competence is shown in children's visual attentiveness and object manipulation. Representational competence is the ability to use one thing (gesture, word or object) to stand for or represent something else and has obvious and strong links with later symbolic representation in the form of role play, language, mathematics and the arts. Through their pretend play, schemas and multi-modal activities, we can see how young children move from personal meaning making to shared understandings of symbolic systems and build on this in the resources and experiences we provide. In the extracts above, James shows exploratory competence in the behaviours he displays when manipulating the marbles. Roxanne, by contrast, demonstrates representational competence when she uses a wooden brick as a mobile phone, and pretends to write a list. The development of both exploratory and representational competence depends on the support of parents and other adults, but that support is best given in the form of joint and reciprocal play. This happens, for example, in the home corner, when an adult takes turns to stir and taste the imaginary soup rather than simply hand over the spoon or ask the child questions about the realistic features of the soup (Campbell 2002). Entering into the imaginary world created by the child and engaging in joint play appears to lead to more extended play and language. Similarly, adults who offer babies and toddlers a 'secure base' from which to engage with an environment that stimulates exploratory activity can help children to become confident learners. For example, Goldschmeid's work on treasure baskets and heuristic play, where the adult adopts the role of silent partner 'provides young children with a secure base to venture from and playfully explore the environment, whilst the safe haven provides them with a refuge when that environment causes them any distress' (Rose and Rogers 2012).

To become confident learners, children need to gain mastery of their environment through play and exploration. This might mean that they use materials in ways that adults have not considered, climb higher on the climbing frame than an adult might feel comfortable with and explore ideas that are challenging to adults such as death, violence and sex. But for children to achieve both representational and exploratory competence through play, they need adults who allow for the sometimes 'messy' outcomes of exploratory play and support children to take risks that give 'stretch' to their capabilities. It is through such play that young children are likely to develop a greater sense of self-worth and autonomy.

From playful beginnings: attachment and attunement

The ability to play and to respond to playful interactions from others is present from birth. In these early interactions lie the seeds of secure attachment and effective learning which cut across and influence all developmental domains. One of the earliest ways in which babies come to understand their place in the world is through the process of attachment to the primary caregiver, an idea initially suggested in the work of John Bowlby (1969). **Attachment** is a **relational** process where strong affectional ties are established between one person and another (Rose and Rogers 2012). In early years settings this role is taken by the key person.

Rose and Rogers (2012) state that secure attachment is achieved through adults being empathetically responsive (Underdown 2007), by looking closely for verbal and non-verbal signals from the child that reflect how the child is feeling and what their needs and interests might be. This is 'attunement', a term which refers to the deep, genuine and significant connection established with another human (typically but not exclusively with the primary caregiver). Attunement between baby and caregiver creates a context for reciprocal connectedness that powerfully influences the synaptic make-up of the brain and provides the foundation for learning and well-being.

In summary, according to Arredondo and Edwards (2000), attunement depends on the following key elements:

- Emotional availability of the adult
- High degree of flexibility from the adult
- Display of a range of affect (emotion)
- Capacity for genuine playfulness
- Initiation of affectionate interactions
- Sense of humour
- Patience

Once again we see that 'genuine playfulness' features in positive interactions with babies. Moreover, it is through this early reciprocal play that the foundations are laid for babies to see that they exist in the world separately to other people. The feedback they receive from the caregiver is vitally important in affirming their place in the world and in encouraging subsequent attempts to communicate. The pleasure and affirmation that stems from these playful interactions encourages babies to repeat actions and sounds and to search out the caregiver.

The age of discovery! The case of heuristic play and treasure baskets (Goldschmied)

Exploratory play appears to be most prevalent in what Piaget described as the sensori-motor period typically from birth through to 2 years (1978). Babies try to make sense of the world in many ways – through grasping, sucking, banging and throwing objects. Through sensory and exploratory play, babies and young infants construct schemas, or 'patterns of repeatable actions that lead to early categories and then to logical classifications' (Athey 2007: 49). Building up a body of schemas through exploratory play enables children to learn about cause and effect, to test the properties of objects, and through their increasing mobility, to become spatially aware. In exploratory play, children rely on adults to provide an environment that affords interesting materials and objects for exploration and discovery, but also through interaction with and encouragement from other people. As babies become able to sit up and manipulate objects, the world takes on a different perspective and they gain greater independence in their play. A particular approach to sensori-motor play was developed by Elinor Goldschmied (1987), beginning with so-called 'treasure baskets' or collections of a range of everyday objects contained in a basket which provide multi-sensory experiences and encourage opportunities for hand/eye co-ordination (Rose and Rogers 2012). Goldschmied assigns the adult a passive rather than active role in heuristic play acting as a 'secure base' and 'safe haven' from which the child can explore. Child-led exploration allows for children's innate curiosity to flourish and supports their emerging sense of control and self-efficacy. Equally, however, adults might take a more proactive stance while children are exploring as Dowling suggests (2006). 'Scaffolding' children's learning, through approaches such as 'sustained shared thinking', allow for a dialogue to develop centered on the activity. However, it is important not simply to ask questions about the properties of the objects. What colour is it? How many? Is it heavy? But also to join in with modelling ways of exploring and affirming children's actions as in the example of James and his dad. Open-ended questions, such as 'Can you tell me, how does it feel when you hold it?' or contributions such as 'I like the warm feeling of that, what do you think' and 'I wonder what will happen if I put that on top?' are more beneficial to extending learning (Siraj-Blatchford and Manni 2008) whereas closed questions when overused may shut down possibilities for exploratory and playful behaviours. Knowing when to step back and allow the child to explore alone is important too.

From these early explorations and playful interactions, babies begin to build a bank of experiences and associated images from which they come to make sense of the world around them. Although research is unclear about the precise age at which babies begin to hold on to mental representations, it is certainly present in infants from around 5 months. We call this **object permanence** or, put simply, the ability to remember something that is no longer present. We believe that this ability to hold images in our heads is particularly human. Imagine if we couldn't do this. Of course, you couldn't imagine at all without this powerful capacity for remembering or for mental representation. Remembering something that is absent in this way is quite distinct from recognition of something when it is present. These mental representations enable children to remember and recall images of familiar people or things even in their absence. Without this capacity children would not be able to develop imitative and pretend play. However, a second capacity which develops in the second year of life enables children to move beyond mental representations to more complex, social imaginative activity. This is the development of a 'theory of mind.'

Developing a theory of mind in the context of play

Developing a 'theory of mind', that is, knowing that someone else thinks differently from you, is a vital human skill which has particular relevance for the ability of children to engage in play, and particularly pretend play. As we saw in the example of Roxanne and the café, being in role, acting out the thoughts and feelings of others, and negotiating role-play plots all require that children understand perspectives and experiences different from their own. Shared pretence, then, may be a particularly significant spur for the development and consolidation of theory of mind skills (Dunn 2004). As far as we know, babies in the first year of life do not engage in pretend play (Gopnik et al. 2001; Campbell 2002). In the second year of life, we see the emergence of imitative behaviours and early pretence. For example, at 18 months Laura imitates her mother by 'combing' her hair with a comb she finds on a table. Later at 24 months Laura is playing 'mums and babies' with her sister, Kara, aged 4. Laura pretends to comb her hair with a wooden brick that she finds in the toy box. She shows that she can substitute one thing for another, a vital skill in the development of symbolic thought which provides the foundation for later learning across all subjects. This type of play develops rapidly over the next few years and becomes increasingly elaborate and varied. Between the ages of about 3 and 5 years we see significant changes in the nature and quality of pretend play as children begin to organise and assign roles to others as well as adopt roles themselves. Their play becomes increasingly social and complex.

Key points to consider in the development of play and exploration include:

- Play helps children to develop a sense of self and the world around them and appears to be linked to the development of theory of mind.
- Through playful interactions and exploration babies and young children begin to build up a mental model of themselves as separate from others.
- Children's emerging sense of self is enhanced or reduced by the feedback the young child receives from those around them.
- Object permanence and theory of mind skills are essential to the growth of imagination, play and problem solving.
- Children aged 24 months to 5 years engage in more social pretend play than any other kind of play!
- Social pretend play between children builds social, communication and intellectual skills.
- The ability to move beyond the here and now, between belief and make-believe, is a uniquely human activity.
- Children aged 3 to 5 years engage in more pretend play than any other form of play.
- From about the age of 4 years, children begin to assign roles as well as adopt roles.
- Children from around 3 to 5 years have a strong desire to self-generate themes in play.

Outdoor play, rules and risk taking

It is Sabina's first day at nursery. She is wearing a beautiful velvet dress with matching slippers. Her mum is with her helping her to settle in. Together they move to the outdoor area. A group of children are playing around a large 'puddle' into which water from a pump overflows. One child is pouring water into the puddle from a can. Another is pumping the water, while another is wearing wellington boots and runs through the puddle splashing and laughing. The nursery teacher is talking quietly to the children about what they are doing. Sabina watches for a while then runs through the puddle with obvious pleasure. She is still wearing her velvet slippers.

What is interesting about this brief observation is the reaction of the adults. We might have expected Sabina's mother or the teacher to have tried to stop her or reacted loudly or even reprimanded her. Instead, the teacher calmly suggested that Sabina might like to come inside and find some boots. It was the experience that was important at that moment and, of course, the slippers could be dried out. So often we curtail children's explorations because concerns over mess, safety and noise take precedence. In so doing we might actually discourage children from 'having a go'.

The outdoors offers a range of different learning opportunities and characteristics to the indoors – not least because it offers children freedom to be more active, noisy and exploratory than is possible in indoor spaces. In addition to the obvious physical benefits of being in the outdoors, such activity offers young children a range of multi-sensory, first-hand experiences such as feeling the effects of the weather and related temperatures, coming into direct contact with the textures and smells of natural materials such as grass, ice, earth, water and wood, as in the case of Sabina. Grassy banks, garden areas, walls, fences, and tarmac surfaces provide an interesting array of features, textures and mini environments for children to explore. A small grassy hill or a few shrubs can be transformed into mountains and forests as children play (Rogers and Evans 2008). Open-ended resources, such as large boxes, drapes and large construction materials, encourage children to create imaginary worlds and develop complex narratives. The outdoors has equal value to the indoor classroom and, where possible, children should be able to move seamlessly between the two environments, in what we call 'free-flow' play. Such play enables children to combine elements of indoor and outdoor learning, to mix resources in creative and innovative ways and develop a sense of place and space. Young children need to create and explore their own places through the use of open-ended and suggestive (rather than overly prescriptive) props and materials and there are obvious limitations to what is possible indoors, in terms of space, noise level and the nature of the resources. The outdoor environment allows children to play on a larger scale and to explore a wider range of resources.

Much of what has been said about playing and exploring in this chapter applies to the outdoor environment and, in particular, the need for adults to interact in ways which allow children to take the lead and which foster confidence and enjoyment. But there are also different challenges inherent in outdoor spaces. Play and exploration, particularly in outdoor spaces, by its very nature involves children taking risks which push them beyond their current capabilities and challenge them physically, socially and cognitively. For adults, managing risk is challenging too and may lead to anxieties about how far they can allow children to explore and push boundaries. Certain types of play can also pose a risk to adults' own boundaries about what is acceptable behaviour, particularly within the heavily regulated classroom. This is why we see differing levels of tolerance of physical, noisy play in indoor and outdoor spaces (Rogers et al. 2017). As children develop, they move from a situation of dependence and adult-managed experiences to independence and self-management. Gill (2007) argues that there is growing evidence to suggest that in the developed Western world an increasingly regulated, risk-averse approach is severely limiting children's opportunities to practise some of the vital skills which would enable them to make this move and to exercise good judgement about what constitutes risk and danger. Recent research by Waite et al. (2017) notes that adults in early years settings may hold an exaggerated view of what constitutes a risk to young children, stemming from their own personal anxiety about potentially threatening situations, about the potential for disorder within the group and a genuine anxiety about litigation while in *loco parentis*. Clearly, the views held by adults will strongly influence the nature of provision and the extent to which children have licence to explore their environment. Indeed, several research studies confirm that opportunities afforded to children to take risks is highly dependent on how risk is viewed by adults (Stephenson 2003; Waters and Begley 2007; Waite 2017). A study of practitioner beliefs about risk in play in Australia and Norway (Little et al. 2012) demonstrated that where there were shared views on the benefits of risk and in how risk was understood, there were significant differences between the countries in how risk was enacted in practice. Perhaps unsurprisingly, the Australian educators felt more constrained by the regulatory and pedagogical context that arose from it. By contrast, the regulatory environment in which the Norwegian practitioners operated provided greater flexibility, allowing these practitioners to exercise their own professional judgement to manage children's risky play.

For some adults, the pedagogic challenge may stem from their personal attitude towards the outdoors. Inclement weather conditions and the often physical, risky and boisterous nature of outdoor play can be off-putting for some adults. Adult attitudes to outdoor play may also be gendered, expecting and encouraging more physical and messy play for boys than girls (Tovey 2010). Adults may perceive that girls are in need of greater protection outdoors from potential threats such as accidents, bad weather and strangers. The study of outdoor learning in Foundation Stage and Year 1 classes by Waite et al. (2017) found that the dominant form of interaction in the outdoor areas was for the purpose of preventing risk through admonishment or curtailing children's activity. How can we ensure that young children have ample opportunities to take risks and maximise the impact of the outdoor learning environment?

Tovey (2010) suggests that rather than emphasise risk assessment, we need to embrace risk as an essential part of play pedagogy. In keeping with the over-riding message in this chapter, children need time, space and flexible resources to develop outdoor play that allow for risk-taking but so that it does not become the main or leading focus of planning for the outdoor play. Playing and Exploring in the EYFS promotes the view that children should have opportunities to:

- initiate activities;
- seek challenge;
- show a can-do attitude;
- take a risk, engaging in new experiences and learning by trial and error.

Outdoor spaces offer children freedom to explore and test out their capabilities which often exceed our expectations. But, to achieve this, children need adults who enjoy the outdoors, and understand the wide-ranging benefits it brings.

Valuing children's play and exploration

This chapter has emphasised the importance of establishing playful relationships with babies and young children to help establish positive feelings about learning and to encourage them to explore the world with increasing autonomy, confidence and feelings of self-worth. As children approach the end of the EYFS and 'school readiness' becomes more pressing, it is easy to view play instrumentally, as a vehicle through which to deliver the prescribed curriculum and assess the concepts, skills and knowledge children have acquired (Bradbury 2019). This may mean that the type of free-flow, flexible play that we see more commonly in nursery settings where children have extended periods to choose play partners, resources and spaces, are increasingly interrupted by the demands of more formal learning activities such as phonics and reading with an adult (Roscoe 2020).

In this example Yelda expresses her frustrations at the fact that a role-play episode has come to an end, as she and her peers were each asked to take part in an adult-led task (either involving assessment or teaching of skills). Her comments reveal how important it can be for children to return to their play, even if they are asked to leave it for a short period of time. A reduction in the amount of time they have to engage in and develop their play can also result in children not fully reaping the benefits of participation in either activity and lead to feelings of frustration.

Yelda: I didn't play. I do that quickly [writing], but I didn't play.
Me: When?
Yelda: Mrs Tanveer call me. I didn't play…Sabah don't want to play now. She's writing; where's Mary?
Me: There [table one].
Yelda: All them not playing me now.
Me: How about later…when they're free?
Yelda: Noooo…is snack now. Mrs Terry tell me.

(Roscoe 2020: 211)

On the surface, the pedagogy in this classroom appeared to be play-based. However closer observation showed that pedagogy emphasised 'school readiness' and teacher-led activity as children approached the end of their Reception year. Play functioned as a holding task, rather than an activity valued as an important context for children's learning.

Final thoughts

At the time of writing, children, their families and teachers are navigating the challenges of working and playing in the midst of the Covid-19 pandemic. Restrictions on domestic spaces to play, social distancing and home schooling will impact in different ways on children accessing play. The ways in which the pandemic has both exacerbated and uncovered inequality has led to the concept of lost learning. How and in what ways that lost learning will be conceptualised and recovered for young children remains to be seen. A renewed appreciation of the importance of the outdoors, play and creativity to health and well-being may also play a part in our journey back from the effects of the pandemic and the very tangible ways it has altered our day-to-day lives and working practices. It remains to be seen if, in the post-pandemic world, play is further marginalised in order to recover lost school learning or if the time has come to recognise more fully that, in order to thrive and cope with adversity, we need opportunities to engage in less formal, more creative and nature-based activity.

Key messages

Developing a pedagogy which supports play and exploration means:

- giving children real choice about where, with whom, what and how they play;
- providing flexible spaces (indoors and outdoors) and extended periods of *uninterrupted* time to play, to revisit, rebuild and recreate ideas with adults and children;
- tuning into and following children's ideas;
- showing children that we are interested in their play through playful interactions, co-construction, consultation and negotiation, observation and feedback;
- being knowledgeable advocates for play and exploration.

References

Anning, A. (2015) Play and the legislated curriculum, in J. Moyles (ed.) *The Excellence of Play*, 4th edn. Maidenhead: Open University Press.

Arredondo, D. and Edwards, L.P (2000) Attachment, bonding and reciprocal connectedness, *Journal for the Center for Families, Children and the Courts,* 1: 109–127.

Athey, C. (2007) *Extending Thought in Young Children*, 2nd edn. London: Paul Chapman.

Bornstein, M., Haynes, M., Watson, A. and Painter, K. (1996) Solitary and collaborative pretense play in early childhood: Sources of individual variation in the development of representational competence, *Child Development*, 67, 6: 2910–2929.

Bowlby, J. (1969) *Attachment and Loss. Vol 1: Attachment*. New York: Basic Books.

Bradbury, A. (2019) Datafied at four: The role of data in the 'schoolification' of early childhood education in England, *Learning, Media and Technology*, 44(1): 7–21.

Brown, S. (2009) *Play: How It Shapes the Brain, Opens the Imagination and Invigorates the Soul*. New York: Penguin.

Campbell, S. (2002) *Behavior Problems in Preschool Children: Clinical and Developmental Issues*. New York: Guilford Press.

DfE (Department for Education) (2021) *Statutory framework for the early years foundation stage: Setting the standards for learning, development and care for children from birth to five*. Available at: https://assets.publishing.service.gov.uk/government/uploads/system/uploads/attachment_data/file/974907/EYFS_framework_-_March_2021.pdf (accessed 20 April 2021).

Dowling, M. (2006) *Supporting Young Children's Sustained Shared Thinking: Training Materials*. St Albans: Early Education (The British Association for Early Childhood Education).

Dunn, J. (2004) *Children's Friendships: The Beginnings of Intimacy*. Oxford: Wiley-Blackwell.

Early Education (2021) *Birth to 5 Matters: Non-statutory guidance for the Early Years Foundation Stage*, published on behalf of the Early Years Coalition, St. Albans: Early Education. Available at: www.birthto5matters.org.uk/wp-content/uploads/2021/04/Birthto5Matters-download.pdf (accessed 23 April 2021).

Gill, T. (2007) *No Fear: Growing Up in a Risk-averse Society*. London: Calouste Gulbenkian Foundation.

Goldschmeid, E. (1987) *Infants at work*. VHS video, London: National Children's Bureau.

Goncu, A. and Gaskins, S. (eds) (2006) *Play and Development: Evolutionary, Sociocultural and Functional Perspectives*. Mahwah, NJ: Lawrence Erlbaum Associates.

Gopnik, A., Meltzoff, A. and Kuhl, P. (2001) *How Babies Think*. London: Wiedenfeld and Nicolson.

Hughes, B. (1996) *A Playworker's Taxonomy of Play Types*. London: Playlink.

Hutt, S., Hutt, C., Tyler, S. and Christopherson, H. (1989) *Play, Exploration and Learning: A Natural History of the Pre-School*. London: Routledge.

Klocker, N. (2007) An example of 'thing' agency: Child domestic workers in Tanzania, in R. Panelli, S. Punch and E. Robson (eds) *Global Perspectives on Rural Childhood and Youth*. Abingdon: Routledge.

Laevers, F. (1993) Deep level learning: An exemplary application on the area of physical knowledge, *European Early Childhood Education Research Journal*, 1(1): 53–68.

Little, H. Sandseter, E. and Wyver, A. (2012) Early childhood teachers' beliefs about children's risky play in Australia and Norway, *Contemporary Issues in Early Childhood*, 13 (4): 300–316.

Piaget, J. (1978) *The Development of Thought*. Oxford: Blackwell.

Roberts-Holmes, G. (2015) The 'datafication' of early years pedagogy: 'If the teaching is good, the data should be good and if there's bad teaching, there is bad data', *Journal of Education Policy*, 30(3): 302–315.

Rogers, S. (2010) Powerful pedagogies and playful resistance: Researching children's perspectives, in E. Brooker and S. Edwards (eds) *Engaging Play*. Maidenhead: Open University Press.

Rogers, S. and Evans, J. (2008) *Inside Role-Play in Early Education*. London: Routledge.

Rogers, S., Waite, S. and Evans, J. (2017) Outdoor pedagogies in support of transition from Foundation Stage to Year 1, in S. Waite (ed.) *Children Learning Outside the Classroom From Birth to Eleven*, 2nd edn. London: Sage.

Roscoe, S.B. (2020) *Play in an English Reception Classroom: How Children Navigate Classroom Rules During their Self-initiated Play*. Doctor of Philosophy Thesis. University College London. Available at: https://discovery.ucl.ac.uk/id/eprint/10092952/ (accessed 11 Sep 2020).

Rose, J. and Rogers, S. (2012) *The Role of the Adult in Early Years Settings*. Maidenhead: Open University Press.

Roulstone, S., Law, J., Rush, R., Clegg, J. and Peters, T. (2011) *The role of language in children's early educational outcomes*, DFE Research Brief 134. Available at: www.education.gov.uk/publications/eOrderingDownload/DFE-RB134.pdf (accessed December 2012).

Siraj-Blatchford, I. and Manni, L. (2008) 'Would you like to tidy up now?' An analysis of adult questioning in the English Foundation Stage, *Early Years*, 28.1, 5–22.

Shore, C. (1998) Play and language: Individual differences as evidence of development and style, in D. Fromberg and D. Bergen (eds) *Play from Birth to Twelve: Contexts, Perspectives and Meanings*. London: Routledge.

Smith, P.K. (2010) *Children and Play*. Oxford: Wiley-Blackwell.

Stephenson, A. (2003) Physical risk-taking: dangerous or endangered? *Early Years*, 23 (1): 35–43.

Tovey, H. (2010) Playing on the edge: Perceptions of risk and danger in outdoor play, in P. Broadhead, J. Howard and E. Wood. (eds) *Play and Learning in the Early Years*. London: Sage

Underdown, A. (2007) *Young Children's Health and Well-being*. Maidenhead: Open University Press.

Vygtosky, L. (1978) *Mind in Society: The Development of Higher Psychological Processes*. Cambridge, MA: Harvard University Press.

Waite, S. (ed.) (2017) *Learning Outside the Classroom: From Birth to Eleven*, 2nd edn. London: Sage.

Waters, J. and Begley, S. (2007) Supporting the development of risk-taking behaviours in the early years: An exploratory study, *Education 3–13*, 35 (4): 365–77.

Wood, E. (2013) *Play, Learning and the Early Childhood Curriculum*, 3rd edn. London: Sage.

4 Active learning

Nancy Stewart

Chapter summary

- Learning is not a passive process. Once a child is engaged in learning opportunities, deep learning requires motivation to actively exert effort, maintain focus and involvement, and persevere in the face of difficulties.
- This chapter examines the roots of motivation to learn, as well as factors that affect the quality of motivation including goal orientation, intrinsic and extrinsic motivators, and growth mindsets versus fixed mindsets.
- Ways adults play a key role in supporting children to maintain strong motivation to learn are outlined.

Introduction

The most effective learning involves energy and commitment from the learner. Children learn as they interact with people and things, but while they may not recognise this as learning at the time, they are far from passively and unconsciously soaking up knowledge and understanding. Central to working with the characteristics of effective learning is understanding that children, as the agents of their own learning, must be willing to actively expend mental and physical effort in the process.

Adults may be skilful at providing opportunities and supporting children to learn, but learning can never be done for another person. This chapter is about how children actively conduct their own learning. Learning theories have moved beyond the transmission model of teaching and learning which assumes knowledge and understanding can be directly transferred from the more knowledgeable person. Instead, social constructivist theory explains that while a more expert partner opens doors to new possibilities and supports use of these new approaches, the learner must actually do the work of mentally interpreting and linking the new input to existing understandings. This may involve building new concepts or restructuring existing understanding as required to make the learning usable for the individual. The learner, then, is not a passive recipient of their learning but is the active agent in the process.

The active part children play in their learning goes far beyond the physical activity which is a natural element of being a young child. Moving and physically experiencing the world are prime sources of gathering information and of stretching competence, independence and understanding. The term 'active learning' is sometimes used in this sense: children learn by doing, and so learning opportunities should be hands-on and involve concrete materials and movement rather passive abstract experiences. In terms of the characteristics of effective learning, however, the focus on hands-on physical experience sits more clearly within the strand of playing and exploring.

Engaging in experiences through movement and the senses is an essential part of children's learning and development – but it is not enough. The three characteristics of effective learning in the Early Years Foundation Stage can be described as 'ready, willing and able'. Children playing and exploring are having the experiences that give the raw material for them to learn from; they are *ready* to learn. They must also be *willing* (active learning) and *able* (creating and thinking critically).

It is possible for children to be 'hands-on, brains-off'. A newspaper report on a newly opened interactive museum display described children's use of the buttons and flashing lights: 'Children flit; they see a button, press it and move on to the next, without pausing to reflect on what has happened. It just becomes a button-pressing experience rather than true interactive learning' (Hall 1995). Children may move so quickly between activities that the possibilities for learning are limited. They can also be physically active in ways which are routine and repetitive without bringing real discovery or thought to bear.

Lilian Katz (2000: 394) draws a clear distinction between shallow engagement and the quality of involvement that leads to learning, warning against confusing amusement and fun with education:

> Take care not to confuse what is exciting, amusing, and fun with what is educative. Excitement is appropriate for entertainment and special occasions; it is short-lived pleasure — easy come, easy go. But what is educative requires sustained effort and involvement, often includes many routine elements, and offers long-term deep satisfaction rather than momentary fun and excitement.'

To be an effective learner requires more than superficial engagement in an experience. It requires becoming involved and concentrating, expending effort, persevering with an activity even when it is difficult or not turning out to plan. This active involvement is driven by the desire to satisfy a goal, whether the goal at the time is experiencing competence in the activity or building understanding. 'Active learning' in this chapter, then, refers not primarily to physical engagement but to the way the learner is actively committed to the learning process. In other words, the child has the will – the motivation – to expend energy and effort to learn.

Motivation

Motivation can be considered as the driving force that both propels and maintains interest and engagement toward achieving a goal. Martha Bronson (2000: 5) outlines the importance of motivation for self-regulating learners: 'It gets physical, social, and cognitive activities started and keeps them going by providing both the direction or goal for action and the force necessary to sustain effort. Motivation is at the centre of self-regulation and must be considered in relation to the development of all forms of voluntary control.'

Developing the will to strive toward personal goals has a resounding lifelong impact and is linked to achieving success in learning as well as other endeavours. Of course, people do not maintain a uniform level of motivation toward all activities – we are all much more highly motivated to do some things than others, and we become more particular about where we aim our motivation as we grow older. An orientation to motivation, however, does seem to be something that is developed in the early years as children develop attitudes and habits of mind which carry through into their later experiences. Motivation in childhood has been found to predict motivation and success later in life and, while not uniform across areas of endeavour, there remains a more generalised level of motivation (Gottfried et al. 2001; Lai 2011: 14). Through early experiences that promote the development of healthy, balanced neurological systems, motivation becomes an approach to experience that children develop and carry with them over time and across contexts such as home, school or in relationships (Grolnick et al. 1999; National Scientific Council on the Developing Child 2018).

It may be that motivation becomes an approach to experience that children develop and carry with them over time and across contexts such as home, school, or in relationships (Grolnick et al. 1999).

Early years practitioners who understand the importance of children's motivation will be concerned to identify what this quality of active learning looks like in action, and what their role is in protecting and fostering children's natural motivation to learn. When helping children to be strong learners is a clear goal of the adult, this will help to guide decisions about why, whether, when and how to intervene and interact with children in their learning.

Sources of motivation

The amount of effort and persistence the youngest children bring to their experiences is phenomenal, and results in enormous amounts of learning in the first years of life that we never again match as we grow older. From helpless infants who are encountering the world of time, space, objects and other people for the first time, children push themselves to attempt, to practise and to master physical skills, communication with others, and understanding what things are and how things work. What is it that pushes babies to learn? And how can we build on that natural impetus to support children to remain strong and committed learners, and avoid giving negative messages that risk shutting down learning capacity?

Self-determination theorists propose that innate needs, part of the inborn psychological nature of human beings, lie at the root of motivation. These are described as the need to feel **competent**, to have **autonomy**, and to be **related to others** (Deci and Ryan 1985).

It is easy to see how the need for feeling competent to manage our world and our lives would support us to master new skills and build understanding, from egging a baby on to take up new challenges to spurring us on to further learning at any stage. Adults who support children's need for competence provide stimulation both in relationships and environments, provoking children to engage with the next challenge on their horizon (Perry 2015).

The need for autonomy, or being in control of our own decisions and actions, is concerned with needing to feel that we are agents in our own lives and not simply passive recipients of what life brings. The more children have autonomous experiences, where they are aware that they are making choices and making things happen in their world, the more they will repeat and seek out those satisfying experiences. From the baby who is able to see a toy move in response when they wave their hands or knows they can elicit a response from an adult in response to their noises, to an older child who makes choices about their activities and is encouraged to do things in their own ways, children who know they have autonomy play an active part in their learning. They avoid the demotivation of learned helplessness, where a lack of opportunity to exercise autonomy results in the belief that nothing they can do makes any difference.

The need for warm, caring relationships with others is fundamental to being human, and is well-recognised in theories of attachment for its emotional impact as well as its impact on development and learning. The relational and emotional aspects of motivation come into play in determining whether children feel safe and secure enough to explore, to take risks, and have the emotional resilience to bounce back from set-backs. The need for relationships – for a sense of belonging – also motivates children to take part in the social interactions that enable them to co-construct their understanding, and to begin to identify with and be motivated toward the goals of those with whom they connect.

The desire to satisfy these innate psychological needs arises within the learner, and so can be seen as an internal source of motivation – leading to **intrinsic motivation**. There are other sources of intrinsic motivation, as well, including the person feeling interest or curiosity and enjoyment in the experience itself. Deci and Ryan propose that interest and enjoyment are intrinsic motivators, as long as the essential underlying needs for competence, autonomy and relatedness are satisfied within the activity. If the experience denies satisfaction of these needs, however, then interest alone will not maintain motivation. It is as if competence, autonomy and relatedness are basic necessary nutrients for psychological development, as food is for life and physical growth. We will follow interesting pursuits when we are not hungry, but if we are starving we soon lose interest in anything but the need for food. Their definition of intrinsically motivated behaviours is 'those that are freely engaged out of interest without the necessity of separable consequences, and, to be maintained, they require satisfaction of the needs for autonomy and competence' (Deci and Ryan 2000: 233).

Intrinsic motivation, which arises from within the individual and where the activity itself brings satisfaction, can be seen in contrast to **extrinsic motivation**, which relates to behaviour arising from factors outside the person and outside the behaviour itself. Behaviourist theory holds that development and learning occur primarily in response to factors from outside of the individual. Some of these external factors are described as positive or negative reinforcements, where behaviour is more likely to be repeated if it is met with a reinforcement. A positive reinforcement occurs when a child learns that something good happens when they do a certain behaviour (such as people give pleasant attention when a baby smiles), and a negative reinforcement is learning that something unpleasant stops in response to a behaviour (for example, being left alone in your cot will stop when you cry for attention). These reinforcers are consequences of the behaviour and are quite different from the rewards and punishments that occur not as a natural consequence, but are administered by someone else and are separate from the activity itself.

Children certainly can and do learn behaviours through reinforcements, and their ability to make the association between their behaviour and the reinforcement or external rewards can be used to shape behaviours that are seen as desirable. This is, however, an essentially passive view of children's development and learning – with children simply noticing the patterns between what they do and the response, and passively receiving the set of reinforcers that is available to them. It certainly cannot account for the enormous explosion of learning that young children engage in.

While there are both intrinsic and extrinsic sources of motivation, for children to become self-regulating learners there are significant advantages in supporting an orientation to intrinsic motivation. Intrinsic motivation is associated with higher achievement, welcoming challenge, becoming more involved in learning, using strategies more effectively, greater persistence and developing deeper understanding that can be applied across situations. When external motivation causes someone to take on an activity not for its own sake, but in order to gain an unrelated reward, the person does not bring the energising focus of interest, curiosity and enjoyment, nor commitment to the activity itself. Instead, the focus is on the reward, so that doing just enough to get by can be substituted for doing all that the person has the potential to do. Intrinsic motivation has emerged as an important phenomenon for educators – a natural wellspring of learning and achievement that can be systematically catalysed or undermined by parent and teacher practices, according to Ryan and Stiller (1991). Exploring how early years practice can support children as active learners will require attention to maintaining that vital wellspring.

Goal orientation – mastery or performance?

Motivation is not a generalised feeling, but always has a direction toward a goal. The type of goal someone sets strongly affects how they approach their activities, and researchers have identified the qualities and effects of two basic categories of goal: **mastery goals** and **performance goals**. Mastery goals are sometimes called 'learning goals', because the person's goal is to increase their competence to the best of their ability. Success is seen within the personal *process* of improvement. With performance goals, on the other hand, the person wants to show their competence to a standard relative to other people, with the end *product* determining success. In a sense, a mastery goal is never reached because we can always learn more, and this orientation pulls the learner forward to achieve more in the long term. A performance goal, however, is short term and may be met even when it is not stretching for the individual – performance can be 'good enough' to get by without the person reaching their potential. In fact, you may prefer to manage an easy task that will make you look good rather than take the risk of failing on a more challenging task.

There are many other advantages to mastery goals. People with a mastery goal focus on the task, while those with a performance goal focus on their self-image and are distracted by measuring how well they are doing compared to others. Those who hold a mastery goal are more likely to become more deeply involved in their activities, using deep processing so that they are able to truly own the learning, while a performance goal means one is more likely to engage just on the surface of the task. People with a mastery orientation are more likely to persevere in the face of difficulty, interpreting failure in terms of not having made enough effort and so responding by trying harder (Cerasoli and Ford 2014). Performance-oriented people are less likely to persevere because they tend to respond to failure by assuming they lack the ability, and so feel helpless to do anything about it (Dweck and Leggett 1988; Elliott et al. 2011).

Interestingly, people with a mastery orientation have greater access to an important source of learning – collaborating with other people. Co-constructing knowledge and understanding through working together and sustained shared thinking with peers is an important arena for children's learning; the skill of collaboration remains critical for success in adult occupations and is highly valued by employers. People with a mastery orientation readily share ideas and work together with others, because their focus is on quality of learning in the task. Performance-oriented people, however, are competing with others, want to be seen to be right and as more competent than others, and so do not readily explore ideas together (Darnon et al. 2006).

The links between the type of goal and intrinsic and extrinsic motivation are clear: mastery goals are pursued with intrinsic motivation toward the internal satisfaction of increased competence, while performance goals are pursued for extrinsic reward such as a certain ranking, mark or praise. While recent and current research demonstrates the limiting nature of performance goals and extrinsic rewards compared to a mastery orientation, Ruedy and Nirenberg

(1990: 238) quote the ancient Chinese sage Chuang Tzu who described the difference thousands of years ago in a poem entitled 'The Need to Win':

When an archer is shooting for nothing

He has all his skill.

If he shoots for a brass buckle

He is already nervous.

When shooting for a prize of gold, the archer's skill can be seriously undermined:

He goes blind

Or sees two targets –

He goes out of his mind!

His skill has not changed. But the prize

Divides him. He cares.

He thinks more of winning

Than of shooting –

And the need to win

Drains him of power.

Retaining children's power to learn must be a central goal of early education, and using external motivators and focusing on the end result rather than the process risks distracting children from their powerful internal drives to learn.

Growth and fixed mindsets

One way to describe the cluster of motivational attitudes and approaches that support learning power is the concept of a growth mindset, developed by researcher Carol Dweck (Dweck 2006). Through her research with children as young as four, Dweck has identified a belief held by some people that intelligence and ability are not fixed but grow through effort and practice. This growth mindset leads to a mastery orientation, to welcoming and enjoying challenges as an opportunity to improve, and to facing difficulty by using greater effort or changing strategy.

The opposite is a fixed mindset, characterised by the belief that intelligence and ability are fixed and cannot be changed. According to this mindset, an individual may or may not have particular talents and abilities – finding a task easy to do indicates that they happen to be good at it, while if it is difficult this means they are not good at it. The fixed mindset leads to people avoiding challenges which might prove difficult and so give uncomfortable messages about a lack of ability, preferring to repeat the same level of unchallenging tasks. The person with a fixed mindset experiences a sense of helplessness in the face of challenge and believes there is nothing they can do to deal with the obstacle. This feeling of a lack of autonomy, of having no power in the situation, is enough to turn someone with a fixed mindset away from potential learning opportunities.

Where do different mindsets come from? Dweck and her colleagues have identified the effect of subtle messages adults give to children which result in either a growth or fixed mindset. In their experiments, when children succeed at a relatively easy puzzle task and are praised for their effort (that is, the active role they took in their success) they then show a growth mindset; they attribute difficulties with harder puzzles to needing more effort, and they are interested to work with more challenging puzzles. But when the children are praised for their ability to solve the easy puzzles ('you must be really good at these' – that is, the passive role of happening to have that ability) they then show a fixed mindset and interpret not succeeding with harder puzzles to mean that they are not good at puzzles after all. They choose not to try harder puzzles, but to return to the easy level where they can expect success. Dweck has found evidence of growth or fixed mindsets in children as young as age 4 and has identified links between the type of praise parents give their children between ages 1 and 3 with their mindset and desire for challenge 5 years later.

Active learning in the EYFS

Active learning in the characteristics of effective learning in the Early Years Foundation Stage is outlined in three strands:

- being involved and concentrating;
- keeping trying;
- enjoying achieving what they set out to do.

These describe the way children are motivated agents in their learning, and each can be enhanced by skilful and sensitive adults through their interactions with children and through providing an environment geared to learning.

Being involved and concentrating

Children may show interest in an activity or a phenomenon for any number of reasons. It may be simply a novelty that attracts attention for a brief exploration, with initial interest being easily satisfied. Or perhaps the activity is simply fun – it may offer a wonderful feeling of stretching physical capacities, or be pleasurable for its sensual qualities, or be enjoyable and rewarding for its social involvement with others. Perhaps it is satisfying because it involves repeating a familiar activity or skill, which brings a sense of security or confidence in having mastery.

A brief and superficial interest, however, is unlikely to lead to learning that takes the child to new levels of understanding. Deep learning results when the learner explores and tests many facets of the experience, relating the experience to previous understanding and building the robust mental links that allow them to use the new information, applying it in new situations. This focused attention and energy is what is meant by involvement and concentration.

Concentration versus development of attention

Babies and young children are sometimes described as being unable to concentrate, but nothing could be further from the truth. The degree of focus and sustained attention even quite young babies can bring to an object of interest can be striking to a quiet observer. There is, however, a developmental element to attention, with neurological maturation gradually enabling children more purposefully to control their attention.

A young baby will be immediately distracted by a more dominant stimulus – so talking to the concentrating baby can end the period of attention to the object of their interest. Gradually children develop the ability to resist distractions, but still need to pay attention to one thing at a time and cannot easily shift their attention at will. Eventually, children become able to shift attention from one focus to another and back again, to pay attention to more than one thing at the same time, and finally to purposefully maintain focus for brief periods on something that is not of their own choosing.

Since children can concentrate on and become deeply involved in the experiences that they feel drawn to, long before they can concentrate at will on something of someone else's choice, it is important to recognise that children choosing their own focus of learning is an important element of their will to learn.

Involvement in learning

Involvement in learning is rooted in true curiosity, which brings together an initial arousal of interest in something new with a deeper need to understand. Piaget's theories of assimilation and accommodation describe cognitive development as a response to taking in new information that may not fit with existing mental structures – our current hypotheses about what is and how things work. That cognitive dissonance is uncomfortable and it causes us to try to resolve the inconsistency by seeking more information. We investigate to find out whether we can after all assimilate the new phenomenon into what we already understand, or whether we will need to shift our mental map to fit the new information. For people to show real curiosity leading to sustained involvement they must both be open to something new and determined to understand – in other words, have the clear mastery goal of increasing knowledge.

Ferre Laevers, whose Leuven scale for involvement offers a clear way to observe the quality of children's involvement in their activity, has described the importance of children learning through deep involvement. He believes that nurturing the child's exploratory drive promotes 'deep-level' learning as opposed to more superficial learning which the child is unable to use in real-life situations (Laevers 1993). The involvement signals are useful indicators of intense mental activity which indicates that learning and development is taking place. Laevers identifies observable signals including the child's concentration, energy, creativity, facial expression and posture, persistence, precision, reaction time, language and satisfaction. These can be observed in children of any age, in any context, and are interpreted according to descriptors of five levels from extremely low to extremely high involvement. This provides a tool for understanding and reflecting on practice and provision for a group as a whole, and for identifying individual children who demonstrate lower levels of involvement with the aim of considering what could be done to support greater involvement.

Laevers (2005: 4) describes involvement as 'strong motivation, fascination and total implication; there is no distance between person and activity, no calculation of possible benefits'. The crucial point is that the satisfaction that goes along with involvement stems from one source, the exploratory drive. He goes on to explain that the exploratory drive is 'the need to get a better grip on reality, the intrinsic interest in how things and people are, the urge to experience and figure things out (p. 4)'.

Involvement is similar to the concept of 'flow' in adults in states of optimal experience, developed by Mihalyi Csikszentmihalyi (2000). In a state of flow the experience becomes its own reward as the person becomes lost in the process, experiencing deep concentration and enjoyment, clarity about their goals and progress in what they are doing, no fear of failure, a feeling of control and interest in the activity for its own sake. Flow has been associated with increased performance in work, education and sports. Flow is associated with a strong sense of autonomy, being more likely in people who feel they can control events and so can concentrate on internal drives rather than be concerned with the external demands of others. People with a strong flow motivation show a mastery orientation, associating learning with feelings of curiosity, interest, excitement, concentration, absorption, challenge and the need to seek and master difficulties. Flow is connected with embracing challenge and enjoying the process but is decreased when there is pressure to achieve and when there are external tangible rewards. Research has demonstrated that in adults flow motivation remains stable over time (Baumann and Sheffer 2010), so helping children to develop these dispositions could be expected to have far-reaching effects in the long term.

Well-being

Along with the scale describing involvement levels, Ferre Laevers' well-being scale works in tandem to support full understanding of children's learning. Using both scales together recognises that emotional and physical well-being is a necessary pre-condition for learning. As Laevers (2005: 4) explains, in order to ascertain the degree of children's well-being 'we first have to explore the degree in which children do feel at ease, act spontaneously, show vitality and self-confidence'. By doing this we find out if their physical needs and 'the need for tenderness and affection, the need for safety and clarity, the need for social recognition, the need to feel competent and the need for meaning in life and moral value are satisfied (p. 4).'

The adult role in children's involvement

The EYFS themes of Enabling Environments and Positive Relationships offer a useful framework for considering the role of the adult. An environment which supports emotional well-being will be first on the agenda in any consideration of good practice. Considering the needs of each child to build relationships with warm, consistent and responsive adults as well as with peers should be seen as a foundation for supporting children's involvement in their learning.

Children making their own choices is a key factor in children's levels of involvement, highlighting the importance of a learning environment which includes plenty of opportunity for children freely to initiate their own activities. In the autonomous opportunity to choose, plan and lead their own activity children are able to focus at the edge of their competence, finding their own challenges.

Although adults can and do plan activities with specific learning objectives geared to what they have observed of children's interests and current learning, they can never accurately fascinate and challenge all the children in a group. In self-selected activities, however, each individual child can focus on what is currently of most personal interest and can explore and repeat investigations to satisfy deep curiosity and a need for mastery. Adults can support children's absorptions by noticing what is fascinating to a child and plan to introduce into the environment resources and opportunities that will further challenge the child to engage more and develop their understanding.

Along with choice and well-planned, stimulating resources, an enabling environment will offer uninterrupted periods of time and space which free children to follow their ideas and become deeply involved.

Child-initiated activity does not imply a lack of interaction with supportive adults. Children may be supported to focus and maintain attention in a number of ways, through contingent response based on observing the individual child. Adults may sometimes support children to focus their attention, for instance, by offering non-directive stimulation. Researchers have found that babies who focus more successfully on their play have mothers who frequently stimulate their attention in a non-obtrusive way, helping draw their attention back from passing distractions and effectively teaching the child to focus their own attention (Carlton and Winsler 1998). At times where a child is clearly involved and concentrating, the sensitive adult might make the decision to guard the learning moment and avoid distracting the child's attention.

Practitioners who are aware that their stimulation and talk can be important supports for children's learning may sometimes feel an onus to interact almost constantly with children – but this can become interference rather than support. It is important for adults to observe carefully, ask themselves whether their interaction would be of use and in what way, and only then decide whether to become involved in the child's activity. One possibility is to become involved afterwards and talk with the child about their experience as a review rather than at the moment of concentration.

Where a child's interest is fleeting, renewed focus might be stimulated by playing alongside, modelling possibilities, introducing new elements or resources, and refocusing through shared attention. A child who is over-stimulated and too excited to pay attention may be supported by offering a calmer environment or an island of calm in a one-to-one interaction.

As well as helping children to experience the innate satisfaction from states of deep involvement and concentration, a further aim of effective adult support is for children gradually to become aware of and able to regulate their own learning – including knowing how important their concentration is. Children are very sensitive to what adults value, and adults can communicate the importance of committing energy and focus to activities by explicitly acknowledging when they have observed children showing deep curiosity and involvement. Children need to know that adults value the process of wondering, of losing yourself in something interesting which can grow increasingly complex, rather than looking for quick answers or showing interest in products only (Perry 2015).

Keeping on trying

We learn from having a go at new things and giving the new experiences our full concentration. If we stay within the safe zone of what we already know how to do, we are sure to be successful – but we don't learn anything new. It is only from meeting a challenge just beyond what we can currently do that we have the opportunity to develop new skills and understanding, and this carries a built-in risk that we won't be successful in our efforts. It may require several trial-and-error attempts, learning each time from what went wrong, before we achieve our goal. It may be that in unsuccessful attempts we didn't apply enough effort, or concentration, or needed to stick with it longer.

Persisting in the face of difficulties is an essential ability for strong learners. The most successful people do not find that everything comes easily but are familiar with trying hard and bouncing back from setbacks. This resilience is summed up in the familiar phrase, 'If at first you don't succeed, try, try again'.

Babies and young children are carried through early challenges by their power of perseverance, practising each stage of their emerging skills until they are successful. A baby balancing on unsteady legs, taking the first few tentative steps before toppling to the floor, doesn't give up and decide to rely on cruising along holding on to the furniture for the rest of her life.

Maintaining the ability to persevere when things don't go well is rooted in a strong sense of autonomy, competence and a growth mindset, and in emotional well-being:

- believing that trying again, trying harder or in a different way will make a difference (my decisions and actions make a difference);
- not being afraid of errors (I can learn from what doesn't work);
- not being afraid of difficulty (I can improve with effort, and difficulty doesn't mean that I'm no good at this).

The adult role in children keeping on trying

While babies persevere in repeating their efforts to drive their development and learning, differences in persistence appear very early. There may be some temperamental factors, but research has shown that adult interaction affects how persistent children are toward reaching their goals. One study illustrated the importance of both the quality of interaction within a relationship and the opportunities in the environment. Babies who were more persistent and focused on goals at 6 months were found to be more competent at 13 months – and these were the babies who experienced more stimulation and responsiveness from their mothers and had experiences of responsive toys (Yarrow et al. 1982).

Another study, which looked at parenting styles and babies' persistence and competence at 12 and 20 months, concluded that the mothers' attitudes and behaviour affected their babies' persistence at mastering their environment. Babies were more persistent when their mothers sensitively supported babies' autonomy in their activities, responding to their child's attempts rather than attempting to control them (Grolnick et al. 1984). Adults who model effort and persistence in the face of difficulties also support the growth of persistence in babies (Leonard et al. 2017).

Educators and parents are often encouraged to ensure that children are successful in their efforts and never left to fail, based on the assumption that self-esteem will suffer if children do not always experience themselves as able. The relevance of self-esteem to learning is questionable in any case, as repeated studies have found either no link or even a negative association (Baumeister et al. 2003). Self-esteem – holding oneself in high regard which may not be rooted in the reality of one's attributes – is not the same thing as a sense of self-efficacy as described by Albert Bandura (1994). Self-efficacy is a belief in one's abilities to reach a goal in a particular situation and is based on experience of what one can do, including one's ability to manage challenging tasks and situations.

There is a fine line between scaffolding children to work successfully within their zone of proximal development and over-supporting children so that they never face real difficulty. Children need opportunities to struggle, to find that things go wrong, and to learn that persistence often pays off. Very able children for whom everything comes easily in their early education often under-achieve when they hit later challenges, through never having had opportunities to develop emotional resilience and strategies for dealing with difficulty.

Guy Claxton (2006) cautions against too carefully scaffolding children's learning: 'Helping (children) learn better is not the same as helping them become better learners. Effective support can easily create dependency, unless the teacher is continually looking for opportunities to dismantle the scaffolding, and build students' disposition to do their own supporting.' Gunilla Dahlberg (2000) quotes Eric Bronfenbrenner's comment which recognises that careful scaffolding can limit children's possibilities: 'For upbringing to be successful, there needs to be at least one crazy uncle around who astonishes'. As well as offering un-dreamed-of possibility thinking to support children's creativity, the 'crazy uncle' will not carefully scaffold opportunities for children but is likely to take them beyond their comfort zone, providing valuable experience of the risks and thrills that attend working in uncharted territory.

Adults can be effective at supporting children's persistence when they:

- ensure the learning environment offers challenge so that children can find their own challenges in play;
- introduce stimulation and manageable challenge;
- offer encouragement and sensitive support as they allow children to remain in conditions of uncertainty and difficulty when they grapple with challenges.

Adults could remind themselves to keep their own goal firmly in mind: not to ensure children do not make errors or face problems nor to solve the problems for the child, but to support children to know that they can learn from their errors and face problems with a belief in the power of their own efforts.

Enjoying achieving what they set out to do

Having become interested enough to expend effort and energy in deep involvement, and persevered even if things didn't go smoothly, active learners will continue to be drawn to learning experiences through receiving the satisfaction of reaching their own goals. This reflects the importance of intrinsic motivation where the experience brings its own reward.

Satisfaction of the need to feel competent is a strong motivator, and the reward comes when we know we are making progress at the edge of our competence. Even very young children begin to evaluate progress toward their own goals. Two-year-olds know their capabilities, and show more pride with success in difficult tasks, and more shame in failing to manage easy tasks (Lewis et al. 1992).

The emotional component of intrinsic mastery motivation is strong. Alison Gopnik (Gopnik et al. 1999: 162) describes the 'distinctive joy' of babies and young children who have made sense of a puzzling situation, while Pen Green practitioners talk about toddlers showing 'chuffedness' at their achievements. This sense of internal satisfaction when children have met their own goals is quite different from what occurs when children achieve a goal set by adults, encouraged and rewarded through extrinsic motivators (Elliott et al. 2011).

Linked to the questionable emphasis on promoting self-esteem, it is common for early years practitioners to encourage positive behaviours by providing children with liberal amounts of praise and other rewards such as stickers. There is a danger, however, that this approach could backfire and lower children's intrinsic motivation (Theodotou 2014). Managing children's behaviour through positive rewards is rooted in an assumption that children are not motivated unless the motivation is provided from outside and conveys a message to children that the goal is set and performance is judged by the adult – in other words, it harms the child's sense of autonomy to choose their own goals and to find satisfaction in the process of mastery. Studies have shown that the child then identifies less with the activity and becomes less motivated to participate. As Bandura (1994: 220) explains:

> goals can be applied in ways that breed dislikes rather than nurture interests. Personal standards promote interest when they create challenges and serve as guides for aspirations. But if goals assigned by others impose constraints and performance burdens, the pursuit can become aversive.

Children do, of course, value the positive response of others – which lays a responsibility on adults to respond wisely. Injudicious use of praise and reward can divert a child from a mastery orientation, and intrinsic pleasure in the activity, and encourage turning instead toward a performance orientation and extrinsic motivation. So, while praise and rewards may seem to gain a desired response from the child and bring good feelings in the short-term, the longer term effects can be to reduce a child's internal sense of control, confidence in their own processes and judgements, and ultimate learning power.

The adult role in children enjoying what they set out to achieve

The use of tangible extrinsic rewards, such as stickers or star charts, should be a prime target for a re-think in early years practice, as their regular use has been shown to strongly reduce young children's intrinsic motivation. It is again important for adults to keep their own goal in mind: not to train children to perform when someone will reward them, but to support children to reward and strengthen the drive within themselves.

There may be a useful role for such external motivators if used only occasionally, for a short period, or for a specific purpose. In situations where adults may decide that external motivation has a place, there is a distinction to be made between rewards which are doled out in the gift of someone else and not directly linked to the activity itself, and consequences linked to a behaviour which can be used as reinforcers. For example, a child with additional needs who is reluctant to try to walk may be encouraged to take a few steps by the adult placing a sweet at intervals just out of the child's reach. Reaching the chocolate is an immediate reinforcer of what walking can do and will encourage the child to step toward the next one. Here the child can see that walking itself can give power and have a benefit, which is preferable to the adult saying, 'Take three steps and then I will give you a sweet.' The hope is that the child will learn that walking is a useful skill, and the reinforcers can be withdrawn as soon as possible.

Praise is often used as an external motivator, and there is no doubt that people value positive responses from others. But positive feedback includes showing genuine interest and engaging in the detail of what a child has done.

Carol Dweck (2006: 205) cautions, 'Remember that praising children's intelligence or talent, tempting as it is, sends a fixed-mindset message. It makes their confidence and motivation more fragile. Instead, try to focus on the processes they used – their strategies, effort, or choices. Practice working the process praise into your interactions with your children.'

Praise that is an empty comment, such as 'well done', 'good girl', 'that's lovely', or labelling children, such as saying 'you're so clever', 'you're very good at that' can decrease intrinsic motivation. On the other hand, where praise gives clear feedback about the child's process in the activity it has been shown to improve intrinsic motivation – it makes it clear that the child's own actions make the difference, and so supports the child's autonomy. Praise should be specific, linked to the child's behaviour and pointing out aspects that are important in successful learning – how the learner is involved, concentrates, persists, uses different strategies, problem-solves and has ideas. Feedback can also involve a specific discussion about the competence shown, not as a judgement by the adult but as an opportunity to consider the child's role as the active agent – what has been achieved, what can be learned from problems, or how the child might approach it another time.

Travelling with a different view

Active learning describes the way strong learners engage with the people, things and events they encounter. In the context of warm social interactions with peers and adults, children are motivated by the enjoyment and sense of belonging together and experience their own autonomy while gradually beginning to identify with the values and goals of the group. Active, self-regulated learning arising from intrinsic motivation has been seen to occur most often in small group situations, as well as in play (Timmons et al. 2016). Establishing an orientation to active learning in the early years is an important potential for early education, and as such straddles the dual nature of childhood as both being and becoming: though being an active learner is a foundation for a lifetime, it is built in the rich here-and-now quality of how children experience their childhood. As described by British philosopher RS Peters (1965: 110), 'To be educated is not to have arrived at a destination; it is to travel with a different view. What is required is not feverish preparation for something that lies ahead, but to work with a precision, passion, and taste at worthwhile things that lie at hand.'

Key messages

- Intrinsic motivation to learn can arise from innate needs for competence, autonomy and relationships. Motivation will be continually strengthened when children have regular experiences of mastering challenges, making their own choices and making things happen, and engaging with others in warm, supportive relationships.
- Environments and relationships which support emotional well-being and offer sensitive stimulation and scaffolding help children to become deeply involved, and to persevere in the face of setbacks.
- Opportunity to choose, plan and lead their own activity enables children to determine their own goals, find their own challenges focusing growth at the edge of their competence, and to build autonomy and self-regulation.
- When adults limit the use of external motivators and focus more on processes than products, they avoid distracting children from their powerful internal drives to learn, while regular use of rewards and injudicious praise has been shown to reduce young children's intrinsic motivation. Rather than training children to meet external goals, retaining children's power to learn must be a central goal of early education.

References

Bandura, A (1994) Self-efficacy, in V.S. Ramachaudran (ed.), *Encylopedia of Human Behaviour, Vol. 4.* New York: Academic Press.

Baumann, N. and Scheffer, D (2010) Seeking flow in the achievement domain: The achievement flow motive behind flow experience, *Motivation and Emotion,* 34.

Baumeister, R., Campbell, J., Krueger, J. and Vohs, K. (2003) Does high self-esteem cause better performance, interpersonal success, happiness, or healthier lifestyles? *Psychological Science in the Public Interest* Vol. 4, No. 1, May 2003, American Psychological Society.

Bronson, M. (2000) *Self-Regulation in Early Childhood: Nature and Nurture.* New York: The Guilford Press.

Carlton, M. and Winsler, A. (1998) Fostering intrinsic motivation in early childhood classrooms, *Early Childhood Education Journal,* 25 (3): 162–163.

Cerasoli, C.P. and Ford, M.T. (2014) Intrinsic motivation, performance, and the mediating role of mastery goal orientation: a test of self-determination theory. *Journal of Psychology* 148(3): 267–86. doi:10.1080/00223980.2013.783778

Claxton, G. (2006) Expanding the capacity to learn: A new end for education? *British Educational Research Association Annual Conference,* 6 September 2006.

Csikszentmihalyi, M. (2000) *Beyond Boredom and Anxiety: Experiencing Flow in Work and Play.* San Francisco: Jossey-Bass.

Dahlberg, G. (2000) Early childhood pedagogy in a changing world: A practice-oriented research project troubling dominant discourses, *Policy, Practice and Politics, NZEI Te Riu Roa Early Childhood Millennium Conference Proceedings,* 19.

Darnon, C., Muller, D., Schrager, S. and Pannuzzo, N. (2006) Mastery and performance goals predict epistemic and relational conflict regulation, *Journal of Educational Psychology,* 98(4): 766–776.

Deci, E. and Ryan, R.M. (1985) *Intrinsic Motivation and Self-determination in human Behavior.* New York: Plenum.

Deci, E. and Ryan, R. (2000) The 'what' and 'why' of goal pursuits: Human needs and the self-determination of behavior, *Psychological Inquiry*, 11(4): 227–268.

Dweck, C. (2006) *Mindset.* New York: Random House.

Dweck, C. and Leggett, E. (1988) A social-cognitive approach to motivation and personality, *Psychological Review*, 95: 256–73.

Elliot, A.J., Thrash, T.M. and Muyarama, K. (2011) A longitudinal analysis of self-regulation and well-being: Avoidance personal goals, avoidance coping, stress generation, and subjective well-being. *Journal of Personality*, 79: 643–674. doi: 10.1111/j.1467-6494.2011.00694.

Gopnik, A., Meltzoff, A. and Kuhl, P. (1999) *How Babies Think.* London: Phoenix.

Gottfried, A., Fleming, J. and Gottfried, A. (2001) Continuity of academic intrinsic motivation from childhood through late adolescence: A longitudinal study, *Journal of Educational Psychology*, 9(1): 3–13.

Grolnick, W., Bridges, L. and Frodi, A. (1984) Maternal control style and the mastery motivation of one-year-olds, *Infant Mental Health Journal*, 5: 72–82.

Grolnick, W., Kurowski C. and Gurland, S. (1999) Family processes and the development of children's self-regulation, *Educational Psychologist*, 34(1): 3–14.

Hall, D. (1995) Children: Hands on, brains off? *The Independent*, 22 October 1995.

Katz, L. (2000) Last class notes, in D. Rothenberg (ed.) *Proceedings of the Lilian Katz Symposium 5 November 2000*, Issues in Early Childhood Education.

Lai, E. (2011) *Motivation: A Literature Review*, Pearson Research Report. http://images.pearsonassessments.com/images/tmrs/Motivation_Review_final.pdf (accessed 11 October 2021).

Laevers, F. (1993) Deep level learning: An exemplary application on the area of physical knowledge, *European Early Childhood Research Journal 1993*, 1(1):53–68.

Laevers, F. (2005) *Deep-level-learning and the Experiential Approach in Early Childhood and Primary Education.* Leuven: University of Leuven, Research Centre for Early Childhood and Primary Education.

Leonard, J.A., Lee, Y. and Schulz, L.E. (2017) Infants make more attempts to achieve a goal when they see adults persist, *Science*, 357(6357): 1290–1294.

Lewis, M., Alessandri, S. and Sullivan, M. (1992) Differences in shame and pride as a function of children's gender and task difficulty, *Child Development*, 63: 630–638.

National Scientific Council on the Developing Child (2018) *Understanding Motivation: Building the brain architecture that supports learning, health, and community participation, Working Paper No. 14.* Retrieved from www.developingchild.harvard.edu

Peters, R. S. (1965) Education as initiation, in R. D. Archambault (ed.), *Philosophical Analysis and Education.* London: Routledge & Kegan Paul.

Perry, N.E. (2013) Understanding classroom processes that support children's self-regulation of learning, *British Journal of Educational Psychology monograph*, 11(10): 45–68.

Ruedy, E. and Nirenberg, S. (1990) *Where Do I Put the Decimal Point? How to conquer Math Anxiety and Increase Your Facility with Numbers.* New York: Henry Holt and Company.

Ryan, R. and Stiller, J. (1991) The social contexts of internalization: Parent and teacher influences on autonomy, motivation and learning, in M.L. Maehr and P. Pitrich (eds) *Advances in Motivation and Achievement: Vol. 7: Goals and Self-regulatory Processes.* Greenwich, CT: Jai Press.

Theodotou, E. (2014) Early years education: Are young students intrinsically or extrinsically motivated towards school activities? A discussion about the effects of rewards on young children's learning, *Research In Teacher Education*, 4(1): 17–21. https://files.eric.ed.gov/fulltext/ED560161.pdf

Timmons, K., Pelletier, J. and Corter, C. (2016) Understanding children's self-regulation within different classroom contexts, *Early Child Development and Care*, 186(2): 249–267, DOI: 10.1080/03004430.2015.1027699

Yarrow, L., Morgan, G., Jennings, K., Harmon, R. and Gaiter, J. (1982) Infants' persistence at tasks: Relationships to cognitive functioning and early experience, *Infant Behavior and Development*, 5(2–4): 131–141.

5 Thinking creatively and critically

Di Chilvers

Chapter summary

- Children's thinking is often seen as superficial and mainly aligned to knowledge and knowing. This chapter shows how young children are competent and capable deep thinkers and learners, using complex strategies in their play and conversational talk.
- It looks at the processes involved in the development of children's creative and critical thinking – through the language of thinking.
- Examples of children's creative and critical thinking are used to make connections between theory, research and practice.

Introduction

Here are two examples of everyday conversations that children have with each other and with adults which make their creativity and critical thinking visible

> Corey and Alfie (6 years old) are having a reflective conversation with Amy, their teacher, whilst looking at a Floor Book from their Reception year when they were 5. They are drawn into some of the pages which documented previous, mathematical learning about subtraction as they played with their favourite dinosaurs, making them disappear and then appear.
>
> Amy: So are you learning about subtraction here?
> Corey: Yes.
> Alfie: We didn't call it subtraction in Reception, we called it 'taking away' in Reception.
> Corey: Yeah (*he laughs*). You're making my memory come back.
>
> (Corey, Alfie and Amy are at Prince Edwards Primary School, Sheffield)

William (4 years old) is talking to Iva (the adult) about the meaning of zero, an interest which began with the 'Zero Project'.

Iva asked the children:	If I have zero friends what does it mean?
William:	'You are lonely'. Don't you have really any friends Iva?
Iva:	I have many friends; I have all of you. Is zero friends a lot or not?
William:	It means no friends!
William counted out loud for himself:	1,2,3,4,5,6,7,8,9 … I have 9 friends. How many friends do you have Iva?
Iva:	I have 7 friends (*she shows her fingers*)
William:	I have much more than you.

(William and Iva are at Puss in Boots Nursery in Camden, London)

These everyday observations of young children engaged in conversations about their play, ideas and questions illustrate well their capacity to become involved in thoughtful, imaginative and creative thinking. While the three EYFS characteristics of 'playing and exploring', 'active learning' and 'creating and thinking critically' may be viewed separately in the documentation, the reality for children (and adults) is that they are all intrinsically meshed together, with connections running between them that are hard to separate out. With this in mind, adults always need to remember that the tangle of young children's thinking, learning and development is there for a reason – it's how they think and learn best. What the three characteristics do is help us to 'untangle' what we have seen and observed in order to make sense of the complexities of children's learning and development, while always remembering that children's thinking needs to remain tangled in order for it to make sense to them. This is all about seeing young children's learning and development as a holistic process.

The characteristic of thinking creatively and critically is 'untangled' further as it is broken down into the following aspects (Early Education 2021: 42):

- **having their own ideas**, which involves children being curious and imaginative, prepared to 'have a go' at solving problems and to find new ways to do things;
- **making links** where children notice patterns in the ways things happen and in their experiences, make predictions about what may happen and test their ideas. Children develop ideas of grouping and categorising, sequencing and cause and effect;
- **working with ideas**, which includes children planning how to approach a task, solve a problem or reach a goal. They check how things are going and can change strategy if appropriate as well as review how well the approach worked.

All these aspects weave together as children play and explore and learn actively. By being authentic partners in thinking and learning, they have a central part to play in their own learning and development. In the observations at the beginning of this chapter we see children having their own ideas, making links and choosing ways to do things. Observations like this are a window into the way children's minds are working and enable us to tune into their thought processes and emerging understanding of the complicated world they inhabit. Their thoughts and ideas are creative and unique to them, which, as Drummond et al. suggest, is a privilege to witness and be part of. 'When we work with children, when we play and talk with them, when we watch them and everything they do, we are witnessing a fascinating and inspiring process: we are seeing young children learn' (Drummond et al. 1993: 5). They go on to suggest that it is through these observations in everyday practice that we think about what we see, and 'strive to understand it and then put our understanding to good use' (p. 5).

The language of thinking

Both before and after birth children's brains develop and their early experiences combine to construct their thinking, understanding and knowledge. There is clear evidence now that children's early experiences – particularly those connected to attachment, nurturing and attunement – will shape their future engagement in learning (Gopnik et al. 1999; Karmiloff-Smith, 2010; Whitebread 2012; Harvard University Center on the Developing Child 2018, 2020). Children's thinking and learning are often viewed and interpreted in isolation from their emotional and social well-being with little understanding of the connections in the brain and the fine networks that are forged through these early experiences. Disconnecting these naturally formed bonds through a compartmentalised view of children's learning, and focusing on what they learn rather than how they learn, creates a superficial and simple view of teaching, and runs the risk of disempowering children as thinkers and learners. Children's social and emotional development supports them in the process of thinking of ideas, solving problems, making links and choosing strategies in all sorts of complex, sophisticated and above all, connected ways. We saw how children make these connections in their conversational talk and play at the beginning of this chapter.

These processes can be described as the child's *language for thinking*, since constructing and then communicating thinking and creative ideas are a form of expression; they are ways of making thinking visible. For example, children who are pre-verbal or have no spoken language can all communicate their thinking through action. It is no coincidence that babies and toddlers have an innate drive and instinctual need to explore, play and follow their spontaneous, 'in the moment', urges. We can see this particularly in early schematic behaviours as children become fascinated with objects that roll, spin and pop up. We can also see it in the children's conversations (above) as they follow their emerging ideas, that are sparked off by each other and supported by the adult.

Creative and critical thinking as a process

The view of thinking and learning as a process is grounded in the theories of Bruner, Vygotsky and Malaguzzi as they made the case for children's thinking unfolding alongside their first-hand experiences, in a social context and as part of their mental architecture (Harvard University Center on the Developing Child 2020), with periods of challenge and struggle which, if supported, build and extend their thinking and learning in meaningful ways. Babies and young children are involved in this process right from the start as they instinctively explore the people, places and things within their immediate world, 'hoovering' up experiences which they then accumulate and add to previous ones. Many readers will be familiar with Reggio Emilia pedagogy where the message is clear: *all* children are competent and creative thinkers and learners. This belief forms the basis of their early years philosophy which includes the principle that children's development grows from their emergent and ongoing ideas as part of a process of co-constructing learning (Edwards et al. 1998; Rinaldi 2006).

In this process of co-construction, which is more effective when undertaken in collaboration with other children and adults, children's thinking is tried and tested with problems created and solved in a familiar and safe context. If we watch this process, we see the unique ways in which children are creatively making sense of their world in genuinely thoughtful ways, as Corey, Alfie and William do through their conversations at the beginning of this chapter. It makes perfect sense for William to say that Iva will be lonely if she doesn't have any friends when they are talking about the meaning of zero; a thought which she values and respects through her considered response. 'Creativity is part of the process through which children begin to find out they have something unique to "say" in words, dance, music, or hatching out their theory' (Bruce 2004: 14).

The process of creative and critical thinking has been unravelled in various theories in the early twentieth century, and more recently in work undertaken by Robson (2006), Fumoto et al. (2012) Craft (2012) and Chilvers (2013). Robson (2006: 172) builds on the ideas of Meadows (1993) and Claxton (1998) when she describes the creative process of thinking in four steps: **familiarisation, incubation, insight** and **verification** (see Table 5.1). This is not a neat sequential process; it is a messy weaving together of ideas and experiences which, as they flow, create more complex thinking and understanding. This is the creative and critical thinking process which will be used throughout life. However, while the four steps of familiarisation, incubation, insight and verification offer us a framework for understanding children's creating and thinking critically there are other connected elements to consider.

The language of the imagination

Imagination is fundamental to children's creative and critical thinking; it is a significant part of the language of thinking which enables children to create and visualise their own ideas in unique and imaginative ways, as well as being

Table 5.1 Familiarisation, incubation, insight and verification

	Explanation	In practice
Familiarisation	Information gathering, acquiring expertise, testing out ideas Becoming familiar with people, places and things and finding out about the immediate world around you Collaborating and playing with others as a social, communicative process	We can clearly see these actions and thoughts as children play and experiment Babies sensory exploration of objects as they put everything into their mouths; toddlers repetitive actions, curiosity and beginning to question by pointing and asking why?; older children puzzling out and problem solving to find out how to make things work and recreate their ideas Corey, Alfie and William are interacting and shaping their ideas as they talk – one child's idea and understandings spark off another's
Incubation	A period of absorption, reflection and thinking; taking time to process the idea or information and make sense of it in order to make it your own. Time to generate even more ideas, develop your own perspective and have an opportunity to think about your thinking This can often be a solitary process where children digest what they have experienced. Bruce (2004) refers to this as incubating and hatching your ideas with an important period of 'simmering'	Babies, toddlers and young children all need the time and space to think, play and repeat. It is important to make sure that they have the time and space to do this both on their own and with others Observation of children's facial expressions, body posture and complete involvement as they ponder and mull over their actions and thinking will give us the clues to their creativity, as long as we are observing them while they are engrossed in their own activities Corey, Alfie and William have clearly incubated and simmered their ideas, digesting the information they already have, thinking about and trying to make sense of it by asking thoughtful questions

	Explanation	In practice
Insight	A connection is made and children reach that moment of 'illumination' or 'insight' This could happen in a flash or may be more of a gentle unfolding of understanding; in either case the child's thinking has deepened	Observation of child-led play and activities (including babies and toddlers) shows us the moment when something has happened. We saw this moment of 'illumination' very clearly as Corey happily points out 'You're making my memory come back'. With babies and toddlers, insight often comes with actions, e.g. knowing that the doll has not completely disappeared when mummy hides it behind her back
Verification	Children check out their thinking and re-test it in other contexts in order to establish and refine their understanding	Children (including babies and toddlers) use play to verify their thinking and understanding. If we observe how children are interpreting their thinking through their play we can verify our understanding (and judgements) as to their progress. For example William in his conversation with Iva is using his previously acquired understanding and experiences to inform his thinking and his mature sensitivity to the situation

able to engage in complex processes of thinking which involve memory, perception and abstract thinking. By deconstructing William's conversation with Iva, we can gain an insight into these complex processes and develop a better understanding of why being able to play and talk in an imaginative way is essential 'brain exercise' for becoming a creative and critical thinker.

The 'zero project' began as a possibility question posed by Iva: 'What is zero and what does it mean?'. The question becomes a provocation for thinking and encouraging the children to have their own ideas and imaginative possibilities of the concept of zero which they talk about together at length. Duffy (1998) explains this process as children visualising and creating exciting possibilities from the ideas they have in order to make meaning of their thinking; a creative process which is essential to creators of IT software, innovative design and engineering. If there are no limits on children's imagination and their creative possibilities then their thinking can flow as they familiarise and incubate the experience.

Csikszentmihalyi (1996) has written at length about the 'state of flow' in humans' ability to become so engrossed in what they are doing that they become unaware of time, cannot be distracted and are fully focused on the task in hand. It is at moments like this that children's thinking and learning move into another dimension and become more meaningful, eventually leading to higher levels of 'mastery' and understanding. Laevers (2005) has also made the connection between children's involvement in their play/activities and their flow of concentration, persistence and energy, which he describes as 'intense mental activity' leading to deeper levels of thinking and learning. (See Chapter 4 for more on the importance of involvement and persistence.)

It is through imaginative play that children make meaning of their (and others') ideas and are able to think things through as they simmer or incubate their thinking and refine and extend what they know. Claxton (2000) refers to children having a 'learning toolkit' which expands throughout life and contains the critical components of being a confident and capable 'learner'. He includes imagination (which he describes as 'the ability to extend what we know and can do by creating imaginary worlds.') in the tool kit for the following reasons:

> You can play and push things to the limit and test your understanding to destruction. You can weave new patterns inside your mind from the different bits of information that you've picked up from the world around you.
>
> (Claxton 2000: 6)

The combination of the flow of thinking, deep involvement and imagination all contribute to the child's repertoire of learning, deepening their understanding and moving their learning into much more sophisticated zones of thinking, particularly sustained shared thinking. For example, as William and Iva's conversation develops and she asks, 'If I have zero friends what does it mean?', William becomes concerned about Iva being lonely and how important it is to have friends. His thinking is supported through imagining, in abstract form, counting out loud, the number of friends he has compared to Iva and being sensitive to Iva's feelings and well-being. Siraj-Blatchford et al. (2002) explain this collaborative, co-constructed process as 'when an adult and a child or two children work together in an intellectual way to solve a problem, clarify a concept, evaluate activities or extend a narrative' (p. 8).

The REPEY project (Siraj-Blatchford et al. 2002: 12) gave clear evidence that child-initiated play alongside 'teacher-initiated group work' were the 'main vehicles for learning', especially if they were embedded in play that had been started by the child/children. Other research (Siraj-Blatchford 2008; Whitebread 2012; Fisher 2016) has shown us that young children become more involved and engrossed in learning if they are encouraged and allowed to follow their interests, either as a group or individually. When this happens, they will concentrate for much longer periods, persist at challenges and look for ways to do things by using reasoning and problem-solving skills.

Imaginative play – moving from concrete to symbolic thinking

The language of imaginative thinking takes children from their current, in the moment, concrete experiences, to those which are much more sophisticated and abstract; the roots of this being in children's play: 'the projection into an imaginary world stretches their conceptual abilities and involves a development in their abstract thought. The complexity involved in this process makes imagination the highest level of early development (Vygotsky 1978)' (Duffy 1998: 53).

The complexity begins early on as children represent their ideas through play, for example an older baby plays hidey-boo and claps to show enjoyment, repeating the game by covering their eyes, or a toddler begins to feed the dolly and rock it to sleep (see Chapter 3 for more detail on this process). For older children, the play becomes more complex and imaginative as objects and materials are given meaning. For example, the box is a roller coaster, a piece of fabric becomes an invisible cloak and the red water is a potion. Children become increasingly creative in the ways that they attach meaning to objects, as long as the objects leave room for the imagination. They are learning about the ways in which meaning can be attached to all kinds of things.

Children then need to make the connection between their own meanings and marks/symbols and those which are created by the culture and systems around them. For example, cultures imbue meaning into symbols which represent sounds, letters and words, so the word 'house' is agreed to mean a place you might live, though it becomes more complicated when they are also called 'bungalows', 'terraces' and 'flats', etc. but generally everyone understands what these words mean. There is also the symbolic language of mathematics, music and the modern abstractness of text messaging. Children have to make sense of the meaning and not just the word and they have to learn how to read and write using the agreed symbols. The more opportunities that children have to think flexibly and play imaginatively in this representational way, the more confidently they can make the leap from concrete to symbolic forms of thinking.

Children have a complex system of symbols with which to become familiar yet they eagerly embrace the challenges involved by being curious, motivated and connected to wanting to make sense of it all. Playing imaginatively is one of the most important opportunities we can provide to help them in this quest; however, imaginative play is often marginalised and seen as a frivolous activity which you can engage in when all the 'real work' is done. Even when there is clear evidence to support the value of play (Ofsted 2015), many children are channelled early into the formal aspects of literacy and numeracy at the very time when they need to be following the pathways of familiarisation, incubation, insight and verification. Some questions to reflect on are:

- What status does imaginative play have in your setting or school?
- What opportunities are there for all the children to engage in imaginative play both indoors and outdoors?
- Whose imagination are you following – the children's or your own? Who decides?
- How much time are children given to think about and incubate their imaginative ideas?
- Are the materials you offer open-ended with imaginative possibilities?
- Are children using imaginative language and asking imaginative and creative questions like Corey, Alfie and William?
- How often are children able to reflect upon and revisit their thinking like Corey and Alfie as they look at the Floor Book together?

The language of reflection – being creative and critical

Creative thinking could be described as the zone in which children's ideas and thoughts blossom and emerge in unique and genuine ways, especially through rich and varied imaginative play, while critical thinking is more aligned to the processes that support creative thinking. Both types of thinking require opportunities to reflect and think in a metacognitive way.

Metacognition can be explained as 'thinking about thinking' (Robson 2006: 82), 'knowing what to do when you don't know what to do' (Claxton 1999) and 'spontaneous wonderings' (Donaldson 1978). It is how children become aware of themselves as thinkers and how they reflect on their thinking, but in order to do this they have to have their thinking and ideas recognised and acknowledged by the people around them.

Metacognition was evident as Corey and Alfie looked at the Floor Book together, reflecting on their thinking and learning from the previous year. Reflection and metacognition become a cycle which deepens critical thinking through making connections in the brain. As we saw, the boys are confident with their new language of 'subtraction' recognising that the term 'taking away' was a more simplistic term used when they were younger.

Reflection is an integral part of pedagogy in Reggio Emilia philosophy where children constantly share and discuss their ideas and thinking in collaborative partnerships; metacognitive discussions are a regular part of the day and emerge out of the children's current ideas. The following is a conversation between a group of children (all aged 5) in a Reggio Emilia pre-school. They are talking about the city and how it is connected through the piazzas or squares.

Giacomo: In the squares there are people talking

Simone: There are pretty squares and ugly ones. Then there are some squares for parked cars and for soccer players

Giacomo: I think they don't work well because the people don't know where to be

Then they discuss the role of the streets

Simone: Cities are all connected by the streets and the railroads, right. Giacomo?

Giacomo: Well, yeah, the streets are important for keeping the city together and for making it work

Emiliano: We need to see if it's all connected

Simone: Like in real cities

Giacomo concludes that they 'need to make sure that the whole city is connected and that nobody gets lost.'

The boys' discussion and co-construction makes them think about some complex social and strategic issues – how to make the roads work! They are busy talking, reflecting and symbolising their ideas in drawing and mapping out the roads, the piazzas and the city of Reggio Emilia. They bounce ideas backwards and forwards and even ask each other questions to verify their thinking. These metacognitive discussions begin early on in the Reggio pre-schools and are probably one of the main reasons why the children, in the main, are such creative and critical thinkers as they are supported to follow their own ideas and their flow of thought.

In Reggio pedagogy, reflective practice and metacognitive thinking are also supported through the process of documentation, where children's unfolding ideas and hypotheses are captured through a process of observation, documenting the flow of children's play/activities as a narrative, interpreting what has been observed by making informed judgements and keeping children's thinking, interests, ideas and talk central. The documentation weaves together teaching, learning, assessment and planning to make the process of thinking and understanding relevant and meaningful to the children as Rinaldi (in

Giudici et al. 2001: 84) explains that it is impossible to document without observing and interpreting:

> Observation, documentation and interpretation are woven together into what I would define as a 'spiral movement', in which none of these actions can be separated out from the others. By means of documenting, the thinking – or the interpretation – of the documenter becomes tangible and capable of being interpreted.

In practice, the process of documentation is undertaken with the children; for example as the children continued to explore their city of Reggio, the practitioners were recording the conversations they had, taking sequences of photographs to document the narrative of the children's thinking as it evolved, photocopying drawings and maps in stages as the children kept coming back to add more and refine them and generally gathering together evidence of the children's ideas, conversations and thinking. This was then brought together by the practitioners to reflect upon and decide ways in which to support and extend the thinking. It is then re-presented to the children and referred to as they take their learning forwards. The children reflect on previous experiences, discuss them and move onto other ideas in a cycle of metacognitive thinking just as Corey and Alfie have done with the Floor Book. This review process is also central to the HighScope approach (Holt 2010) and illustrates very well how practitioners can effectively support the processes involved in the EYFS strand of creating and thinking critically – 'working with ideas' (critical thinking) – (Early Education 2021: 54):

- planning, making decisions about how to approach a task, solve a problem and reach a goal;
- checking how well their activities are going;
- flexibly changing strategy as needed;
- reviewing how well the approach worked.

The language of possibility thinking

Craft (2010: 20) describes possibility thinking as 'allowing us to transform *what is* to *what might be*' (original emphasis) in order to develop ideas and thinking through a process of questioning, self-expression, imagining, collaborative view sharing and taking risks.' For example, the possibility question 'What is zero and what does it mean?' empowers the children to *play* with their ideas and possibilities, then rephrase them as William did in his conversation with Iva. Possibility thinking and possibility questions become an important tool for both adults and children to grow creative and critical thinking for lifelong learning.

The seven points shown in Table 5.2 have been identified by Craft (Craft et al. 2007; Craft 2012) as being the key features of possibility thinking; they

Table 5.2 Seven key features of possibility thinking

Feature	How does this connect to the examples?
Question posing and question responding – finding the perfect possibility question which is neither too narrow (closed) nor too broad (too general), both of which would affect children's creative and critical thinking. Questions have different roles: Leading questions will drive the children's activity – with more control from the question asker (child or adult)	In the 'zero project' Iva asks the children a leading question 'If you have zero friends what does it mean?' this sparks the children's thinking. She then uses a follow-through question 'Is zero friends a lot or not?'
Service questions enable children to develop strategies to help them undertake the leading question Follow-through questions are the finer questions which help to fulfil an idea	William asks a service question so that he can find out more to inform his answer, 'Don't you have really any friends Iva?' which Iva follows up with 'I have 7 friends' and shows 7 fingers
Play – which is open-ended, creative and imaginative with adults who participate and become involved as play partners, 'offering possibilities in terms of where children might take their play' (Craft 2012: 57). Play with high cognitive challenge such as playing with the concept of zero on the exploration table Providing props, continuous provision, plenty of time and space	The children have been playing with materials on the 'exploration table' which offer many open-ended possibilities for talking and thinking about zero. The adult observed the children as they followed their creative ideas through their play and, collaborative dialogue
Immersion – or incubation. Time to become lost in the play and involved in a safe and secure enabling environment with practitioners who respect, support and value children's ideas and thinking	The children's ideas about zero are followed by the adults who write them down and take photographs so they can document their creative and critical thinking. These are shared back with the children through a learning story or floor book with time to talk and engage in further creative and critical thinking. Any pre-defined planning is dropped in order to follow the flow of talking and thinking

(Continued)

Table 5.2 (Continued)

Feature	How does this connect to the examples?
Innovation – or insight. Children make connections between their ideas which support the development of their understanding and take their thinking forward	Corey and Alfie make many connections as they reflect on their previous learning in the Floor Book. They reach a eureka moment which is captured as Corey laughs and says: 'Yeah. You're making my memory come back'
Being imaginative. See above – children need to engage in imagining what might be – the possibilities. Taking ownership of their ideas and translating them through their play	Thinking about what 'zero' means is an imaginative exploration to experience and understand a complex concept. As the children played and talked together, they imagined all sorts of scenarios including their thoughts about Iva and her friends. These are the children's ideas translated through their talk and play
Self-determination and risk taking. Children become deeply involved and self-motivated with adults encouraging children to try things out and 'have a go' in a safe and supportive enabling environment	We see and hear Alfie, Corey and William's determination, involvement and motivation as they imagine, think and talk in open-ended and creative ways

Source: Adapted from Craft et al. (2007) and Craft (2012).

all connect to the examples of children's creating and thinking critically at the beginning of this chapter. Craft's research has shown that where children were able to weave in and out of these features in their play and early experiences, their creativity and critical thinking moved to deeper levels of involvement and learning, particularly in being able to communicate and generate more ideas and discuss them with others, become self-motivated and self-determined, engage in collaborative thinking and learning and take their ideas forward into unknown territory. Children had a sense of agency and control over their learning which supported their belief and confidence in themselves as creative and critical thinkers (Craft et al. 2007; Craft 2012).

The language of conversation to support the co-construction of thinking

In the examples at the beginning of the chapter the children articulate thinking through their inquisitive conversations and the questions they have for each other and the adults. While spoken language isn't the only way to communicate your thinking (remember the 'hundred languages of children' – Edwards et al. 1998) it is certainly one of the best ways to share what is happening in your head in a social and reflective way. Talking clarifies thinking and can lead to the generation of even more ideas, which in itself is creative and the kind of lifelong learning skill that all children need to have in the present and the future.

Conversational talk (Hirsh-Pasek 2018) is particularly influential in constructing creative and critical thinking because of its informality and context in everyday experiences which are rich in opportunities. Importantly, the conversations which *children start* are usually the ones that will develop into powerful and creative learning experiences. (See Chapter 7 for examples of how to support children's conversation.) They mainly originate when children are involved in play, cannot be predicted or planned for, but provide a good foundation for learning which can be extended by the children or a sensitive adult who has observed, listened and then participated (Siraj-Blatchford et al. 2002). It is the 'serve and return' (Harvard University Center on the Developing Child 2018) model of co-construction which Loris Malaguzzi (Edwards et al. 1998) describes as a game of 'ping pong' (table tennis) and is created when the conversation flows from one aspect to another, with the participants batting ideas, possibility questions and thinking to each other in such a way that no one misses the ball! As a result, creative thinking is co-constructed in a situation of 'joint involvement' or sustained shared thinking.

The following points, adapted from Chilvers 2006, highlight some of the finer detail of creative, conversational language where children can:

- **formulate ideas:** talking generates ideas and thinking at any age. A baby will babble with delight as she controls a game of 'I drop the rattle and you pick it up' and a 3-year-old will chatter as he tries to work out how to make the wheels turn on the car he has just made. Sensitive support from an adult and repetition of single words will help this babble and chatter become words and logical thought.

- **confirm and clarify what they think:** by talking about experiences, including learning, young children can reaffirm themselves and gain confidence in what they are doing. They can check and re-check their ideas collaboratively.

- **reflect:** speaking involves reflection – thinking, for example, about past experiences or what they have just done and engaging in conversation. 'I remember when …' or 'When I was a baby did I …?', 'The last time I did this it …' or 'You're making my memory come back …'.

- **make their ideas and thinking visible:** in a conversation the child's ideas and thinking are made visible and are usually related to something which is of interest to them and based in the reality and context of their lives, e.g. 'Why does the snow disappear?' Or 'Why can't I jump as high as the cat?' It is only by giving children endless opportunities to talk that we can begin to understand what is going on in their heads. We also need to pay attention to where they are going next to support their developing language and thought – often by modelling the process ourselves.

- **build their confidence and self-esteem:** confidence and self-esteem arise out of being listened to and accepted. One of the key ways in which this happens is through children's conversation. If children's own conversations are accepted, they quickly learn that their views, ideas and talk are valued. Through conversation children gain affirmation and the courage to contribute as well as being able to express their own needs, wishes and thoughts. They will become more in touch with themselves and develop a sense of positive well-being.

Observing the language of thinking

If we are expecting children to become more reflective and engage in metacognition as part of the development of their creative and critical thinking, then it seems only fair that the people who work with them also pursue this goal. Observing children's thinking, ideas and interests unfold is one of the most effective ways to do this as adults are involved in the reflective observation cycle seen in Figure 5.1 (Early Education 2012). This cycle is explored in more detail in Chapter 6.

Observation is the adult's opportunity to watch children's creative and critical thinking unfold, which usually happens in moments which are spontaneous, unplanned and start from the child/children. If we really want to understand how the child is thinking, and what they know and understand, we just have to watch them and document it in some way.

Figure 5.1 The Observation, Assessment and Planning Cycle

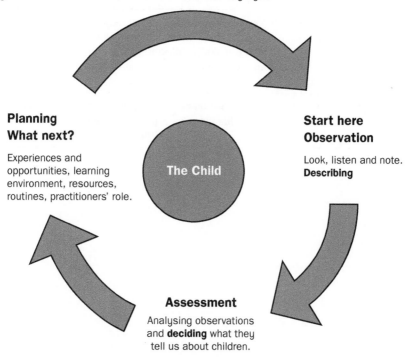

Planning
What next?

Experiences and
opportunities, learning
environment, resources,
routines, practitioners' role.

The Child

Start here
Observation

Look, listen and note.
Describing

Assessment
Analysing observations
and **deciding** what they
tell us about children.

Source: Early Education (2012). (Reproduced under the terms of the open Government Licence.)

> Integral to achieving this, it seems to us, is reflective practice, in which *teachers stand back,* to consider what children are telling them though their engagement in the classroom. It also involves *documenting these moments* in some way.
>
> (Craft et al. 2007: 9, original emphasis)

It is important to remember that it is the process or narrative of the child/children's creating and thinking critically which needs to be observed and recorded. Taking single snapshots at the beginning and/or end will not illustrate the whole picture; it is the 'bit in the middle' that tells the story of the thinking and provides those incredible moments when you have witnessed children reaching a point of understanding and real mastery.

Assessment is the way that we make sense of what we have seen. At this point we are trying to unpick the holistic nature of children's thinking, development and learning; looking for the language of thinking as well as the 'tools' children use for thinking, such as problem setting and problem solving, hypothesising and reasoning, asking questions and possibility thinking. It is only then that we can make an informed, professional judgement about children's progress, especially about *how* they are learning as well as what they are learning. Table 5.3 may be helpful in clarifying your own thinking and understanding of these critical aspects of young children's development.

Table 5.3   Observing the language of thinking

As you observe children in their play, indoors and outdoors, did you see children using the language of thinking? Note down what you saw, take sequenced photographs or film and use this to make an informed judgement about children's progress. Think about the following and discuss it together with others in your setting or school.

Aspects/processes	What does this mean?	Did you see this happening as you observed the children? What did it look like?
Familiarisation		
Incubation		
Insight		
Verification		
Imaginative play		
Imaginative play – moving from concrete to symbolic thinking		
Reflection		
Metacognition		
Possibility thinking		
Conversational language and co-construction		

Planning is the way in which children's development is supported and taken forward and should be a collaborative partnership approach between the adult leading the way and planning play, activities and focused groups and children initiating ideas and being creative. If this doesn't happen and the adult is planning and structuring every minute of the day there will be few, if any, opportunities for children to undertake their own journeys in creative and critical thinking.

Final thoughts

The language of children's thinking is the foundation of children's creative and critical thinking, on which they can grow in confidence, self-assurance and well-being with a real belief in themselves as competent and capable thinkers and learners. They are also the lifelong learning attitudes, skills and dispositions we would want people to have for the future. 'In the early 21st century we recognise that being creative is one of the defining characteristics of all human beings' (Craft 2010: 2).

> **Key messages of this chapter**
>
> - Children's creative and critical thinking is at the centre of their development and learning.
> - The language of creativity and critical thinking is visible in many forms which all weave together through children's imaginative play, conversational serve and return talk, co-construction, reflection, metacognition and possibility thinking.
> - Adults working with young children need to be creative and critical thinkers reflecting on how children are developing and learning through observing, interpreting and understanding learning

References

Bruce, T. (2004) *Cultivating Creativity in Babies, Toddlers and Young Children*. London: Hodder and Stoughton.

Chilvers, D. (2013) *Creating and Thinking Critically: A Practical Guide to How Babies and Young Children Learn*. London: Practical Pre-school Books.

Chilvers, D. (2006) *Young Children Talking: The Art of Conversation and Why Children Need to Chatter*. London: Early Education.

Claxton, G. (1998) *Hare Brain, Tortoise Mind*. London: Fourth Estate.

Claxton, G. (1999) *Wise Up: Learning to Live the Learning Life*. Stafford: Network Educational Press Ltd.

Claxton, G. (2000) A sure start for an uncertain world. Transcript of a lecture, *Early Education Journal*, Spring 2000. London: Early Education.

Craft, A. (2010) Teaching for possibility thinking – what is it and how do we do it? *Learning Matters*, 15(1): 19–23.

Craft, A. (2012) Child-initiated play and professional creativity: Enabling four-year-olds' possibility thinking, *Thinking Skills and Creativity Journal*, 7: 48–61.

Craft, A., Cremin, T., Burnard, P. and Chappell, K. (2007) Developing creative learning through possibility thinking with children aged 3–7, in A. Craft, T. Cremin and P. Burnard (eds) *Creative Learning 3–11 and How We Document It*. London: Trentham Books.

Csikszentmihalyi, M. (1996) *Creativity*. New York: HarperCollins.

Donaldson, M. (1978) *Children's Minds*. London: Fontana Press.

Drummond, M.J., Rouse, D. and Pugh, G. (1993) *Making Assessment Work: Values and Principles in Assessing Young Children's Learning*. London: NES Arnold/National Children's Bureau.

Duffy, B. (1998) *Supporting Creativity and Imagination in the Early Years*. Buckingham: Open University Press.

Early Education (2012) *Development Matters*. London: Early Education.

Early Education (2021) *Birth to 5 Matters: Non-statutory guidance for the Early Years Foundation Stage*, published on behalf of the Early Years Coalition, St.Albans: Early Education. Available at: www.birthto5matters.org.uk/wp-content/uploads/2021/04/Birthto5Matters-download.pdf (accessed 23 April 2021).

Edwards, C., Gandini, L. and Forman, G. (1998) *The Hundred Languages of Children, The Reggio Emilia Approach – Advanced Reflections,* 2nd edn. Westport, CT: Ablex Publishing.

Fisher. J. (2016) *Interacting or Interfering? Improving Interactions in the Early Years.* Maidenhead: Open University Press.

Fumoto, H., Robson,S., Greenfield, S. and Hargreaves, D. (2012) *Young Children's Creative Thinking.* London: Sage.

Giudici, C., Rinaldi, C. and Krechevsky, M. (eds) (2001) *Making Learning Visible. Children as Individual and Group Learners,* Reggio Emilia, Reggio Children (www.reggiochildren.it).

Gopnik, A., Meltzoff, A. and Khul, P. (1999) *How Babies Think: The Science of Early Childhood.* London: Weidenfeld and Nicolson.

Harvard University Center on the Developing Child (2018) *Serve and Return,* online resource. Available at: https://developingchild.harvard.edu/science/key-concepts/serve-and-return/ (accessed 20 March 2021).

Harvard University Center on the Developing Child (2020) *Brain Architecture,* online resource. Available at: https://developingchild.harvard.edu/science/key-concepts/brain-architecture/ (accessed (20 April 2021).

Hirsh-Pasek, K. (2018) PEDAL Seminar, A Prescription for Play: Why play fosters social and cognitive development, University of Cambridge. Available at: https://sms.cam.ac.uk/media/2833460 (accessed 20 April 2021).

Holt, V. (2010) *Bringing the High Scope Approach to Your Early Years Practice,* 2nd edn. London: Routledge.

Karmiloff-Smith, A. (2010) Neuro-imaging of the developing brain, taking 'developing' seriously, *Human Brain Mapping* 31:934–41. Available at: https://onlinelibrary.wiley.com/doi/epdf/10.1002/hbm.21074 (accessed 5 May 2021).

Laevers, F. (2005) *Deep-level-learning and the Experiential Approach in Early Childhood and Primary Education.* Leuven: Katholieke Universiteit.

Meadows, S. (1993) *The Child as Thinker.* London: Routledge.

Ofsted (2015) Teaching and play in the early years – a balancing act? A good practice survey to explore perceptions of teaching and play in the early years (Reference no: 150085). Available at: https://assets.publishing.service.gov.uk/government/uploads/system/uploads/attachment_data/file/444147/Teaching-and-play-in-the-early-years-a-balancing-act.pdf (accessed 20April 2021).

Rinaldi, C. (2006) *In Dialogue with Reggio Emilia: Listening, Researching and Learning.* London: Routledge.

Robson, S. (2006) *Developing Thinking and Understanding in Young Children.* London: Routledge.

Siraj-Blatchford, I. (2008) Understanding the relationship between curriculum, pedagogy and progression in learning in early childhood, *Hong Kong Journal of Early Childhood,* 7(2): 3–13.

Siraj-Blatchford, I., Sylva, K., Muttock, S., Gilden, R. and Bell, D. (2002) *Researching Effective Pedagogy in the Early Years (REPEY),* DfES Research Report RR356. London: DfES.

Vygtosky, L. (1978) *Mind in Society: The Development of Higher Psychological Processes.* Cambridge, MA: Harvard University.

Whitebread, D. (2012) *Developmental Psychology and Early Childhood Education.* London: Sage.

6 Observing, assessing and planning for how young children are learning

Judith Dancer and Helen Moylett

Chapter summary

- This chapter explores the observation, assessment and planning cycle and how it can support and extend children's learning.
- It focuses particularly on the assessment of *how* children learn and provides opportunities to reflect on practical examples demonstrating the principles which underpin effective formative and summative assessment.
- Flexible planning, which keeps at its heart the need to tune into children's current enthusiasms and fascinations, is illustrated and discussed as well as the implications of engaging parents in statutory summative assessment at age 2 and at the end of the Reception year.

Introduction

So how do playing and exploring, active learning and thinking creatively and critically (the characteristics of effective learning) fit in to the 'big picture' of observation, assessment and planning and the principles which underpin the process?

The diagram on page 3 of *Development Matters* (Early Education 2012; reproduced as Figure 6.1 below) gives a clear overview of the observation, assessment and planning process, starting with, and *keeping* the child at the heart. Observation is the starting point for all assessment and planning.

Observing: describing what is happening

Assessing: analysing observations and deciding what they tell us about children

Figure 6.1 The Observation, Assessment and Planning Cycle

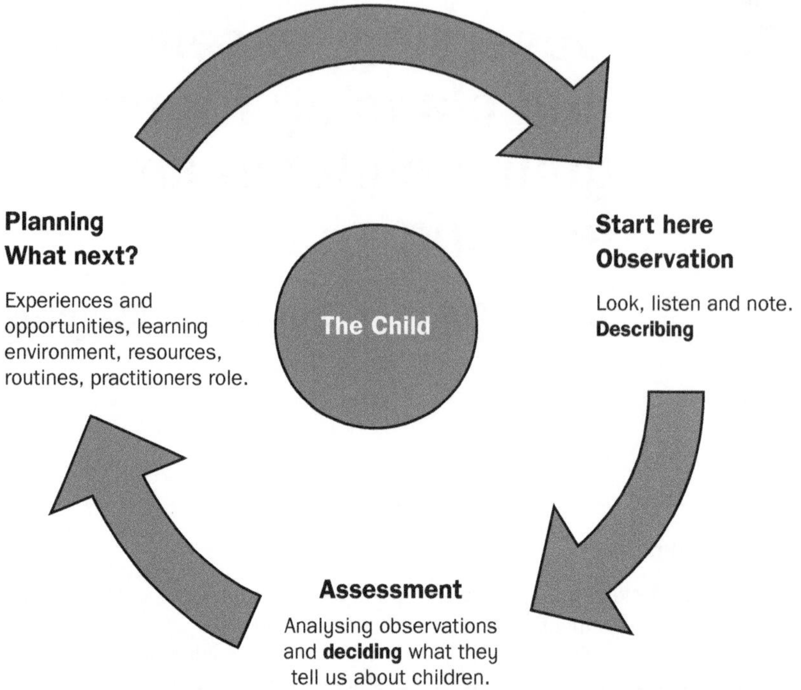

**Planning
What next?**

Experiences and
opportunities, learning
environment, resources,
routines, practitioners role.

The Child

**Start here
Observation**

Look, listen and note.
Describing

Assessment

Analysing observations
and **deciding** what they
tell us about children.

Source: Early Education (2012). (Reproduced under the terms of the Open Government Licence.)

Planning: what next? Using observations and assessments to inform: experiences and opportunities; the indoor and outdoor learning environments; routines; resources and the role of the practitioner.

As we consider how the characteristics of effective learning fit within this observation, assessment and planning process, it is worth reflecting on how the process can be interpreted for both formative and summative assessment.

- **Formative assessment**, or assessment for learning, is where assessment is part of and supports learning and teaching.
- **Summative assessment**, the periodic summary of formative assessments, which makes statements about children's achievements.

The cycle is often thought of in terms of written observations and assessments used to inform planning for the next day or the next week. But, as was identified in Learning, Playing and Interacting (DCSF 2009: 23), we need to think about how the process works on an ongoing, daily basis for babies and young children who are very much learning in the here and now and the adult makes a difference where children are, seizing the 'teachable moment':

By using this cycle on a moment-by-moment basis, the adult will be always alert to individual children (observation), always thinking about what it tells us about their thinking (assessment), always ready to respond using appropriate strategies at the right moment supporting children's well-being and learning (planning for the next moment).

Principles underpinning effective observation, assessment and planning

So, the very first thing we need to do is to keep the child at the heart of the observation, assessment and planning process. We need to observe children, analyse our observations in order to plan to build on what they know and can do, and support the ways in which they are learning. The second thing we need to remember is that observation, assessment and planning should not generate mountains of paperwork or electronic data. Third, the process should not detract from the core business of working with young children – that of extending their learning, interacting and offering appropriate challenge and support. As the EYFS Statutory Framework 2021, 2.2 clearly states: 'Assessment should not entail prolonged breaks from interaction with children nor require excessive paperwork'.

A fourth key principle is the need to involve families in the observation, assessment and planning process – not as passive 'receivers' of a summative assessment at key stages. It is worth revisiting Principles into Practice card 3.1 (DCSF 2008a), which reminds us that the child should be the starting point for all observation, assessment and planning, and that families should be involved:

Starting with the child

- observe children to find out about their needs, what they are interested in and what they can do
- note children's responses in different situations
- analyse your observation and highlight children's achievements or their need for further support
- involve parents as part of the ongoing observation and assessment process

---

If these four key principles are kept at the forefront, everything else should fall into place. Practitioners should not be led by formats and paperwork, and observations should certainly not be content driven. There is a danger that if the focus of summative assessment is solely on *what* children learn, *how* they are learning may be neglected and yet we know that the foundations of all learning is being laid in children's playing and exploring, active learning and thinking critically and creatively. (See all previous chapters).

If we are to be able to give a clear summary of how children are learning, then observations of how they are learning need to be core to everyday practice. Most local authorities give a strong steer on the importance of this. Many have developed pro formas and guidance to support the Progress Check at Two and the majority include not only the three prime areas, but also a commentary on the characteristics of effective learning. In some local authorities this has become part of a suite of materials supporting practitioners throughout the EYFS, offering guidance for summative assessment, based on observation, until the end of the Reception year and emphasising the importance of the characteristics of effective learning as well as including families in the process.

Observing

If observations of the child are at the heart of the observation, assessment and planning process, we need to consider how this works in practice. Practitioners may use many formats for recording what they see and hear children doing. Some of these observations may be long, planned observations and, as is increasingly popular, many may be 'spontaneous', short observations of key moments of significant achievement.

But sometimes we are so focused on 'learning intentions', that we miss the key, significant learning that is going on all around us. We may be so busy 'observing' how children are ordering numbers from zero to ten, as they peg number cards they have made onto a washing line as part of an adult planned experience, that we fail to observe how they are approaching the process. So we may miss:

Flavia: Piling the number cards up, then collecting another set from the maths learning zone and matching the numerals – putting a '2' with a '2' and a '3' with a '3'. Then shuffling all the cards and dealing them out to friends.

Serge: Sorting the cards into piles of 'even' and 'odd' numbers – counting in twos out loud. Walking away, still chanting 'two, four, six, eight, who do we appreciate?'.

Charlotte: Singing 'Ten in a Bed', as she fixes the cards to the line, and calling to Charlene 'come and play 10 in a bed with me, bring the babies'. Spending over 20 minutes pegging up the cards, laying them in a row and matching one toy to each, singing and laughing.

Rifat: Struggling with using the pegs to fix the cards onto the washing line. Looking hard at the pegs, practising opening and closing them with two hands, and watching other children. Then having another go and beaming as the card remains fixed to the line.

Milo: Refusing to join in with the activity when invited by the practitioner, but later returning, when the adult and group of children leave. Looking at the cards and fixing the '4' card onto the line – between the '7' and '8', saying 'Four, I four'.

So, in focusing so narrowly on the planned learning intentions, a practitioner could miss significant learning in other areas of learning and development – Rifat's physical development, Charlotte's development in the expressive arts, Serge's personal, social and emotional development. What's more, really important information about *how* children learn could be missed too. If we look harder, we can see that we could make comments about the children's approaches to learning:

Flavia: The way that Flavia is thinking and learning – *'having her own ideas'* about how to use the resource and putting them into practice **(thinking creatively and critically)**.

Serge: The way Serge is thinking and *'making links'* in his learning – how he is thinking about the oral 'counting in twos' activity earlier in the week **(thinking creatively and critically)**.

Charlotte: The way Charlotte continues to be *motivated* by a task she sets herself – how she is *'involved and concentrating'* for a prolonged period **(active learning)**.

Rifat: The way Rifat exhibits his *motivation* – how he *'keeps on trying'* and *'enjoys achieving what he sets out to do'* **(active learning)**.

Milo: The way Milo becomes *engaged* in the experience, after initial reluctance – being willing to *'have a go'* away from the group **(playing and exploring)**.

So those practitioners who are really watching and listening to children, with eyes wide open and ears alert, can find out a lot about *how* they are learning as well as what they are learning, as long as flexibility is intrinsic to the ethos of the setting. They can see *how* children are playing and exploring **(engagement)**, learning actively **(motivation)** and thinking creatively and critically **(thinking)** – in short, how they exhibit being 'ready, willing and able' to learn.

It is worth reflecting on the fascinating 'Invisible Gorilla' experiment (Chabris and Simons 2011). In the original video footage, observers are asked to focus on a particular task – counting the number of basketball passes. Part way through the game, a person in a gorilla costume walks onto the court, and off again. About half of all observers are so focused on their task of counting, that they completely miss the 'gorilla'. We too, can be so focused on what we want, or expect to observe, that we fail to notice the *real* learning going on throughout the indoor and outdoor provision. We need to remember the importance of:

- observing children as a natural part of all normal activity;
- interpreting children's actions and words to try to understand the child's thinking and learning;

- being sensitive to the child's thinking and learning when deciding when to interact and when to value the child's independent activity;
- joining in play and child-initiated activity following children's agendas;
- scaffolding children's learning through talk, discussing strategies and ideas, suggesting possibilities and modelling approaches;
- providing brief, well-planned, focused learning opportunities in response to observed interests, learning and development.

When we respond to children's independent activities, and accept their invitations to become co-players, we become engrossed in participant observations and notice significant events:

Sebastian: We will see how Sebastian notices the markings on a pebble, and sets out to make a collection of pebbles in a bucket, involving adults and peers, digging in the outside area. We will find out how he is showing curiosity about objects; using his senses to explore the world around him; initiating activities; maintaining focus for a period of time; not easily distracted; finding new ways to do things and making decisions about how to approach a task – **finding out and exploring, choosing ways to do things** and **enjoying what he sets out to do**.

Remi: We will notice that although Remi first gets really upset that the tower of empty boxes he is building collapses, he goes on to learn from his early attempts, draws in peers and develops ways to build a stable base, starting again several times until he succeeds. We'll notice that he then moves onto constructing with crates outdoors, and applies what he has learnt there too. We will find out how he is showing particular interests; seeking challenge; showing a 'can do' attitude; paying attention to details; persisting when challenges occur; bouncing back after difficulties; finding ways to solve problems and changing strategy as needed – **finding out and exploring, choosing ways to do things** and **enjoying what he sets out to do**.

Rima: We will notice that Rima collects some empty boxes from the creative workshop, gathers up wrapping paper, string and ribbons and struggles with different ways to wrap 'parcels', making labels. We will see when she gestures and invites friends to a 'party' and sets up a picnic on the grass outdoors – playing 'pass the parcel' and 'musical bumps'. We will find out how she is acting out experiences with other people; taking on a role in her play; learning by trial and error; maintaining focus on an activity for a period of time; showing high levels of energy and fascination; thinking of ideas and reviewing how well an approach is working – **finding out and exploring, choosing ways to do things** and **enjoying what she sets out to do**.

Practitioners who create a learning environment which values *how* children learn as well as *what* they are learning will be able to make meaningful, significant observations which will support effective assessment and impact on ongoing planning.

Assessing

Assessment is all about reflecting on observations and other knowledge of a child to decide what it means in terms of the child's interests, current focus of learning, ways of thinking, emotional response and level of development. Quite simply, assessment involves the practitioner making an informed judgement about the child's learning.

In England the EYFS Statutory Framework (2021) requires early years practitioners to review children's progress and share a summary with parents at two points: in the prime areas between the ages of 24 and 36 months (the Progress Check at Age Two), and at the end of the EYFS (the EYFS Profile).

Assessment plays an important part in helping parents, carers and practitioners to recognise children's progress, understand their needs, and to plan activities and support. Ongoing assessment (also known as formative assessment) is an integral part of the learning and development process. 'It involves practitioners knowing children's level of achievement and interests and then shaping learning experiences for each child reflecting that knowledge. In their interactions with children, practitioners should respond to their own day-to-day observations about children's progress, and observations that parents and carers share' (DfE 2021: 2.2).

Statutory assessment

Progress Check at Age Two

When a child is aged between 2 and 3 years, practitioners must review their progress and provide parents and/or carers with a short, written summary of their child's development in personal, social and emotional development, communication and language and physical development.

Beyond these areas, it is for practitioners to decide what the written summary should include, reflecting the development level and needs of the individual child.

The National Children's Bureau non-statutory guidance (NCB 2012: 3) explains that the progress check:

- should be completed by a practitioner who knows the child well and works directly with them in the setting. This should normally be the child's key person;
- arises from the ongoing observational assessments carried out as part of everyday practice in the setting;
- is based on skills, knowledge, understanding and behaviour that the child demonstrates consistently and independently;

- takes account of the views and contributions of parents;
- takes into account the views of other practitioners and, where relevant, other professionals working with the child;
- enables children to contribute actively to the process.

Although there is no statutory obligation to include a commentary on the characteristics of effective learning in the Progress Check at Age Two, one example shared in the non-statutory guidance, from the Early Learning Consultancy (NCB 2012: 27), includes such a commentary, as do many local authority examples.

An informative paragraph, written in collaboration with parents, will capture the essence of the way in which a child is learning as a 'snapshot' at some time between the ages of 24 and 36 months. For example:

I am Unique – Shaun

Playing and exploring

Finding out and exploring; playing with what they know; being willing to 'have a go'

Active learning

Being involved and concentrating; enjoying achieving what they set out to do; keeping on trying

Creating and thinking critically

Having their own ideas; making links; choosing ways to do things

Shaun is very eager to explore all the centre provision – moving between being indoors and outdoors. He has a real 'can do' attitude and loves to challenge his physical abilities – he recently discovered how to hop after watching older children and persisted until he could use both legs. One of Shaun's favourite activities is painting with water and large brushes. He really engages in this open-ended activity and maintains focus for long periods. He finds the water butt tap difficult to turn on, but really persists.

I am Unique – Carla

Playing and exploring

Finding out and exploring; playing with what they know; being willing to 'have a go'

Active learning

Being involved and concentrating; enjoying achieving what they set out to do; keeping on trying

Creating and thinking critically

Having their own ideas; making links; choosing ways to do things
Carla really likes small things – she picks them up and trickles them between her fingers. When she is outdoors, she loves to make collections of twigs, pebbles and leaves. Most recently she likes to put these in a particular saucepan and stir with a wooden spoon from the home corner. She has begun to offer favourite friends and her key person 'dinner', pretending the leaves and twigs are food and taking on roles in her play. Carla is very eager to take off and put on her own clothes – and persists even when her shoes are difficult to put back on.

Early Years Foundation Stage Profile

In England the EYFS Profile is completed in the final term of the year in which the child reaches age 5 years, and no later than 30 June in that term. The profile provides parents and carers, practitioners and teachers with a well-rounded picture of a child's knowledge, understanding and abilities. In addition to an assessment for each of the 17 early learning goals (ELGs) in which practitioners must indicate whether children are meeting expected levels of development, practitioners may choose to provide a short commentary on each child's skills and abilities in relation to the three key characteristics of effective learning.

This commentary was previously mandatory and has now become optional, which is most unfortunate given the fundamental nature of the characteristics to children's learning in all areas. The most useful commentary about the characteristics of effective learning will summarise the way a child learns within the school, but also reflect parental views of how the child is learning at home. When families have been involved in discussions about *how* their child is learning throughout the EYFS, they will be well placed to contribute in a meaningful way.

Chaz, 4 years 11 months

EYFS: characteristics of effective learning

Playing and exploring

Finding out and exploring; playing with what they know; being willing to 'have a go'
Chaz has a particular interest in outdoor play. Most recently he loves to take on the role of 'Merlin', initiating activities and drawing his friends into his play, acting out their experiences in their play. He uses branches as 'wands' and makes collections of natural objects for magic potions, pretending these objects are magical items.

Active learning

Being involved and concentrating; enjoying achieving what they set out to do; keeping on trying
Chaz focuses on preferred activities for long periods of time and is not easily engaged by adults when he is choosing to 'mix potions', 'cast spells' or planning 'rescue missions' across the climbing frame and in the wooded area. Chaz sets challenges for himself and others – most recently using the tyres, blankets and logs to create 'stepping stones' across a 'river'. He really persists with these self-identified challenges and shows great satisfaction in meeting his own goals.

Thinking creatively and critically

Having their own ideas; making links; choosing ways to do things
Chaz is beginning to make links in his learning. Most recently he was trying to move a builders' bucket filled with wet mud. He couldn't move it on his own, and actually sat down and looked for a few minutes before emptying some of the mud into a box. He moved the bucket and refilled – predicting what would happen, trying out his idea and solving his problem. Later he used a different strategy – asking his friend to help him put the bucket on the wheeled toy to move it.

Mei-Xing, 5 years 8 months

EYFS: characteristics of effective learning

Playing and exploring

Finding out and exploring; playing with what they know; being willing to 'have a go'
Mei-Xing engages in a wide range of activities, both indoors and outdoors. She has a particular interest in role play and imaginative play. Mei-Xing spends a lot of time being 'mum', using dolls as her twins sisters and engaging her two close friends H and K-L in her play themes. Mei-Xing is very interested in people – she loves visitors and always approaches them with confidence, asking questions about their family, where they live and what they do.

Active learning

Being involved and concentrating; enjoying achieving what they set out to do; keeping on trying
Mei-Xing is fascinated by small things and particularly likes to find tiny things in the dry sand – she sieves for nuggets and 'treasure' and use tweezers to move items into treasure boxes, sometimes focusing on this activity

for prolonged periods. Mei-Xing pays attention to very small details when involved in one of her passions – fixing shiny, glittery objects onto small pieces of card to create greetings cards. She recently found out how to make a 'pop-up' card and persisted, even when she found the cutting for the hinge challenging. When she cut right across the card first time, she used masking tape to fix the card and was extremely satisfied when the card opened and 'popped up'.

Thinking creatively and critically

Having their own ideas; making links; choosing ways to do things.

Mei-Xing spends long periods watching other children when they are doing something new and unusual. She often takes an idea and innovates – for example, making a 'double zig-zag' book when her story about her family was too long for eight pictures. She tried out her idea for the book first and only fixed it when she was sure it would work. She then showed her best friend H how to make the book. When she tried to make a stapled book and realised it wouldn't work, she approached C, her key person, for support. She knew she couldn't use masking tape for all the pages and worked with C for a long time, eventually making a 'staple-less' book together.

Planning

No plan written weeks in advance can include a group's interest in a spider's web on a frosty morning or a particular child's interest in transporting small objects in a favourite blue bucket, yet it is these interests which may lead to some powerful learning. Plans should therefore be flexible enough to adapt to circumstances.

(DCSF 2008b: 12)

Planning involves deciding what to provide next to support the child's learning, informed by what the practitioner finds out about the child from the assessment process. Effective planning includes a wide range of ways of interacting through which practitioners can support and extend learning.

Effective planning should:

- ensure children are excited to learn and effectively supported;
- identify opportunities to explore ideas, resources, experiences;
- be developmentally appropriate;
- provide a tool kit for adults – but be enabling not restrictive.

As long ago as 2001, the Qualifications and Curriculum Authority (QCA) emphasised the need to identify *how* children learn, stressing that children who are educated in:

a learning environment that is vibrant, purposeful, challenging and supportive stand the best chance of developing into confident and successful learners. Effective learning environments are created over time as a result of
practitioners and parents working together, thinking and talking about children's learning and planning how to promote it.

The document goes on to say that:

Good planning is the key to making children's learning effective, exciting,
varied and progressive. Good planning enables practitioners to build up
knowledge about *how* individual children learn and make progress. It also
provides opportunities for practitioners to think and talk about how to sustain
a successful learning environment.

(QCA 2001: 2, original emphasis)

Practitioners need to ensure coverage of the seven areas of learning and development over a period of time. But what is absolutely essential is planning to
create a rich, vibrant learning environment which supports children's own
interests and supports the characteristics of effective learning: an indoor and
outdoor environment which motivates and engages children and supports the
ways in which they think, helping them to develop their own 'tool kit' for
learning.

A well-planned environment should include the following:

- Open-ended, accessible resources which can be used in a variety of diverse
  ways – for example, two sets of wooden blocks of different sizes, which fit
  together, will offer children more options than a complex construction kit
  which can only be fitted together in one way.
- Resources which reflect children's current interests and enthusiasms – if a
  group of children are fascinated by superheroes, support this interest
  through open-ended resources which can be used as cloaks, or provide
  superhero comics and images.
- Spaces which can be used in different ways, so that children can make links
  within their learning. Rigidly defined areas can be limiting. For example,
  provide rugs, duvet covers and blankets which children can use indoors and
  outdoors to define their own learning areas and spaces.
- Quiet spaces, which are visually calm. Limit noise by keeping adult voices
  low, rather than speaking over children. Make sure children have lots of
  space and time outdoors to be loud and physical, but also quiet, serene
  spaces outdoors.
- Familiar, favourite resources but also, on a regular basis, novel and unusual
  resources to investigate and explore, particularly those linked to their
  current interests.
- Resources which arouse children's curiosity and intrinsically motivate
  children, promoting deep involvement.

- Flexible routines which ensure children have opportunities to become deeply involved – no more stopping playing to 'go out to play'.
- Opportunities for children to revisit activities over a period of time. For example, where possible, the flexibility of leaving large constructions out to be developed over days, rather than 'tidied up' every session.

Adult-initiated activities

Adult-initiated activities build on children's current interests. However, they are also planned because familiar adults have good reasons to expect that this experience will engage the children. Young children cannot ask to do something again, or develop their own version, until they have that first time experience. The best plans are flexible; there is scope for the children to influence the details and adults can respond to what actually happens.

(Stevens 2012: 2)

When planning adult-initiated experiences, practitioners need to ensure that activities motivate and engage children – open activities will offer children more opportunities to find their own ways to represent and develop their own ideas, not simply reproducing someone else's ideas.

The Cambridgeshire Independent Learning Project (C.Ind.Le; Whitebread et al. 2008, see Chapter 2) found examples of children showing characteristics of effective learning in all sorts of contexts, but they identified that they were most common in certain situations, in particular:

- children initiating activities (setting personally meaningful goals and challenges);
- opportunities to work in unsupervised groups (self-directed learning; resolving problems for themselves);
- extensive collaboration and talk (visible learning; making strategies and decisions explicit).

Practitioners, should reflect on the daily opportunities children have to engage in these sorts of activities. Effective planning should include specific examples of things adults could do (positive relationships) and provide (enabling environments), having made particular observations of the ways in which individual children are currently learning.

Consider then, the approach practitioners take to planning adult-initiated activities for a small group of children. One common approach may be to plan a specific activity, which offers opportunities for assessment. The practitioner plans an activity, based on observations of the children, identifying a learning intention of '*Counts up to three or four objects by saying one number name for each item*'. Building on the children's interests in rhymes, the practitioner provides five green speckled frogs, a log and some crepe paper 'lily pad' leaves.

The children engage in counting the frogs, some counting three or four frogs, saying one number name for each. The children are engaged, the practitioner makes observations and assesses their achievement in that particular aspect of learning and development.

But consider the limitations of the activity, and how these could be avoided. If the children are fascinated by the number rhyme 'Five Little Speckled Frogs', then make a collection of all sorts of frogs – wooden, fabric, plastic, in different shapes, sizes and colours. Introduce these in wicker baskets, alongside logs and natural objects. Observe how the children investigate and explore the resources. Note how they 'count up to three or four objects by saying one number name for each item' but notice so much more as well. The observations will show not only the children's achievements in one aspect of mathematics but *how* they solve mathematical problems they have identified themselves, and *how* they are learning:

Sabiha: Notice the descriptive and comparative language Sabiha uses as she sorts the frogs. Notice the words she uses to compare the size of the sets she creates: 'there are more green frogs, there's millions. No, not millions, one, two, three … eleven.' Notice also, how she puts the frogs into sets, starting with materials, then realising this is too complex, debates size and moves on to colour – green, and 'not green'. She *plans, makes decisions about how to approach her self-identified task, solves the problem and reaches her goal.*

Eddie: Notice how Eddie lines the frogs up and counts them, then how he throws them all in the air and tries to count them where they land. When he gets to 'seven', notice his *satisfaction:* 'That's my brother, that is – seven. I be seven too after Christmas.' Notice too how he *makes predictions* and *keeps on trying, showing a belief that a different approach will pay off.*

Each of these approaches to adult-initiated activities will give practitioners opportunities to observe and assess children's achievement in numbers, but one, in its rigidity, may limit children's achievements, and one will offer opportunities for children to exhibit what they know and can do, and how they are learning. The richness of the observations will feed into more accurate assessments and provide deeper insight which will lead to more effective planning.

Planning to enhance provision

Observations of the ways in which children are learning, in specific areas of continuous provision, will impact on the ways in which practitioners plan to enhance the provision. For example, practitioners can support children as they are 'playing with what they know' in the home corner.

Some examples of what adults might provide (**enabling environments**):

- Provide well-organised, accessible, open-ended resources which can be used in different ways. Instead of a plastic iron, plastic cups, a battery-operated pop-up toaster and purpose-made dressing up clothes, add collections of 'real' kitchen utensils – spoons, ladles, barbecue equipment. Add lengths of interesting fabrics like camouflage materials, sheer fabric, netting, shiny and textured fabrics. Or consider adding a collection of shoes and shoe boxes, or hats for a short while.
- Fix a digital photo frame to the wall, with a slide show of children's real experiences – when they visited the farm and the supermarket; when the firefighters, Sally's mum and the baby came to the settings and 'animal man' visited; when they went on a number walk around the local area. Keep the slide show up to date *with* the children. Display still images of different homes.

Some examples of what adults might do (**positive relationships**):

- Act as a co-player with the children in the home corner, sensitively fitting in with their ideas and play themes. Take on a role – as disgruntled teenager, busy mum, or granny visiting from overseas. Act out your own experiences and support them to act out theirs.
- Use an object in unfamiliar ways, pretending it is something else – use a box as a bucket to mop the floor, or as a crib for a baby. Use a block as an iPad, games console or mobile phone – showing what it is by the way it is being used.
- Support children without taking over their play – if they are playing at 'being Uncle Elijah', make comments about what they are doing or, where appropriate, ask open questions to extend the play 'I'm making pancakes for tea because they are my favourite. Do you have a favourite cake, Uncle?'

Key messages

- Keep the child at the heart of the observation, assessment and planning process.
- Avoid lots of paperwork and/or electronic tracking and note children's significant learning – including *how* they are learning – and use this to inform planning.
- Spend as much time as possible interacting with children, acting as co-players, offering challenge and extending their learning.
- Involve families in the process in meaningful ways – in particular around how children are learning at home and their current fascinations.

References

Chabris, C. and Simons, D. (2011) *The Invisible Gorilla*. New York: HarperCollins.

DCSF (Department for Children, Schools and Families) (2008a) *Principles into Practice cards*. Available at https://resources.leicestershire.gov.uk/sites/resource/files/field/pdf/2019/6/14/EYFS-Principles-into-Practice-Cards.pdf (accessed 20 March 2021).

DCSF (Department for Children, Schools and Families) (2008b) *Practice Guidance for the Early Years Foundation Stage*. Available at: www.foundationyears.org.uk/category/library/publications/ (accessed 23 March 2021).

DCSF (Department for Children, Schools and Families) (2009) *Learning, Playing and Interacting: Good Practice in the Early Years Foundation Stage*, 00775-2009BKT-EN. Available at: www. foundationyears.org.uk/wp-content/uploads/2011/10/Learning_Playing_Interacting.pdf (accessed 23 March 2021).

DfE (Department for Education) (2021) *Statutory Framework for the Early Years Foundation Stage: Setting the Standards for Learning, Development and Care for Children from Birth to Five*. Available at: https://assets.publishing.service.gov.uk/government/uploads/system/uploads/attachment_data/file/974907/EYFS_framework_-_March_2021.pdf (accessed 23 March 2021).

Early Education (2012) *Development Matters in the Early Years Foundation Stage*. London: Early Education. Available at: www.early-education.org.uk/sites/default/files/Development%20Matters%20in%20the%20Early%20Years%20Foundation%20Stage%20-%20FINAL.pdf (accessed 23 March 2021).

NCB (National Children's Bureau) (2012) *A Know How Guide: The EYFS Progress Check at Age Two*. Available at: www.foundationyears.org.uk/early-years-foundation-stage-2012/ (accessed March 2021).

Qualifications and Curriculum Authority (QCA) (2001) *Planning for Learning in the Foundation Stage*. London: QCA. Available at: www.educationengland.org.uk/documents/foundationstage/2001-planning-for-learning.pdf (accessed 23 March 2021).

Stevens, J. (2012) *Planning for the Early Years: Storytelling and Storymaking*. London: Practical Preschool Books.

Whitebread, D. with Dawkins, R., Bingham, S., Aguda, A. and Hemming, K. (2008) Organising the early years classroom to encourage independent learning, in D. Whitebread and P. Coltman (eds) *Teaching and Learning in the Early Years*, 3rd edn. London: Routledge.

7 Interacting and talking for learning and thinking

Nancy Stewart and Helen Moylett

Chapter summary

- Thinking is strongly supported by language – putting thoughts into words often through talking aloud to themselves is an early stage in children thinking consciously about ideas. Adults help children by supporting them to talk about their ideas and learning.
- This chapter explores the role of the adult as a communication partner with these young active learners who are playing and exploring and thinking creatively and critically about the people, environments and concepts they encounter.
- It draws on examples from other chapters as well as setting out a practical interaction framework.

Introduction

The main theme of this book is children learning how to learn with adults supporting and extending their learning. It is therefore unsurprising that the role of language is an important sub-theme that runs through all the chapters. Using language enables children to ask questions, tell stories, join in play, make friends, understand adult activities, explore concepts and make sense of the environment. But, most importantly in the context of this book, language changes thinking. Nelson (2007) talks about children as learners embedded in the relationships and interactive language of their everyday environments. In these 'communities of minds' they gain conceptual knowledge, learn about their own minds and update their beliefs. As Gopnik (2009:157) tells us, 'their entire stock of knowledge turns over every few months – they go through whole paradigm shifts between their third and fourth birthday ... Really flexible and innovative adults might change their minds this way two or three times in a lifetime.'

From birth, children are primed to encounter their environment through relating to and communicating with others, and engaging physically in their experiences. Their focus is drawn most strongly to other people, and learning and development occur within the context of relationships. Children cannot learn to communicate, use language or build vocabulary, for instance, just from television; it must be in interaction with other people. In addition, early attachment and emotional well-being is a strong foundation for successful cognitive and physical development. A child who feels emotionally secure and safe is confident to expand the boundaries of exploration and is motivated to reach, move and test physical capacities. They play and move with others, within relationships which establish turn-taking, joint activity, a desire to communicate and understanding of shared meanings of words.

A good knowledge of language development coupled with an awareness of the 'teachable moments' in everyday interactions will support adults in nurturing children's ability to use their developing communication and language skills for thinking, playing, learning and interacting. The influence of educators' beliefs on their interactions has been explored in various studies (Manlove et al. 2008; Degotardi 2010; Salamon and Harrison 2015, for example) but very few have looked specifically at beliefs about language development. Degotardi and Gill (2019) found that the majority of a small sample (n = 59) of infant educators working with children under 2 attributed a relatively passive role to infants' own contributions to their language-learning experiences. In other words, there was often little reference to the power of conversational, 'thinking together' language development. The researchers speculate that this apparent lack of understanding of language learning being a partnership may indicate a training need.

This training need has been identified many times in the UK. Over the years, efforts have been made through national programmes and the current government has an espoused aim to improve early language development. Unfortunately, this rhetoric has not so far been matched by a willingness to improve and fund initial and continuing professional development and the number of well qualified staff in early years settings is declining year on year. Against this background, it is even more important that practitioners are supported in practising positive interactions with young children. Much of what follows is based on the work of the Better Communication Research Programme (2010–12).

A sensitive communication partner

The first step in building communication partner skills is to be sensitively attuned to each child. It truly takes two to talk. The philosopher Wittgenstein has argued that there can be no such thing as a private language belonging to one person alone, and that language can exist only through what happens in the space between people (Candlish and Wrisley 2019). Rather than existing trapped in a solitary world, we take part in a remarkable process of sending and receiving messages from one mind to another. Communication involves taking a concept which exists in my mind, mapping it onto a symbol which I share with you, and you then interpreting that symbol and mapping it onto a concept in your mind. The symbol could be a word, a gesture, a mark or a facial expression. In order to communicate successfully what is in my mind, we both have to be aware of the symbol between us, and trust that the other is matching it to something that is at least similar to what is in our own mind.

If we are both experienced communicators, this can be a fairly equal partnership. But when one of us is just beginning to develop the ability to communicate, then the more experienced partner has a great responsibility not only for enabling the meeting of minds to take place, but also for showing the learner how it is done. Babies and young children have less developed networks of thought; until they develop Theory of Mind (see Chapter 2) they are relatively conscious of their current sensations but less aware of their own thinking. They clearly have a lot to learn about first becoming aware of their own process of thinking, before they are able to find a way to symbolise a thought in order to share it with someone else.

Attunement

A key way that adults help babies and young children become aware of their own thoughts is by acting as a mirror, reflecting back to the child what is in the child's mind. A baby who is vigorously moving an arm up and down may be hardly conscious of deciding to perform the action. But when a watching adult copies the gesture it becomes more apparent to the baby, who may then begin to more consciously experiment with the movement, repeating it and watching for a confirmatory response from the adult. Such a simple but satisfying exchange is only possible when the adult is sufficiently attentive to the baby's signal to pick it up and reflect it back. This is a core element in the process of attunement.

Babies are on the lookout for adults who tune in to them. The instinct to relate to other people is strong because babies have a biological need for someone to care for them. They develop secure emotional attachments to people who can be depended on to recognise, understand and meet their needs. As Sue Rogers and Shabana Roscoe discuss in Chapter 3, this process is intertwined with attunement – a genuine reciprocal connection to another person. Through warm, sensitive, playful interactions, children quickly recognise when someone is on their wavelength. With consistent experience over time, this attunement can build into a secure emotional attachment that supports well-being, learning and development. It is centrally involved in supporting children as communicators and in moving into language.

The most effective communication partners for young children are those who know them well, and so are most attuned to the child's signals and more likely to interpret their messages accurately. By striving to tune in to each individual child, however, skilled and sensitive adults can develop rapport and reciprocal communication with most children. Children are alert for signs that others are with them in the interpersonal space and they will quickly recognise when an adult is picking up their signals. They will also be aware when their thoughts and feelings are not being noticed and so will decline to engage. It is here that the adult bears the primary responsibility for establishing the link. Children are not yet able to interpret the minds of most adults; they may not recognise many of the symbols/words that adults may use, and in any case may not have a mental concept to match what is in the adult's mind. As the more experienced partner, it is the adult's job to meet the child on their own territory. Children are putting out communicative signals all the time, so the adult needs to tune in to catch the child's signals, and then let the child know that they are ready and willing to meet them in the space where communication is shared.

Following the child's lead in interactions and activities is often cited as an important approach for adults to take, in order to foster a sense of agency in the child and allow the child to engage in activities where they are most highly motivated. It is also important because following the child's lead means entering into the child's world in ways which allow communication to flourish. Rather than adopting one way of relating to children, the adult's style of interaction needs to be adjusted for each unique child – like turning the radio dial to pick up the signal from this particular child, at this particular moment. Following the child's lead in interaction means respecting the child's willingness and pace: noticing when your attention is welcomed, waiting to be invited to communicate, using the appropriate level of liveliness or calm, taking turns so that the child is able to continue or end the interaction.

Non-verbal communication

Before we move into talk, we engage in rich communication non-verbally. An invitation to engage might be as simple as purposeful eye contact, which can be answered by an interested facial expression. If the child then looks away the engagement ends, and this is a powerful self-regulation strategy for babies and young children who may be over-stimulated or unsure about the interaction. But a 'conversation' in eye contact, facial expressions and gestures can take place which invites further communication and offers the chance for the adult to begin to supply the language appropriate to the situation.

For a child to be ready to communicate there must be an interested and sensitive partner. Strategies to signal to the child that an adult is ready to enter into a reciprocal interaction, with respect for the child's willingness to engage include:

- **Wait.** Allow time for a child to signal that they are interested in interacting. When an adult starts an uninvited conversation, the effect might be to interrupt what the child is doing or thinking about, and it can feel like an intrusion to the child. This can make children who are more reluctant to communicate withdraw even further. Instead, coming alongside in a 'parallel play' manner, showing interest in the child's activity without saying anything, gives the child confidence and can help them be ready to interact. The child may invite interaction through saying something, or even through eye contact or a smile.

- **Listen, watch.** Observe closely in order to decide what might be in the child's mind, so you will be more likely to understand what it would be most useful to talk about.

- **Follow the child's lead.** Respond in terms of what the child is communicating through their words and actions – what is in their mind – and at the child's pace.

- **Join in and play.** Engaging in the same activity as a child shows interest and enjoyment in their company and their ideas, and episodes of joint attention (see Chapter 2) are powerful opportunities to build communication and language abilities.

- **Be face to face, on the same level.** Simply positioning yourself in this way helps to establish an equal partnership in the exchange, shows you are paying attention and invites interaction.

- **Use and respond to eye contact and gestures.** Be sensitive to all the modes of communication, not just language, to build rapport.

- **Imitate.** Providing a mirror for children's actions and expressions assures them that their signals have been received.

Establishing trust through sensitive interaction strategies such as these is a necessary first step in being an effective communication partner. Further strategies can help to support continued interaction and stimulate growth in abilities and purposes for using language, but use of such scaffolding approaches first depends on the quality of relating to children so that they are interested and happy to engage.

Moving into language: supportive communication partner

When children are happy to engage, they will be confident to try out their developing skills. The adult role is to support that confidence and develop their understandings about communication and language. Adults can do that in a number of ways by continuing the sensitive interactions detailed above and expanding their repertoire to include the following:

- **Using language appropriate to the child's level of understanding.** This will be easier when it is based on attunement and observation as well as knowledge of the child's home language(s) and family circumstances. The aim is to meet the children where they are and use their existing language knowledge as a springboard for development.

- **Commenting** on what the child is doing rather than asking questions. For example, when a child is playing with blocks saying, 'I can see you are working hard to get that straight' rather than 'What are you building?'
- **Limiting the number of closed questions.** It is uncomfortable for anyone to be asked a lot of questions in quick succession. Adults find job interviews stressful because they are required to find the 'right' answers to sometimes unexpected questions. Time for reflection and processing is minimal. So imagine how this feels for a child who is still learning how language works and needs far more time than an adult to process the question asked!
- **Asking open-ended questions.** 'What are you building?', for example, is a closed question, assumes that the child has a clear idea and implicitly demands a short answer to an adult agenda. 'What might happen if that block falls again?' does not put the child 'on the spot' in the same way and is much more of an invitation to reflection, conversation and joint thinking about solutions to a possible problem.
- **Labelling.** Knowing what we call objects, actions and abstract things like feelings is an important part of language learning. When the child says, 'I put the curvy block here over the door' and the adult responds with, 'Oh yes, I can see you have made an arch', the child is acquiring new and useful vocabulary in context. When a child has destroyed a structure that he was making with a friend and the friend is crying, the adult can help by acknowledging and labelling feelings ('You look angry and frustrated', 'You are upset') before going on to support them to solve the problem that caused these emotions. Being able to label feelings helps us to regulate them ourselves.
- **Modelling language in correct forms in response to the child's errors.** Children learning language will make lots of errors and it is not helpful to explicitly correct them. We all become fluent by listening to more competent language users and imitating them. When a young child says 'I goed shops yesterday' the meaning is clear and they are using their grammatical knowledge to make a past participle. These are big positives and the error is minor. They will learn that the correct past participle of go is 'went' if the adult models that in their reply. For example, 'Mummy told me you went to the shops yesterday'.
- **Encouraging turn-taking.** Conversation is often characterised as a process of 'serve and return'. Good conversationalists are aware of this and listen while the other person has their turn and, in their turn, they say something that is related to, or builds on, what was said. The supportive adult communicator can help by regulating the conversation: saying for example, 'Thank you Karim, you gave us three good ideas. Now it's Max's turn and then it will be Raya's.'
- Turn-taking can also be encouraged by **pausing expectantly**. When retelling a favourite story for instance 'Once upon a time there were three ...' or counting '2, 4, 6 ...'.
- **Praising non-verbal communication.** All human beings communicate non-verbally on a spectrum between the very deliberate (such as using

signing) to the often largely unconscious (such as personal mannerisms and resting facial expression). Body language is like a second language and children can be helped to recognise this by drawing attention to it – for example, 'I can tell you are listening carefully, Adiola, because you are looking at me and nodding.'

All of the above strategies, when based on positive relationships and environments described in other chapters in this book based on enabling *how* children learn, will help children to develop their communication and language skills. However, there are some other key strategies that adults should also employ if they are to be stimulating, as well as sensitive and supportive, communication partners.

Extending talk: stimulating communication partner

One of the interesting findings of the Better Communication Research programme (Dockrell et al. 2012) was that, along with encouraging turn-taking and praising non-verbal communication, all the following strategies were generally the least likely to be deployed by the majority of practitioners. This may be because of lack of knowledge about child development and/or an expectation that, once children are talking adequately, there is no more teaching to be done. However, this is far from the reality.

A stimulating communication partner will support and challenge young children to become more and more fluent, giving them more language in which to think and more oral knowledge on which to base their emerging literacy skills.

- **Expand on what the child says.** This can be done by repeating what the child says and adding a bit more information or more relevant words. For example, when a toddler says 'Dinner' the adult responds with 'It is dinner time,' or a child says 'Look new shoes' and the adult smiles and responds with 'Those are new shiny black shoes'. On each occasion a practitioner could just acknowledge the child's utterance with a smile or a 'Yes' but that would be to miss a teachable moment.
- **Model language the child is not yet using.** For example, when talking with a group of 4-year-olds about photos on a theme of feelings the practitioner might say, 'Yes, Ruhksana, he is looking sad. We can tell by the upset expression on his face. Can we find a photo of someone with an angry expression?'
- **Introduce and repeat new words in a range of contexts** and encourage the child to use new words in their own talking. A group of children might be moving on the ground on their fronts and the practitioner might say 'Hey, you are slithering like snakes'. Later she might say 'Here is a story that has a snake in it. I wonder if it will slither along the ground?' The next day she might wonder what it might be like to slither on the slippery floor in the

entrance hall or in a movement session she might suggest slithering along with bouncing, rolling or twisting.

- **Play with language highlighting choices and differences.** A theme throughout this book is the importance of play for children's engagement in learning and thinking. Learning language is no exception to this. Revelling in words and playing with them is an example of the learning power of what Bruce (1991) describes as 'wallowing' in play. Practitioners can lead by example: 'That's a teeny tiny terrapin not a massive, monstrous mammoth' or 'Would you like your juice in the yellow beaker or the red sneaker?'
- **Talk through specific situations providing a 'script'.** This may describe everyday routines and what to say and do. For example, 'First, we give everyone a knife and a fork, then a spoon, then we put out the beakers, one each. Now the table is laid. What do we say to the other children now?' Or it may be preparation for upcoming events that children might need to think about. For example, 'Let's talk about what is going to happen when Maja's mummy brings her new baby sister to visit us.'

How practitioners use all these strategies in their everyday practice will depend on their knowledge of the children and their language communities. Many children are learning English as an additional language and are becoming bi- or multi-lingual. These strategies work for them as well as for mono-lingual children. All young language learners benefit from adults' time, space, patient support and thoughtful provision and interaction. In addition, children learning English as an additional language need acknowledgement of their skills in their home language. Code switching – using words from more than one language – sometimes worries practitioners but is a natural part of learning languages and a strength of bi- and multi-lingualism when one can search for just the right word to express what one is thinking. If it is valued and supported children gain confidence in their communication skills and may help extend the language repertoire of their close practitioners.

Talk throughout the characteristics of effective early learning

Although children are born as powerful learners, the extent to which they maintain and build on the initial drive to expand their world and the capacities to do so is heavily influenced by their experiences. As well as gaining knowledge and understanding in all areas as they interact with objects, events and people, children are also learning more about how to learn. Some of the attributes of a strong learner may be innate, and behaviour supporting learning, such as showing curiosity or determination, may come naturally. At the same time, however, many attitudes and behaviours are strongly influenced by the responses from other people. As with all learning, learning to learn develops in the context of relationships.

We have seen that language is an integral tool for learning and for thinking. Once a label is assigned to an object, a concept, a feeling, behaviour, and so on, these become more concrete and crystallised in the mind as distinct from other objects, concepts, feelings, behaviours, etc. Just as talk involved in co-construction helps clarify and cement understanding in any area, it supports children to become more conscious and in control of their own approaches to learning. Children respond to what they discern is valued by the adults in their lives, so commenting on the processes of learning which a child demonstrates helps the child to understand more clearly what they have done, and that these attitudes and behaviours are seen as important. The contribution of talk to developing the characteristics of effective learning can be seen throughout Playing and Exploring, Active Learning, and Creating and Thinking Critically, as skilful and sensitive adults engage with children in conversational exchanges that are calibrated for the language levels of each child.

Playing and exploring

Talk and play enjoy a strongly reciprocal relationship: talk is often a supportive or even necessary part of play, while play provides a perfect opportunity for developing language skills through the involvement of an expert communication partner. Researchers of this interrelationship of play and talk have concluded, 'Guided play during which adults scaffold child-initiated learning seems ideal for developing language skills. Crucially, during guided play, adults capitalise on teachable moments to support children's learning. Language development seems to thrive particularly well in such settings because children benefit from having an attentive and sensitive adult partner who talks of the things that interest them' (Weisberg et al. 2013, 47).

As pointed out in Chapter 3, adults need to judge carefully when and how they become involved in children's play. For instance, children may be deeply involved in exploratory play through physical observation and experimentation which could be disrupted by an ill-judged attempt at conversation at that moment. On the other hand, this could prove a useful opportunity for using talk to support the learning in an episode of joint attention. An adult can, for example, first move alongside and show interest through body language, or perhaps through imitation of the child's actions. If the child invites the adult to join in verbally or non-verbally, the adult could begin to describe in words what the child is observing, or describe their own parallel experience in a style that models self-talk ('It looks very slippery. Thump! That made a noise').

Comments on the process of exploratory learning are useful to help the child become more aware of using these learning tools, such as 'You are curious about this, aren't you? You're looking very carefully. I wonder … Hmm, that's interesting …'. On the occasions when the adult makes a decision not to become directly involved at the moment of a child's exploratory play, it can be valuable to reflect in similar ways in talking about the experience later ('I noticed you were really interested in that ice ball. What did you find out?').

Talk often takes prime place in representational play, described in the EYFS as 'Playing with what they know'. Language is a key symbolic link which can specify that one thing represents another, with a word almost magically able to turn a child into a dragon or a garden log into a car (see Chapter 5). There is a close relationship between language and pretend play, with both requiring the ability to use a symbol of one thing to stand for another – whether the word 'brick' stands for the object, or the brick itself stands for a telephone. Both language and pretend play usually develop in the second year of life, and the relationship between them has been much discussed and studied. Piaget saw pretend play as supporting the ability to think in symbols, writing, 'One of the purest forms of symbolic thought available to young children, dramatic play contributes strongly to the intellectual development of children' (Piaget 1962) and Vygotsky proposed that language is a central tool of developing thinking, with pretend play offering an ideal context for both.

Dramatic play involves sophisticated use of thought and language. In Rogers' and Roscoe's example (Chapter 3) of children in a role-play café, talk is used to assign roles, to give instructions about how to play, and to speak in role as a customer and as adult staff members. Children move back and forth from being themselves to 'being' someone else, and from acting in role within the agreed context to stepping outside to manage the play. Throughout these elements, children are drawing on and practising their abilities to self-regulate. They need to have flexibility of mind to move in and out of pretence, and to control their behaviour and language appropriately to each circumstance.

Recent research has confirmed the parallel development of dramatic play and language. A study of talk between an adult and child in play found more conversational turns and questions in symbolic play than in play with objects, reflecting the greater complexity in open-endedness and the need to negotiate meanings. A meta-analysis concluded there is evidence of 'significant concurrent and longitudinal associations between symbolic play and language across early development (i.e., 1–6 years)' (Quinn et al. 2018). The more children engage in symbolic play, the more advanced their language development; importantly for developing as learners, both symbolic play and language support the development of self-regulated learning.

Active learning

The role of talk in supporting children to be active agents of their own learning centres largely on articulating the processes involved in learning. Motivation is enhanced by clear commitment to a goal, so encouraging children to state their intentions helps to bring more awareness of an explicit purpose. The plan-do-review cycle offers an ideal opportunity for children to express their own goals.

In addition, the quality of verbal feedback adults give children has a significant effect on whether children maintain intrinsic motivation and a growth mindset where children evaluate their own successes and challenges, rather than moving toward seeking praise from adults for particular approved performance (see Chapter 4).

The three brief interactions in Table 7.1 are examples of adult talk which, although positive in tone (and very common in settings and schools) is likely to encourage performance anxiety and extrinsic motivation.

Table 7.1 Adult talk encouraging extrinsic motivation

Adult says:	Message to child:
Good boy you made that so quickly, you are clever.	I'm good and clever when I do things quickly.
You're so brilliant, I am so proud of you coming first in the race.	I have to come first to be brilliant.
Good girl, I love your picture.	I am a good person when you love what I do.

Adults can support an orientation to intrinsic motivation by commenting on the learning processes a child is employing, and facilitating conversations about challenges, the value of persistence and effort, and a child's own satisfaction with their achievements. When adults consider carefully the sort of praise they give, and focus on the process of learning and the effort children put in, they are enabling confidence and 'growth mindsets' (Dweck 2006). See, for example, Table 7.2 for these alternative examples based on the same scenarios as those in Table 7.1.

Table 7.2 Adult talk encouraging intrinsic motivation

Adult says:	Message to child:
Wow you worked really hard to make that, well done.	My effort is noticed and praised.
You really put your heart and soul into your running, how did it feel?	Running as fast as I could was hard work but it made me feel great – I can evaluate my own efforts.
You really thought about the colours you used. Which part of the picture do you like best?	How I think is valued and I can evaluate the finished result.

Thinking creatively and critically

In the third strand of the Characteristics of Effective Learning, talk takes a particularly powerful role in the processes of children imagining, perceiving and clarifying links in their understanding, and thinking clearly and critically to make and carry out plans and solve problems. Di Chilvers, writing about thinking creatively and critically in Chapter 5 puts strong emphasis on language for thinking, imagining, reflecting, and the pivotal role of the adult engaging in thinking conversations with children. Reciprocal conversations featuring sustained shared thinking are at the centre of supporting children to develop as thinkers.

Following sharing the story of Elmer the patchwork elephant, whose grey-painted disguise washed off in the rain, a group of nursery children and their teacher were talking about the story as they played with toy animals. 'We could paint our animals,' suggested one child. 'How could we test if they would change back, like Elmer?' asked the teacher. 'We could use the watering can, and then the paint would wash off,' said one child. 'Not if we let it dry first,' countered another.

This example shows children transferring ideas from an imaginary tale to their practical activities, and the adult offering support to extend their thinking. The children think of their own ideas, and use prediction based on their experiences – including making links with experiences of some paints which are waterproof once dried.

Of course, pre-verbal children are also engaged in having their own ideas, making links to build understanding, and making decisions about what to do and how to do it. But when adults supply the language to describe these processes as they observe them in action, children gradually develop greater awareness and control of their own thinking – they are developing *metacognition*. Adults can be the narrators of children's thought processes, as far as they can understand them, and also think aloud to demonstrate the nature of their own thinking (e.g. 'I wonder whether we will have time to finish that before lunch', 'I'm trying to remember what we said yesterday...', 'Maybe I could try using this stick ...').

When adults use talk to scaffold children's planning, monitoring their progress and evaluating, they are helping children to learn strategies of thinking critically which can be gradually internalised. A plan-do-review sequence helps children to be thoughtful and purposeful about their activities. Table 7.3 provides some ideas for scaffolding self-regulated learning through talk.

Table 7.3   Scaffolding self-regulated learning

Self-regulated learners ask themselves a 'regulatory checklist' of questions as they plan, monitor, and evaluate their learning.
When adults encourage children to engage in conversation in these areas, they scaffold children's ability to eventually ask themselves a regulatory checklist.

Planning
Experts ask themselves: What is the nature of the task? What is my goal? What kind of information and strategies do I need? How much time and resources will I need?

Scaffold by talking with children about:

- What you are planning to do
- What you will do with it
- What you want it to be like
- Whether you will work with anyone else
- What you need to use
- How you think you will do it
- Whether you will finish it all today
- Whether you need any help

Monitoring
Experts ask themselves: Do I have a clear understanding of what I am doing? Does the task make sense? Am I reaching my goals? Do I need to make changes?

Scaffold by talking with children about:

- What you are doing here
- How this will help you with (your goal)
- Whether it is working out the way you want it to
- The most important thing
- The problem/thing that is hard
- Whether it might be better to think of another way
- Whether you have any different ideas now

Evaluating
Experts ask themselves: Have I reached my goal? What worked? What didn't work? Would I do things differently next time?

Scaffold by talking with children about:

- Whether you did as you planned
- How well it went/ What you think of it
- Whether you concentrated on it for a long time
- What worked well/ What didn't work
- Anything you would do differently if you did it again
- Anything you found out that you didn't know before

Source: Schraw, G. (1998) Promoting general metacognitive awareness. *Instructional Science*, 26(1-2), 113–125.

> **Key messages**
>
> - Children learn to communicate, use language and build vocabulary in inter-action with other people.
> - Early attachment and emotional well-being form a strong foundation for successful cognitive and physical development.
> - When adults understand how to be sensitive, supportive and stimulating communication partners in everyday activities they nurture children's ability to use their developing communication and language skills for thinking, playing, learning and interacting.

References

Better Communication Research Programme (2010–12) For reports see: www.gov.uk/government/collections/better-communication-research-programme and https://warwick.ac.uk/fac/soc/cedar/better/ (accessed 11 October 2021).

Bruce, T. (1991) *Time to Play in Early Childhood.* London: Hodder and Stoughton.

Candlish, S. and Wrisley, G. (2019) Private Language, *The Stanford Encyclopedia of Philosophy* (Fall 2019 Edition), Edward N. Zalta (ed.). Available at: https://plato.stanford.edu/archives/fall2019/entries/private-language (accessed 11 October 2021).

Degotardi, S. (2010) High-quality interactions with infants: Relationships with early-childhood practitioners' interpretations and qualification levels in play and routine contexts, *International Journal of Early Years Education* 18 (1): 27–41.

Degotardi, S. and Gill. A (2019) Infant educators' beliefs about infant language development in long day care settings, *Early Years,* 39:1, 97–113.

Dockrell, J. et al. (2012) Developing a communication supporting classrooms observation tool, DFE-RR247-BCRP8. Available at: www.gov.uk/government/publications/developing-a-communication-supporting-classrooms-observation-tool (accessed 11 October 2021).

Dweck (2006) *Mindset: The New Psychology of Success,* New York: Ballantine Books.

Gopnik, A. (2009) *The Philosophical Baby.* London: The Bodley Head.

Manlove, E.E. et al. (2008) The quality of caregiving in child care: Relations to teacher complexity of thinking and perceived supportiveness of the work environment, *Infant and Child Development* 17: 203–222.

Nelson, K. (2007) *Young Minds in Social Worlds.* Cambridge, MA: Harvard University Press.

Piaget, J. (1962) *Comments on Vygotsky's critical remarks concerning* 'The Language and Thought of the Child' *and* 'Judgment and Reasoning in the Child'. Cambridge, MA: The MIT Press.

Quinn, S., Donelly, S. and Kidd, E. (2018) The relationship between symbolic play and language acquisition: A meta-analytic review, article in press, *Developmental Review,* 49, 121–135. Available at: https://pure.mpg.de/rest/items/item_2602612_8/component/file_3001229/content (accessed 11 November 2021).

Salamon, A. and Harrison, L. (2015) Early childhood educators' conceptions of infants' capabilities: The nexus between beliefs and practice, *Early Years: An International Research Journal,* 35 (3): 273–288.

Weisberg, D.S., Zosh, J., Hirsh-Pasek, K. and Golinkoff, R.M. (2013) Talking it up: Play, language development and the role of adult support, *American Journal of Play,* (6)1:39–54.

8 Affirmative parenting practices: lessons from the High Achieving White Working Class Boys (HAWWC) Project

Chris Pascal and Tony Bertram

Chapter summary

- The evidence from the Early Years Foundation Stage Profile (EYFSP) shows that boys consistently achieve less well than girls. Moreover, alongside the real and persistent underachievement in education of many children from Gypsy, Roma and Traveller, Black and other minority ethnic communities, white working-class underachievement in education is also persistent and evidence consistently shows that recent reforms have done little for many children from these communities, especially boys.
- This chapter is based on research with those who have succeeded 'against the odds' and highlights the central role of the characteristics of effective learning in the parenting and home learning experiences that have been a central feature of their lives from birth. It demonstrates that the 'academic resilience' of these young boys has been supported and sustained by the 'parenting resilience' of their prime carer. There are also positive messages for narrowing the achievement gap suffered by children from other groups.

Introduction

The critical role of a supportive home learning environment and positive parenting in giving children a strong start to their future is well established and found to be more powerful than socio-economic status or parental qualifications, reinforcing the message from the original EPPE study (Sylva et al. 2010) that 'what parents do much with their children is more important than who they are' (Barbour 2020). However, much less is known about how parents create the home learning experiences that lead to such positive outcomes for children, especially in less advantaged families. There is also an inclination to view parents from certain underachieving communities rather negatively and to hold a rather deficit view of their parenting. Addressing this gap in knowledge and challenging the negative stereotyping of these parents was the primary aim of the High Achieving White Working Class (HAWWC) Boys Project. This chapter presents the knowledge about positive parenting and home learning in low-income households that was generated by the participating children, parents and practitioners who contributed to the HAWWC Boys Project.

We know that white working-class underachievement in education is real and persistent, (Ofsted 2007, 2008, 2013, 2014; Select Committee 2014, 2020; Perera et al. 2016) and evidence consistently shows that white British boys from low-income groups make less progress than most other groups and that recent reforms have done little 'to lift the boats' of many children from these communities. White children who are eligible for free school meals are consistently the lowest performing group in the country, and the difference between their educational performance and that of their more advantaged white peers is larger than for any other ethnic group, especially for boys. The gap exists at age 5 and widens as children get older. The possible causes and contributors to white working-class underachievement are many and various, and include matters in home life, early education and care practices, and wider social policies (Pascal and Bertram 2012). Seminal research by Feinstein et al. (2004) suggested that complex interactions between contexts, behaviours and interactions with parents, carers, settings and practitioners and the dispositions of these young children lead to different outcomes; but currently there is very little qualitative evidence about how these factors operate to support or inhibit achievement in the literature and this study aimed to address this gap in the evidence.

Our research project worked affirmatively with a carefully selected cohort of 30 high-achieving, young, white working-class (HAWWC) boys and their families from three regionally selected, low-income, urban, rural and coastal communities. The cohort provided evidence of positive parenting models in families living with adversity and produced new evidence about how their parenting practices and home learning experiences have supported the achievement of their children which we believe are inspiring for all families with young children. Learning from the parents of these high-achieving young boys was illuminative and encourages us to move away from deficit models of parenting and look more deeply and respectfully at what many low-income families are doing to support their child's learning at home. We believe there are certainly lessons learned which can inform parents and practitioners from all communities.

Key terms and concepts in thinking about affirmative parenting

Our project used an adaptation of the definitions set out in the Select Committee Report (2014) to identify the study target group:

- **Working class:** Traditional notions of what constitutes 'the working class' are based on a categorisation of employment occupations but we have pragmatically used eligibility for free school meals (FSM) as a proxy for working class. The Economic Policy Institute (an American think-tank) describes the practice of using poverty as proxy for class in generally positive terms.
- **White:** 'White' is a broad heading within classifications of ethnicity which can be used to make comparisons against other aggregated groups such as black and Asian. Within the white group the overwhelming majority of children fall into the subgroup of white British, but other subgroups include white Irish, Gypsy/Roma, and 'Other white', which encompasses a range of white mostly European ethnicities. The smaller size and greater complexity of other groups within the 'white' category has led us to focus primarily on the performance of white British children, and this matches the focus of Ofsted's (2013) *Unseen children* report.
- **High achieving:** 'High achieving' can be defined as relative to what a pupil could be predicted to achieve in terms of a comparison with another group, such as children from more prosperous homes, a different ethnic group, or a different part of the country. We used data that was most readily available at the end of the Foundation Stage in 2015 which was the children who had achieved a 'good level of development' in the Early Years Foundation Stage Profile (EYFSP), scoring a minimum of 38 out of 51 on the Profile. Where we refer to high achievement in this report, we therefore mean that attainment is high, judged on the EYFSP assessment, and higher than other comparison groups.

The project evidence also suggests two key concepts which are useful when considering how to improve young children's achievement through a greater understanding of home learning. The case studies reveal that successful white working-class boys demonstrate **'academic resilience'** and successful white working-class parents demonstrate **'parenting resilience'**.

Academic resilience is defined as 'a complex process involving internal and external factors, where a network of bi-directional relationships between child, family, school, peers, neighbourhood and wider society factors come into play to overcome environmental risk experiences' (Rutter 2012: 335). (See also Ungar et al. 2013.)

Parenting resilience is defined as 'the capacity of parents to resist and minimise the impact of risky contextual behaviours and conditions in the home and wider family to allow warm, boundaried parenting behaviours to predominate in their relationship with the child' (Pascal and Bertram 2016: 10).

The literature suggests that both academic and parenting resilience are dynamic and fluctuate within different domains and contexts, as well as within various stages of life, so a child or parent who demonstrates resilience at one stage may not necessarily display this at a different life stage. The issue this raises for the ongoing development of the project is the sustainability of resilience conditions once the child enters primary schooling. In this project we are aware that in the early years of the high-achieving boys' lives, the child and parents in this study have been successful in securing this resilience. The question remains as to how and if this can be sustained as the child moves through primary schooling to their young adulthood.

The literature also points to a number of risk factors which surround young boys and their parents which are associated with educational underachievement and which there is a need for wider social policy to address. These include:

- socio-economic background/poverty
- parent unemployment
- low levels of parental education
- single parenthood
- lack of social support
- inconsistent parenting practices
- family conflicts
- physical illness
- caregiver psychopathology

Several of our HAWWC Boy families were living with these risk factors, as the evidence below reveals. However, there is additional evidence that protective factors are also in play which can mitigate these risk factors. These include the following:

- **For the child:**
  - good cognitive skills (motivation, concentration, memory, self-regulation, etc.);
  - easy temperament (socio-affective competencies: good social competencies, empathy, social cognition, etc.);
  - child's behavioural traits.
- **In the home:**
  - parents' ability to cope with stress;
  - parenting style and behaviour;
  - parents' emotional expression.
- **In the early childhood setting:**
  - positive and close key worker relationship;

○ individualised parenting support with a focus on coping strategies and sensitive parenting skills;

○ stimulating, child-focused early education programme with a focus on improving children's social competencies, emotional and cognitive self-regulation skills.

In our project, these protective factors were very evident in the high-achieving young boys' early lives, and they were clearly active in different degrees in enabling the study boys to develop academic resilience. The case studies reveal that the parents of these boys had managed to facilitate these protective factors in the face of quite considerable adversity in some cases, demonstrating high levels of parenting resilience.

Our evidence from the project has supported the development of a conceptual framework which aims to capture and exemplify the complex network of inter-relationships which are involved in supporting the academic and parenting resilience that underpin young white boys' high achievement. We have called this framework the *HAWWC Circles of Success* and this is represented diagrammatically in Figure 8.1.

This framework has four inner elements and two outer elements, each of which can be seen as actively contributing to the ecological context (Bronfrenbrenner 1979) in which the high-achieving young boy is developing and which play a part in enabling (or inhibiting) his achievement. The four inner elements are:

Figure 8.1 HAWWC Circles of success

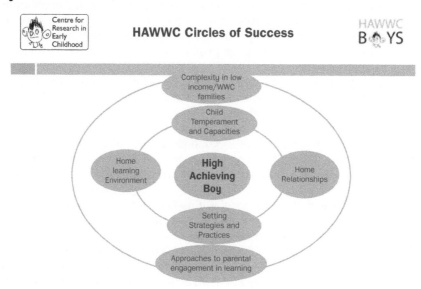

Source: Pascal and Bertram (2016: 13)

- child temperament and capacities;
- home relationships;
- setting strategies and practices;
- home learning environment.

The two outer elements are:

- complexity in low income/white working-class families; and
- approaches to parental engagement in learning.

The evidence from wider literature and extracts from the project case studies for each of these components will be presented below, along with some pointers for action. To set the scene we begin with a challenge to existing stereotypes of low income, white working-class families which the project highlighted.

Challenging stereotypes: complexity in low income/ white working-class families

Official figures show that 'white British' boys in low-income groups are the lowest performing ethnic group in the UK and the difference between their long-term educational achievement and that of their richer white peers is wider than for any other ethnic group. The effects of this class and income difference on their learning are apparent well before nursery school age and are starkly evident on entry to primary school. White boys from low-income families also make less progress than most other groups after entry to school. However, the evidence also reveals that some young white low-income boys are performing as well as, and sometimes much better than, those from more privileged families. As with all groups, it is very important therefore not to homogenise or stereotype families but to see each family within their context, to understand their lived realities and to view them as having significant capacity.

However, it is also true that many white young boys are growing up in families facing a wide range of stressful economic and social challenges and parenting can be much more difficult under such pressures, yet we know parenting styles and interactions are crucial in supporting early learning and sustaining progress. Successful attainment in high achievers appears to be dependent on: the early development of exploratory, self-managing attitudes and the dispositions to learning of these young children; responsive and supportive interactions and relationships in the home; the nature of talk and other home behaviours and experiences; and collaborative interactions between the home and pre-school settings. The overwhelming evidence is that early intervention (critically, between birth and 3 years) both at home and in early childhood settings makes the greatest long-term educative impact on this socially disadvantaged group. We would argue then that focused action supporting parents and early childhood settings is needed to address attainment of young white boys in low-income families, ensuring school readiness and ultimately greater social mobility. We would also argue that the capacity and achievements of many white working-class families can be overlooked when viewing them as a collective. They express the same complexities as families from many other groups, as shown below.

Project findings

Family marital status: There were significant numbers of female single parents rearing these young boys but many do have regular contact with the estranged father. Two-parent families often share parenting responsibilities.

Social isolation: Many families have regular contact with a wider, supportive extended family, particularly grandparents, but some are estranged or geographically distant from family and friends and, in these families, relationships with the HAWWC boy can be intense.

Mental health: Some parents have mental health problems which impact significantly on their parenting capacity and style. The well-being of some parents is significantly enhanced by their close relationship with their bright son.

Employment status: Many low-income families, including single parents, are working full time or accessing training. Some parents, however, positively choose to be at home rather than working during the child's first years and, because of this choice, suffer financial hardship.

Access to childcare and early education: Many of these low-income parents have found funded early education places for their son from 2 years of age. Fewer are accessing childcare prior to 2 years due either to financial constraints or personal preferences.

Case study: Ron

Ron's family situation is complex; his parents have been separated since he was 2 years old but both parents look after him. He spends three days a week with his father and the other four with his mother and maternal grandmother. Occasionally Ron is looked after by his mother's new partner.

Ron's father has high aspirations for his son and they share a close bond. His father, who described his children as 'my whole world' was proud to share with us photographs of displays in his hallway of Ron's work, Father's Day cards, etc.

Reflection/action points

- It is important to recognise and acknowledge the complexity and diversity of 'family' type and circumstances in a non-judgemental way.

- The desire of a parent to be at home with a young boy in the early months of life needs to be acknowledged and supported, as much as the need for support for parental employment.
- Social and emotional support for parents and grandparents is as important as support for boys' learning and development. Learning takes place in a social and emotional context.
- The need for childcare for 'under 3s' depends on particular family circumstances and preferences and is related to parents' employment. The need for educative intervention for targeted users who are most in need is different. It should be recognised and so high-quality, flexible, accessible and affordable services should be aimed at supporting both parents and children. Needs can be complex and require integrated responses from a range of agencies.
- In particular, mental health support for young parents should be made accessible.
- The case for the educational value of accessing funded early education places for boys from 2 years is persuasive.

Child temperament and learning capacities

Certain personality or temperament characteristics, along with certain learning capacities, seem to act as protective factors and increase the resilience of young boys to adversity. Those most frequently observed included sociability, affection, memory, flexibility, reasoning capacity and a sense of humour. Other protective child attributes which can enhance a young boy's capacity to learn include being curious, being socially competent, being an independent learner, and having the ability to focus, concentrate and persist (aspects of active learning). Enjoying dialogue and engaging in sustained talk is associated with higher attainment and development in young boys. An enjoyment of the imagination and stories can facilitate deeper level learning for young boys. Physical outdoor activity is often important in a young boy's explorations, developmental capacity and well-being. As we have seen in other chapters many of these skills, some of which may be inherent as well as learned, are enhanced by the child's relationships and environment. Friendships and attachment to others provide young boys with a sense of belonging, and support their understanding of rules, behaviour expectations and boundaries. These relationships 'anchor' young boys in their social world. Developing a sense of agency and independence provides young boys with a sharpened sense of self-esteem, self-efficacy, self-regulation and capacity for success.

Project findings

Socio-emotional characteristics: The boys have a capacity to make strong and loving attachments to their close family, to make and sustain friendships with their peers and others, to be affectionate, loving, empathetic to others and to 'lead' interactions. These are characteristics associated with high-achieving young boys. Although tantrums and frustrations may appear, they are quickly overcome.

Attitudes and dispositions (the Characteristics of Effective Learning): High-achieving young boys have strong exploratory drive. They are inquisitive, curious, questioning and fascinated by how things and relationships work. They are capable of long periods of concentration, persistence and focus and can become obsessive about things they find interesting. They can memorise and mimic and seek detailed information for things that fascinate which they can retain. They are generally confident, independent, self-motivating and self-sustaining operators within their world, although they also enjoy joint, 'companionable' activity.

Physical capacity: The importance of physical and outdoor activity is evident in the preferred experiences of high-achieving young boys. They enjoy rough and tumble play, movement of all kinds, scooters, trikes, bikes and football and seem to delight in exploring the natural world. They can also get immersed for long periods of quiet, still activities, including puzzles, reading, drawing, Lego® and small world play.

Fascinations and aspirations: Some high-achieving young boys have already developed a prowess for and a deep fascination with an accomplishment such as football, swimming, music, composing, maths or reading, and express a strong motivation to develop this further. This prowess, however, sits in a wider range of achievement not as isolated success.

Case study: Tim

Tim is interested in cars, football, motorsports (an interest of his mother's) and has various temporary obsessions (e.g. the current one is Batman). He loves books and jigsaw puzzles and sees patterns easily. He is a confident and enthusiastic reader, likes riding his bike and swimming. He enjoys being outside but equally 'he loves to watch TV cuddled up to his mum'. He asks a lot of questions and picks things up very quickly; an example is a recent visit to Speedway in Cardiff where he wanted to know all the details of what was going on and had no difficulty in understanding the rules. Until the age of 3, he was fairly shy, and still is in some situations, though generally he is now fairly confident and will engage easily with others. He has good friendships, with a couple of boys in particular, and is popular. While he used to be a follower, his mother now describes him as very independent; 'very much his own man'. He is not an organised child and is untidy with his toys, etc., though he will line up his cars obsessively. He has the capacity to persist in activities and can play for hours at one thing. He has a 'brilliant memory'; an example is his ability to recall details of outings long after they have taken place. His reasoning skills are well developed and he is able to predict consequences of his actions 'but will still carry on'.

Reflection/action points

- Supporting and sustaining strong, secure and trusting attachments of young boys to key adults and peers, both within and outside of their home, is critical to healthy development, resilience and well-being.
- Encouraging a young boy's sociability, friendships and emotional competence is central to their capacity to connect and learn, self-regulate and manage relationships.
- Giving young boys space and time to pursue their interests and develop their fascinations, and supporting their capacity to focus and concentrate for extended periods of time, will enhance their capacity to learn.
- Encouraging the young boy to develop his capacity to 'lead and shape' his learning and engage in sustained dialogues about their interests and passions is hugely beneficial in motivating the child.
- Building in regular and sustained periods of outdoor and physical activity will enhance the young boy's learning, motivation and well-being.

Family relationships and attachments

The early months of a young child's life are very important developmentally but can be very stressful for parents. Many parents need support during these early months in their son's life. Parental health, including mental health and parental resilience in the face of stress and adversity, infuses the home ethos and atmosphere in which the young boy is anchored. Young children need to establish a deep attachment to their main carer(s), who provides the young boy with security, consistency of care and the confidence to trust. These deep psychological roots are linked also to intellectual development. Young boys need at least one person in their lives who would go to unreasonable lengths for them. Young boys can also be an 'anchor' for their parent(s), providing deep meaning and purpose in their lives.

Project findings

Stable, loving, committed and relaxed attachments: The need for strong, secure and relaxed emotional attachments between the main carer(s) and close family and the young boy are essential to the young boy's well-being.

Parents' stress resilience: Stress and mental illness shape and infuse family relationships and interactions. Parents who demonstrate resilience in the face of adversity and have the strength to minimise its impact on their young boy, and protect him from its harmful effects, can minimise its impact on the child, and strengthen the child's ability to cope. Some young boys can also act to protect and provide sanctuary for the parent.

Positive family relationships and interactions: Developing strong and positive relationships with the close and extended family offers the young boy a wider range of social and emotional experiences and access to adults and children at different ages and with different interests. Grandparents often play an important role in the young boy's early life.

Family support: Family support and childcare services can provide a vital additional tier of support for both the young boy and the parent. Accessing this support early can prevent the escalation of need, add a great deal of value to family life and provide the young boy with experiences they might not have in the home. It works best where family, child carers and support agencies are in tune.

Balancing home and work commitments: Balancing home and work commitments can be very difficult for a parent. How this is achieved is a very personal choice. Where parents choose or are required to work, additional care and support is needed to ensure the child continues to thrive and develop and the parent feels secure that the child's needs are being fully met. Where the parent is at home, financial and social support may be needed. Flexible working patterns for both parents can enhance family life and secure family finances.

Case study: Jack

Jack lives with his mother and father with no siblings. His mother is French and has lived in England for ten years. His paternal grandmother, a speech therapist, is a significant figure in his life. Jack's mother describes severe stress in Jack's environment in his early life, when the family's summer holiday letting business was struggling and she was experiencing severe post-natal depression. 'The first three years are a bit blurry. I was not really interested in Jack as a baby and I was really struggling when he had colic and was screaming through the night, but from 3 years old he has been a breath of fresh air, absolutely awesome.' During the difficult times, Jack's father felt excluded and not trusted with the baby, and so she took on the whole burden herself, becoming very depressed and close to tears most of the time. Her mother-in-law was extremely supportive, taking Jack out at every opportunity, whilst never overstepping her place, always respecting the mother's way of doing things but always there when needed, taking Jack to nursery, etc. Sending Jack to nursery at two and a half was 'the best thing I ever did' and it was during this time that Jack began to develop a closeness with his father. Both parents are now working very much as a team in a much happier and settled environment.

Action/reflection points

- Giving parents time and opportunities to establish a close and loving attachment to their son is vital.
- Support to reduce stress levels in the family and build resilience for parents living in challenging circumstances or with mental health needs should be a priority.

- Interaction with siblings, the extended family and wider community provides the young boy with additional stimulation and role models. Grandparents can provide a special relationship which has long-lasting effects.
- Early access to family support, childcare and early education can act to significantly enhance the quality of family life and the development of the young boy.

Home learning environment

Warm, nurturing, attentive, relaxed but 'boundaried', parenting, with regular routines, provides the basic nutrients for optimal development. Parents who enjoy spending time with their son, and support and encourage the young boy's interests and passions encourage self-motivation and self-directed learning. Giving children opportunities to initiate, self-direct and self-manage their activity and to take responsibility for their actions encourages the development of important lifelong learning habits and dispositions, the characteristics or 'super-skills' of learning. Children thrive with regular, familiar routines but which are not rigidly enforced, encouraging a flexible attitude and the capacity to be adaptable. Language development is critical for social and intellectual development and language-rich environments, in which sustained shared dialogues between children and adults predominate with lots of story sharing and creating, provide the optimal conditions for learning to occur.

The mind and the body are inextricably linked and young children need to move to learn. Physical activity and movement, both indoors and outdoors, are essential to healthy development. Children are fundamentally exploratory and curious and seek a broad range of play-based experiences and activities through which they practise and extend their abilities and interests. Young children are born into a digital world and can be seen as 'technology natives'.

Project findings

Warm, nurturing, 'boundaried' parenting: Young boys need warm, caring and intimate parenting and interactions, where rules and behaviour expectations are consistent but not too rigid or onerous. The successful parents in this project were not overtly pushy or domineering. Parenting should meet the young boy's five basic needs:

1 food and warmth;
2 protection and safety;
3 love and a sense of belonging;

4   a feeling of being valued; and

5   a sense of achievable fulfilment, drawing on aspiration and expectations.

Boundaries and order that can come from daily routines such as mealtimes, story times, play times and bedtimes, can be helpful in anchoring the child's day and providing security and structure to daily life.

Sharing time and being attentive: Having regular, one-on-one time, where the young boy is given individual, affectionate attention, sharing activities and interests can deeply impact on the boy's sense of self-esteem, self-worth and well-being. Being 'tuned' into the boy's emotional and cognitive state and needs and being responsive to these gives the child security and the confidence to be independent and exploratory.

Child-initiated activity: Parents of high-achieving young boys follow their son's lead and support their self-directed passions and interests, providing lots of support, encouragement and a playmate. They are not 'pushy' or 'tiger' parents but see their son as competent and with their own agency and play agendas.

Routines: Parents ensure that each day has clearly embedded routines (e.g. getting up, bath time, mealtimes, bedtime, sleep time) and regularity but these are not rigidly imposed and flexibility is also seen as important. Mealtimes often are seen as an important family time when talk is shared and relationships within the family are cemented.

Parent/child talk: Parents of high-achieving boys enjoy their child's company and have talked a lot to their child (engaged in sustained shared dialogues) since birth. Responding to children's curiosity and questions is an important part of the dialogue.

Stories and books: Sharing and creating stories from books and daily life is an important part of daily life for these boys and their parents. Reading together is an important part of daily routines and parents often model reading for pleasure themselves.

Outdoors and physical activity: Being outdoors a lot and sharing walks, playing in the park, on the beach, in the fields or in the garden is an important feature of home life, with lots of dialogue about the natural world. Physical activity is seen as central to child and parent well-being, with football, cycling, wrestling and fishing, from an early age, featuring as important shared activities.

Home activities: A wide range of indoor and outdoor activities are identified as providing the young boy with stimulation and opportunities for both companionable and self-directed learning, including, table games, bricks, jigsaws, drawing, small world play and Lego®. Many parents commented on their son's enjoyment of imaginative and creative play activities, including music making.

Technology: Technology is a present and recognised element in daily home life for most (but not all) the high-achieving children, but 'screen time' is generally monitored and limited.

Case study: Matt

The parental approach is never to push but to 'see what he wants to do and then support him'. The family home is full of books, as both parents are avid readers. Parents read to both boys 'but not excessively' and they have tended not to read the books Matt brings home from school but will instead read *Folk of the Faraway Tree* at bedtime. Neither will they do what home-work Matt is meant to do or push Matt with reading or phonics. Matt has always asked lots of questions so there were always opportunities for sus-tained dialogue. The house is described as 'chaotic' but, within the mess, Matt will always know where his important things are. One important aspect of his early childhood was to go on long walks with his parents during the second period of maternity leave. Matt began to name things on the walks, e.g. saying 'car' when he saw a tractor. The walks were given specific names because of things related to them, e.g. 'chicken walk' or 'Anna walk'. When the younger brother was born, the long walks would help to get him to sleep and Matt would take part, in his pushchair, in all weathers. Both par-ents see these walking experiences as being very significant in Matt's development. He loves physical activity, particularly riding bikes and scoot-ers. He also enjoys writing stories, making up plays and playing the piano. He has a musical ear and says he wants to be a musician. Both boys like dressing up and re-enacting scenes from Spiderman and other superheroes. The parents have resisted anything digital so far and Matt has no access to computers or phones. He repeatedly asks to go on to the CBeebies website but is refused, though he is allowed to watch DVDs. The family have always eaten together, even when the boys were very small, and they feel that this was an important feature of Matt's upbringing. He is very aware of healthy eating and will ask 'Is this healthy?'

Setting strategies and practices

Less advantaged children who access a high-quality, early education pro-gramme achieve better outcomes and enter formal schooling with enhanced school readiness. As we have seen in previous chapters, a play-based, active pedagogy both in the setting and at home which encourages child-initiated activity and offers a broad range of learning experiences provides a stronger foundation for lifelong learning than a narrowly focused, formal, didactic approach. Settings which offer support for parents alongside education and care for children are more effective in developing school readiness and engag-ing families in the educative process at home and at school. An effective local early years system provides an integrated network of support around families, including education and care, community and family activities, parenting sup-port and health advice.

Do you encourage parents to …

- provide positive, warm parenting with regular routines and reasonable expectations for their child can help parents to relax and enjoy their son's company?
- build in daily time for sharing activities and experiences, both indoors and outdoors?
- give extended and sustained time to talk, sharing experiences and celebrating the young boy's achievements?
- get outdoors and move to provide the young boy with a wide range of physical, sensory and cognitive learning opportunities?
- view technology as part of the modern world of childhood but not dominant in daily activities?

Case study: James

From the age of 2 years, James had access to 10 hours pre-school through a children's centre and this was regarded as very important for the mother's health and well-being. Pre-school took place in a church hall in a very family-oriented and loving environment. 'The ladies were mums and grand-mums' and the activities were free-flow, involving computers, music, dancing. Though he didn't settle quickly, he progressed rapidly. 'He had no fear of computers and fixed the pre-school PC!' Progression to pre-school was seamless. During this period, he developed a good relationship with his key person and responded well to the clear behaviour policy. The key person has told his mother 'I've taken my lead from him'. He progressed rapidly, learning to write his name, etc. but his mother feels that a bigger gain was the space and respite offered, and the interaction with other children. The pre-school acknowledged that he was achieving highly at this stage.

Final reflections

Seen in this way, the evidence and actions we identified are optimistic, demonstrating that, even in adversity, excellent parenting is possible and that the resilience the young boys and their parents in our project demonstrate shows the way for others to act. It is also evident from the case studies that this is not about dramatic or extraordinary capacities. Rather, that the required resilience is made of ordinary rather than extraordinary processes. This resilience develops in spite of adversity when basic protective systems in human development are operating to counteract the threats to child's development and parent's capacity to parent. In short, resilience for both young boys and parents is a process that involves ordinary adaptive resources and systems. It is in the grasp of everyone.

Key messages

- Adults' parenting resilience and children's academic resilience are both made of ordinary rather than extraordinary processes. Both of these types of resilience emerge from a process that involves ordinary, adaptable and transferable behaviours and resources which are available to children and their parents.
- The positive parenting practices and home learning experiences which were prevalent in the study's low income, white working-class families provide valuable insights into what might 'narrow the gap' for many other young children from different underachieving groups.

Implications for EY settings

1. There needs to be training for practitioners in anti-discriminatory practice and how to provide individualised parenting support through a warm, responsive, key person system which values parents' social and cultural background and focuses on coping strategies and sensitive parenting skill.
2. Provision of a stimulating, child-focused early education programme with a focus on how children learn and the aim of improving children's social competencies and emotional and cognitive self-regulation skills is essential.

References

Barbour L. (2020) *The home learning environment has never been more important.* London: Sutton Trust. Available at: www.suttontrust.com/news-opinion/all-news-opinion/home-learning/ (accessed 30 October 2021).

Bronfrenbrenner, U. (1979) *The Ecology of Human Development.* Cambridge, MA: Harvard University Press.

Feinstein, L., Duckworth, K. and Sabates, R. (2004) *A model of the intergenerational transmission of educational success: wider benefits of learning* (Research Report 10). London: Institute of Education, Centre for Research on the Wider Benefits of Learning. Available at: https://discovery.ucl.ac.uk/id/eprint/10005977/ (accessed 30 September 2021).

Ofsted (2007) *Narrowing the gap: the inspection of children's services.* London: Ofsted.

Ofsted (2008) *White boys from low-income backgrounds: good practice in schools.* London: Ofsted.

Ofsted (2013) *Unseen children: access and achievement 20 years on.* London: Ofsted.

Ofsted (2014) *Are you ready? Good practice in school readiness.* London: Ofsted.

Pascal C. and Bertram, A.D (2012) *The Potential of Early Education to Impact on Socio-economic Disadvantage.* London: Ofsted.

Pascal, C. and Bertram, T. (2016) *High Achieving White Working Class (HAWWC) Boys Project final report.* Birmingham: Centre for Research in Early Childhood (CREC). Available at: www.crec.co.uk/HAWWC%20Boys/HAWWC%20Boys%20Project%20

Report.pdf (accessed 22 April 2021). Project videos, case studies and information sheets available at: www.crec.co.uk/Default.aspx?PageID=14027591&A=SearchResult&SearchID=3315890&ObjectID=14027591&ObjectType=1 (accessed 20 April 2021).

Perera N., Treadaway M., Johnes B., Sellen P., Hutchinson J. and Mao, L. (2016) *Education in England: Annual Report 2016*. London: Centre Forum.

Rutter M. (2012) Resilience as a dynamic concept, *Developmental Psychopathology*, May 24(2): 335–344.

Select Committee (2014) *Underachievement in Education by White Working-Class Children*. London: HMSO.

Select Committee (2020) *Education and Attainment of White Working-Class Boys*; Hansard, Volume 671. London: HMSO.

Sylva, K., Melhuish, E., Sammons, P., Siraj-Blatchford, I. and Taggart, B. (eds) (2010) *Early Childhood Matters: Evidence from the Effective Preschool and Primary Education Project*. Oxford: Routledge.

Ungar M., Ghazinour M. and Richter J. (2013) Annual Research Review: What is resilience within the social ecology of human development? *Journal of Child Psychology and Psychiatry*, Apr 54(4): 348–366.

Early years settings as lifelong learning communities

Clare Crowther

Chapter summary

- This chapter explores the development of lifelong learning communities in early years settings.
- It draws on a range of case studies illustrating how lifelong learning is embedded in daily practice at three very different early years settings.
- It highlights the characteristics of effective learning and the key role they play in the professional and personal development of educators and, in turn, the development and quality of their settings.
- It explores the importance of team members working collaboratively in the process of creating a lifelong learning community.

Introduction

This is the vision for my workplace: 'Just like the children in our care, we want our staff to hold the "skill, the will and the thrill" to learn more. We want our nurseries to be the best they can be, the best place for our staff to work and train, reaching their fullest potential, holding a strong sense of satisfaction in all they do' (Atelier Nurseries 2021).

We are a learning community, a term which has become more embedded in practice across the early years sector, as settings and providers have needed to develop the training, experiences and opportunities offered to the staff they employ, as well as wanting to develop and enhance the services they offer to children and families.

Over recent years the landscape of the early years sector has changed dramatically. The Childcare Act 2016 brought with it the introduction of the Extended Early Years Entitlement seeing an increase to funded childcare from 15 hours to 30 hours for eligible families.

The introduction of the new Early Years Funding System in 2017 saw a quarter of local authorities drop the funding rates offered to providers. Many settings were already juggling rising business costs and in particular, the National Living Wage which is set to increase to nearly £9.00 per hour in 2021 for staff aged 23 years and over.

In 2020 the funding crisis led to a quarter of responders to an Early Years Alliance poll in England saying it was 'unlikely' that their setting would still be operating in 2021. In addition to the funding concerns, there continue to be significant issues surrounding the recruitment and retention of skilled and qualified practitioners. These challenges have been widely reported and recent research has found that many early years practitioners have left the sector for more highly paid positions with less responsibility (Early Years Workforce Commission 2021).

The recruitment and retention issues paired with low levels of funding have brought the sustainability of settings into question with the shift in government agenda, moving from raising the standard of early years education to ensuring affordable childcare. Setting owners and leaders have needed to refocus their energies and resources into developing a culture of lifelong learning within their settings in order to ensure that high-quality care and education remains at the forefront of their agenda. This is especially vital as we see yet more curriculum changes to the EYFS in 2021.

What does a learning community look like for settings in practice?

The term 'lifelong learning community' encompasses a range of practices, often visible within and facilitated through, the daily provision and leadership of an early years setting. It often summarises the engagement of staff, parents and the wider community in enhancing the learning opportunities of children, their parents and the staff working alongside them.

It describes the variety of ways in which early years practitioners, parents and children work and learn together.

Creating, maintaining and facilitating learning communities

Within the changing landscape of early years provision, it seems important to affirm our understanding of the roles we hold in creating, maintaining and facilitating the learning communities we belong to and lead within the early years sector.

To do this consideration must be given to the culture of the settings we are engaged with. We should question:

- What are the values and principles underpinning the setting's work?
- How and with whom has the philosophy of the setting been developed?
- What pedagogical approaches are taken and how are the characteristics of effective pedagogical practice shared between staff and staff, and staff and families?
- Is there a drive for continuous improvement? How is this shared between all stakeholders?
- What leadership styles are required to develop such a lifelong learning community?
- How are staff encouraged and supported to take joint responsibility for their learning in such a process?
- How are parents engaged with the setting, in order to enhance the home learning environment of their children?

Throughout this chapter, case studies examine the various strategies and approaches adopted within a range of early years settings as they seek to create and maintain lifelong learning communities. Examples are taken from three different settings.

Setting one: Atelier Nursery

Atelier Nursery opened its first site in the city of Bath in September 2012, before expanding and opening its second site in Wiltshire in 2017.

Atelier Nursery strives to provides a careful and seamless balance between the care and education of babies and young children. Each nursery offers thoughtfully designed spaces, which give children the freedom to explore the nursery at their own pace.

Recognising 'play as the language of childhood' and the best way for children to learn, at Atelier children are given the opportunity to gain and embed new skills, develop their understanding, and demonstrate their competencies through carefully planned and purposeful play opportunities.

The philosophy of the setting uses the work of Froebel as its foundation, emphasising the value of play and focusing upon relationships. At Atelier we also recognise the influence of a range of other educationalists and theorists and Atelier has found itself standing on the shoulders of giants such as Vygotsky (1978), Malaguzzi (1993), Athey (1990) and Laevers (2000). Our pedagogy has been developed through experience, research and theory and continues to evolve as the practice across the settings deepens.

At Atelier, what children learn is important, but *how* children learn comes first, both in terms of planning and the approaches undertaken. Through play, children are supported to build their confidence and independence. Through interactions and planning children are empowered to choose, to reason, reflect, imagine and empathise, thus embedding the characteristics for effective learning both now and for the future.

The nurseries implement an informed and successful pedagogy that includes a free-flow, workshop approach and an emotionally enabling environment, in which children are cared for in mixed age, key family groupings (Elfer et al. 2003). Each key family is made up of a group of children from across the age range birth to 4 years. Working in this mixed age approach encourages children to share their nursery experiences alongside each other. Children quickly develop reciprocal relationships that scaffold their individual learning. Building a network of social relationships, children can expand their cultural horizons and build on social capital through friendships and relationships they make with other children from different ages, stages and backgrounds.

The key family approach allows each member of staff to take their time to truly get to know the children in their care. This promotes a strong, secure and genuine bond that enables a 'professional love' (Nutbrown and Page 2008) to develop between the child and their key person.

The staff team have a wealth of qualification and experience, with teachers subtly leading and role modelling practice and a Resident Artist cultivating the creativity of children and staff alike. Leaders and managers support staff in their learning through targeted professional development plans, professional development opportunities and supervision sessions.

Setting two: Snapdragons Nurseries

The first of the Snapdragons Nurseries opened in January 1998 in a farmhouse in Atworth, Wiltshire, in response to local demand for high-quality full day care. It developed an excellent local reputation, and the group has since expanded into Bath, Bristol and two further sites in Wiltshire. The Snapdragons Nursery group has ten nurseries in total and offers 1150 childcare places, employing 345 staff.

Despite its size, Snapdragons remains very much a family-run business that aims to react quickly to local needs but, more importantly, can respond personally to the families that it serves. Like Atelier, the underpinning values of Snapdragons Nurseries see them genuinely wanting their nurseries to be the best, with children's experiences being memorable and fun.

Snapdragons work in partnership with parents to earn their trust and confidence, ensuring that families are happy, understanding how and why practice is undertaken, so that together they can ensure children are happy and confident, engaging with opportunity to maximise their full potential and become well-rounded citizens of the world.

Each of the nurseries uses the Early Years Foundation Stage (DfE 2021) to guide the curriculum offered to the children cared for. Implemented by each child's key person, observation and recognition of each child's stage of development and interest are used to ensure that every child is given the opportunity to learn through high-quality play experiences provided.

In addition to the rich play-based curriculum, at Snapdragons the impact that being outdoors can have on children's learning and development is completely central. Whether within the boundaries of a city or out in the rural wilds, Snapdragons make sure there are plenty of opportunities to take advantage of being outside every day.

Each nursery has its own unique outdoor area and access to natural spaces, a short journey beyond its doors, which allow children to have positive learning experiences in all weathers, throughout the changing seasons.

Setting three: Free Rangers Nursery and Forest School

Free Rangers Forest School offers childcare and education to children from birth to 5 years and cares for and educates up to 105 children on site at any one time. Surrounded by rolling countryside, Free Rangers is located on a former working farm site in Midsomer Norton, north east Somerset, and has exclusive access to 20 acres of land which the children use daily and fully.

The ethos of Free Rangers is very much built on a belief that a child's happiness is the foundation upon which learning will take place. Highly qualified staff nurture every child's self-esteem and self-confidence to ensure they embrace the opportunities on offer at Free Rangers. Staff take their lead from the children. They listen carefully and gently guide each child in a range of directions that will further their learning and development and inspire curiosity and wonderment.

According to their age children are based in one of the three purposefully designed learning spaces, the Hive, Burrow or Den, and are assigned a key person who is the main point of contact for parents and carers.

Forest School is a key approach to learning which underpins the Free Rangers ethos and lies at the heart of the pedagogical practice undertaken.

The principles underpinning the practice at Free Rangers use:

- nature to provide a real context for learning;
- children's preferred learning styles: being active, learning through practical outdoor experiences and employing all their senses;
- nature's resources to facilitate learning.

Aside from ensuring children have fun and connecting with the natural world, these support the development of the characteristics of effective learning, their communication skills and their ability to identify, interpret and manage risk. At Free Rangers children naturally become more inquisitive and learn new levels of perseverance whilst developing physically, socially and emotionally.

Recently Free Rangers have developed their work and created an online network that acts as a childcare collaborative, bringing together parents, practitioners and other sector experts.

The values and principles underpinning a lifelong learning community

The philosophy of any early years setting will be underpinned by the values and principles it holds. These values and principles will shape the culture embedded, practices undertaken and in turn the learning that takes place for the staff, the children and their families.

Each of the settings identified take a unique approach to the care and education of children. Whilst working in different ways, there is however common ground for each of them as they strive to offer high-quality care and education and in turn the development of learning communities. They are also places of trust.

Staff need to be able to trust their peers and their leaders to give helpful, critical feedback on the questions they raise, their practice and the doubts and uncertainties they have. We all strive to create a culture where uncertainty and mistakes are viewed by everyone as an opportunity for learning and development; where positive errors can be made and reflections and processes shared. Working in this way supports staff to understand what quality and excellence means and enables practitioners to improve their judgements, in order to achieve the quality standards identified within the setting.

Embracing the characteristics of effective learning plays a key role in the professional and personal development of educators and, in turn, the development and quality of the settings we lead and work within.

In implementing the chosen philosophy and pedagogical approach of any setting, one can expect significant challenges to arise as the physical, emotional and cognitive demands of working within the sector are truly revealed. Staff will need the opportunity to challenge, debate, question and reflect upon the ways in which they are being asked to work and from this a professional learning community will begin to embed.

Education pioneer Chris Athey discusses the basis for constructivism and, in my view, the underpinning principle of a professional learning community when she states: 'The main value of Froebelian Pedagogy and "Constructivism", the main system of educational research endeavours of the last century, it is quite simple. It is based on the conviction that each individual learner contributes to and collaborates in, his or her own learning' (Athey 2004: 11).

Considering Athey's words, it becomes clear that contribution and collaboration between:

- staff member and staff member
- staff member and parent
- staff and children
- parents and children

are required in order for all stakeholders to have ownership of the philosophy and pedagogy of the setting.

The responsibility of facilitating such relationships that enhance one's own and others' learning initially falls to the leadership team of the setting, who will in turn create the culture required for an effective lifelong learning community.

The role of the leader in developing a learning community

The leadership team are often seen as being responsible for creating and maintaining the vision and ethos of the setting. For it to be implemented effectively, however, the staff team need to have a clear understanding of what their leaders are seeking to achieve and why.

Focus needs to be given to not just what we want our staff to learn but to how we want them to learn it. It is a simple process to share, for example, the setting policies and procedures, but to ensure they are understood, valued and implemented consistently in practice is far from simple and requires a strong leadership team, who are confident in working collaboratively with those they lead.

Within a true learning community, the role of the leader is vast and complex. Leaders coach every team member to achieve self-mastery, to actively look for ways to improve the organisation, to take accountability for making changes, to help other team members learn and focus on developing a culture of growth and professional learning (Sullivan and Glanz 2005).

To be effective, a flexible, responsive and supportive leadership style should be adopted. The use of both transformational and distributive leadership (Law and Glover 2000) that promote contribution and collaboration are key in the facilitating and championing of the processes undertaken within a learning community.

Contribution and collaboration

Within any learning community, it is important that each member of the team can work collaboratively in the process of reflecting on and maintaining or enhancing the vision held for the setting.

Together, staff should take time to reflect upon the personal and professional experiences held between them. The core values that each individual team member brings to the setting should be identified and the influence that these will have on the wider team and its work acknowledged.

As with most teams, staff members will have a diverse range of skills, knowledge and understanding. Recognising this will enable the key elements of practice to be continually debated and improved.

Staff supervision meetings enable the opportunity for leaders to truly get to know their individual staff members, recognise their skills and experiences and together identify the contribution that can be made to collaborative working.

Supervision meetings enable the organisational culture and values to be established, and a commitment to positive working relationships to be fostered, through open communication amongst managers and other staff, promoting high-quality practice.

Supervisions seek to build a culture of honest and constructive shared dialogue in which feedback can be offered and received, enabling the staff team to work towards the improvement of the services offered.

Each of the three nurseries identified in the case studies complete regular supervision sessions with their staff teams. Each setting has created a format and agenda that suits their setting and then implements a structure accordingly.

For Snapdragons, the process is formalised every three months and is based on the visions and values held for the setting. A code of kindness originally created for the children has been adapted for use with the staff team and supports the semi-structured supervision session. Questions are posed to staff relating to their teamwork, and their ability to listen and learn from others as well as their own learning and development, focusing on seeking support and the respect of each other in the sharing of knowledge.

At Atelier, staff supervision sessions seek to complement the facilitated pedagogical conversations already taking place and so focus on the work–life balance of the staff member and any professional or personal issues they are facing. Coaching and guidance are offered, in relation to the role and any specific responsibilities they hold. Shared reflections on how to approach a situation, or perhaps adapt practice styles, are shared and signposting offered.

Peer observation

The use of peer observation can instigate dialogue within staff supervisions and is viewed as a collaborative development activity from which professionals offer mutual support (Bell 2005). Peer observations, when completed sensitively and constructively, enable staff to develop ideas and gather feedback on their interactions and effectiveness.

At Free Rangers, peer observations give staff the opportunity to demonstrate being an 'expert' in their role. Staff observe each other in a learning space that works differently from their usual base room. For example, the Forest School Leader observes in the baby room, or the carpenter will observe in the toddler room.

Once the observations are completed, in a safe space, conversations flow regarding the teaching strategies determined and the interactions that took place. The staff member being observed uses the feedback offered to reflect on their practice and identify ways in which they can develop their professional practice.

The opportunity for mutual learning, however, is not missed and the peer observation process is completed by the swapping of roles. Now acting as an expert in their own role, the staff member is able to explain and explore the learning observed in more depth. For example, sharing the importance of attachment and how this is recognised within the baby room or the underpinning principles of the treasure basket (Goldschmied and Jackson 1994). Working collaboratively, there is a sharing of skills and knowledge to form a shared understanding of how the pedagogy undertaken in one nursery, but two very different spaces, comes together and builds on the children's experiences.

The sensitive yet constructive handling of peer observation demonstrates a respect for the professional practice of others and eases staff's initial hesitance to participate. Gradually, the reviewing of individual practice, as well as the collective, has become the norm.

Across the settings, peer observations have led to higher levels of support and trust between staff and the development of caring yet professional working relationships. Staff are now more comfortable with each other; they openly share in their successes and weaknesses, offering praise and support in the required measure. They steer away from simply being 'nice' recognising that, for professional growth to occur, dialogue cannot be based on shallow responses.

This will at times involve difficult things to say, and difficult things to hear, but as long as conversations are shared in a respectful, empathetic and supportive manner this will support the setting culture to evolve further.

Within the settings, staff now seek to continuously share and grow their understanding and learning, holding the view that:

> We all have something to offer, we can all get better and together we can achieve our aims. I would not want to work at a setting that didn't push you to think and grow in your practice. Working here is really hard work. Nothing stands still and you aren't allowed to just take the easy option. You are always pushed to be the best you can be and do the best you can for the children.
>
> (Extract from a conversation with a staff member regarding their experience of a peer observation that fed into a staff supervision)

The high level of collaboration and mutual respect for each other, evident through supervision and peer observations, is a fundamental requirement in developing practice and in turn a learning community. The learning communities being formed are 'groups of people who share a concern, a set of problems, or passion about a topic, who deepen their knowledge and expertise in this area by interacting on an ongoing basis' (Wenger et al. 2002:4).

Whichever format of staff supervision and peer observation is preferred and adopted, the overarching principle is contribution and collaboration, which in turn leads staff to feeling empowered both for themselves and in the effective completion of the work or learning being undertaken.

The sharing of leadership, power and decision making

The sharing of leadership, power and decision making within a learning community is not always straightforward.

Developing collegial relationships empowers and enables staff, which in turn empowers and enables the children we are working alongside and their families. This heterarchical approach (Frew 2009) recognises the peaks of leadership required across the varying aspects of our practice and the services we may wish to offer.

However, it can also bring challenge to some members of the team, who may have only experienced a more traditional management style, leading to a hierarchical view of the leader being omnicompetent – 'all wise and all competent'. This can lead to some hesitation when staff are given the option of and encouraged to question those who are in a more senior role, in order to make meaning and seek solutions both for themselves as individuals and for the wider team.

Relationships will need to be forged in which everyone is able to contribute, with staff viewing themselves as leaders in their own right. This type of setting culture can be characterised by involvement, openness and trust, with staff feeling a sense of belonging and becoming self-regulated learners.

Whalley (2007) discusses the learning community created at the Pen Green Centre as an environment in which:

- children, parents and staff were encouraged to be good decision makers, able to question, challenge and make choices;
- there were opportunities for staff to become highly trained, reflective practitioners with good levels of support and supervision, in an environment where they could build satisfactory relationships and feel valued personally and professionally;
- staff consulted and felt comfortable with all stakeholders – children, parents, staff, the community, the local authority;
- parents had become advocates for their children and were beginning to share in their understanding of their children's learning at home and with nursery staff.

Whalley states that it is 'recognised that the empowerment of staff will increase as leaders seek "power for" as opposed to "power over" their staff team' (Whalley 2006:9).

Cultivating creativity among the staff team

The concept of a learning community, in which people's new thinking is nurtured and aspirations set free, is a shift from the traditional paradigm. However, many early years settings are now establishing a culture in which people come together to learn and to test ideas and processes, in order to create the outcomes they desire both for the children and for the wider setting.

A leadership team should endeavour to instil creative thinking amongst their staff, generating a sense of excitement and enthusiasm for learning that fosters both engagement and satisfaction. The encouragement of staff to hold high aspirations for themselves and to take responsibility for their own learning will naturally lead to staff questioning how they can improve their practice, increase their knowledge and develop their professional understandings.

One project undertaken during the first National Lockdown in March 2020 at Atelier Nursery, included an optional staff training programme. Led by the resident artist, a range of reflective posts were shared with the staff team, inviting them to explore their own creative thinking. The project sought to nurture the natural curiosity staff members held, inviting them to look at things differently and find new ways to solve problems.

Due to the impact of the pandemic on staff mental health, it was recognised that reflective and mindful practice would be of benefit to the staff team. There had also been previous strategic discussions about how to support staff to recognise and reflect upon their own creativity – an element of our pedagogy we are always seeking to develop. We wanted to challenge the perceptions held by some staff that they weren't creative, both in practice or their thinking.

Each week, posts were shared with the staff team, taking passages from the book *Conscious Creativity* by Philippa Stanton (2018). This felt the most authentic and considerate way to engage staff. The resident artist shared some of her own reflections before attaching activities and exercises for staff to explore. Recognition was given that this opportunity would not be a 'one size fits all'. There were no right answers, but rather starting points or a place to jump off from.

It was suggested that staff start the process by trying to trust themselves and not question their curiosities, but instead follow those thoughts and see what happens. Over the following weeks together staff explored the processes of looking, documenting, texture, the senses, atmosphere, nothingness, light, shadow, abstraction, composition. Little by little, taking it as they wanted, slowly and gently the team found the things that nourished them. Now, back at nursery, we are seeing the impact of this project on our staff and in turn the children they are working alongside, with the conversations and creative thinking across the nursery soaring.

Developing a culture of open dialogue

The joys and challenges of establishing a learning community are vast; there is an ongoing requirement for energy, focus, enthusiasm and, above all, communication.

A learning community requires a culture of open and constructive dialogue, allowing a culture in which the safe and respectful challenging of the working practice of others is acceptable. This open and honest dialogue forces debate within a safe environment, which in turn promotes enquiry, understanding and an appreciation of others. It assists in the formation and effectiveness of the team in meeting the setting's aims, in accepting the challenges faced and in seeking shared solutions and ownership.

One informal strategy used at Atelier Nursery is 'Conversational Café' (Robbins 2001). It promotes experiential learning (Kolb et al. 1995) and provides a holistic model of a learning process which is consistent with the ways in which we see children learn most effectively. It is the simplest of strategies and takes the form of a non-agenda informal meeting in which both staff and parents are invited to participate, rather than required to do so.

Interestingly, the voluntary nature of the experience has immediately led to higher levels of involvement from staff than those seen in formal meetings. The environment is set up to feel relaxed and physically comfortable. The use of a neutral space and consideration as to the timing of the café seeks to promote staff well-being and a sense of value.

A discussion topic may be decided prior to the meeting, thus determining those who wish to be involved. Alternatively, regular cafés take place that offer opportunity to discuss more generic issues, such as the development of learning spaces, or the implementation of policy and procedure, as well as our responses to the pressures, critical incidents or the learning currently taking place within the nursery.

Team members participating within conversational café and reflective conversations are able to seek affirmation and solution. They are able to create new pathways of thinking, within shared practice, creatively approaching their work while maintaining the vision and shared values of the nursery. They play with ideas and explore ways of moving forward, creating and thinking critically at their own level as well as showing the skills involved in active learning.

Creating opportunities for further learning

In order to maintain and further develop the lifelong learning communities created within our settings, it is important to identify and reflect on how we are embedding learning in practice. As setting leaders we need to promote the characteristics of lifelong learning amongst our teams. We need to look at how the characteristics of engagement, motivation and thinking are encouraged and facilitated within the context of the relationships held and the environments we are working within.

Each of the settings are using a variety of opportunities to embed the characteristics of effective learning with staff. At Snapdragons, the largest of the three settings by far, bite-sized, online training sessions have been created by the Quality and Training Manager. These 45-minute snapshot training opportunities came about after recognition was given to the challenge of accessing high-quality training for staff that related to the setting's own practice.

It was acknowledged that engagement levels amongst staff were high and that they were wanting to learn. Embracing this will to learn, the Quality and Training Manager needed to find a solution that met the challenge of working with such a large and diverse team. Each staff member held a differing level of qualification and had different experience and needs. However, for any training to impact on practice, several staff would need to access the same training. The challenge began!

Enabling staff to access external training was going to be both challenging and financially expensive. Staff had already completed a full working day and their well-being would be affected if after-hours training became the expectation.

As such, a fully accessible programme needed to be created that allowed staff to 'dip in and out' of a range of training programmes that suited the staff whilst meeting the setting's needs. A catalogue of training was designed and created, including video tutorials, pre-recorded webinars and simply signposting staff to a resource bank of articles and seminars, all of which were followed up by a practice quiz or reflective question.

For all setting leaders the training of our staff is crucial, as we need to ensure that our settings are meeting both the educational and statutory requirements as a minimum. Most of us want our practice to be at the forefront of international early years provision, with staff feeling satisfied and equally challenged. To achieve this, the use of pedagogical conversations is an additional approach taken. Seeking to complement the training opportunities offered to our staff teams, pedagogical conversations offer staff and leaders the opportunity to come together and reflect on practice, prompt debate, and offer guidance to less experienced staff through informal coaching.

The use of pedagogical conversations

At Atelier Nursery, each room team meets once a week to discuss the observations they have gathered of the children accessing the provision they lead. These observations are used to identify children's interests and to plan for future learning opportunities that are purposeful and seek to extend the children's current skills, knowledge and understanding whilst also offering opportunities to consolidate prior learning.

Each of these team times is led by a senior member of staff who acts as a pedagogical leader for the nursery. They hold the role of drawing together all children's experiences, while subtly and seamlessly ensuring all areas of learning and development are promoted.

The pedagogical leaders facilitate the reflection of the staff team. Asking open-ended questions, they seek to develop the practice undertaken at the nursery. Acting as a critical friend, (Butler et al. 2011) they are a sounding board for team members, whilst subtly coaching practitioners to deepen their own learning and to role model possibility thinking.

Facilitating the dialogue of metacognition allows staff to regulate their thinking, developing critical thinking processes including the ability to:

- identify problems and questions;
- gather information and opinions;

- analyse the information collected and establish its significance;
- make a decision or reach a conclusion and then communicate this effectively to others.

Taking time to discuss, examine and plan for children's learning in this way encourages the opportunity for staff to share in their own experiences. Essentially these meetings are being led by the people who take part in them, reinforcing the contribution and collaboration required for success.

This approach is also adopted at Free Rangers, where staff draw on the wealth of knowledge across the team, in a secure environment which generates a sense of trust, allowing the team to feel safe to discuss different areas of their practice, thus reinforcing the underpinning principles of the learning community.

When choosing to work in this way, ring fencing non-contact time for staff such as team times is essential, as this time allows for a shared reflection upon practice. Ideally this time is in addition to the staff supervision meetings, complementing the opportunity for the organisational culture and values to be established. Commitment to positive working relationships is fostered through open communication amongst all staff, so as to continually promote high-quality practice.

Of course, to truly represent a lifelong learning community within an early years setting, the pedagogical conversations need to extend to the parents and carers of the children we care for.

Engaging parents within the learning community

Research and policy inform us that when parents are involved in their children's learning, both the children and the parents are likely to benefit. Therefore, the next stage in embedding a learning community at an early years setting should be the full inclusion of parents.

It is reported (Sylva et al. 2004) that the participation of parents within children's learning can lead to:

- enhanced self-esteem;
- improved achieved and attainment levels;
- improved relationships between child and parent;
- improved understanding of the educational process and curriculum.

Historically, early years settings have participated in parent evenings, parent one-to-one meetings and encouraged parents to spend time in the setting whenever they could. This, in addition to regular newsletters and communication books exploring the child's daily routine, was deemed sufficient.

All of these methods enable parents to have a greater awareness of what their child is experiencing on a surface level. However, no one strategy allows for a depth of understanding as to how their child might be learning or how as parents they can support and extend this. Or, indeed, how as practitioners we can learn from the observations being captured at home.

As early years educators we need to reflect upon the elements of our practice that require development in order to truly facilitate a learning community that embraces the partnership roles held between the setting and parent. Points to consider may include:

- What is the most effective way to have a dialogue with parents about their child's learning at home and the nursery?
- How can you make this dialogue accessible to all, in a range of formats that meet the needs of our families?
- How can you develop a shared understanding of the theoretical concepts underpinning children's learning?
- How can you develop a shared understanding of how best to support children's learning in both the nursery and the home environment?

Each of the three settings has identified ways of working that meets the varying needs of their families and communities. For Free Rangers, the use of social media has been key in sharing short narratives of the children's daily experiences and raising the profile of the work undertaken by the staff team, by linking posts to other organisations and current research. Working in this way provides an open-ended dialogue, inviting parents to learn more whilst bringing value to the learning undertaken.

Seeking to engage with the wider community and raise the importance of early education, Free Rangers has also launched the *Free Rangers Magazine*. It is a not-for-profit incentive that celebrates outdoor learning and holistic living by sharing in real stories and inspirational articles that underpin the ethos of the nursery and can be purchased in the local area.

At Snapdragons, a focus on engaging the families of some of the most vulnerable children was undertaken at the Shirehampton nursery, where many of the children were in receipt of a funded place or had been referred by the local Children's Centres. A high number of children learning English as an Additional Language (EAL) were registered and a large percentage of the cohort were children with Special Educational Needs and/or Disabilities (SEND). The nursery staff quickly found themselves struggling with the ratio of 1:8 when potentially two-thirds of those children had specific support plans or additional care requirements. Engaging with these families took time, as trust needed to be built and language barriers overcome. Theraplay strategies, such as Sunshine Circles, were implemented to support both the children with SEND, and those needing support in developing social interaction, attachment and resilience. Repeating these sessions weekly became an effective intervention for the children but also offered an invaluable way of engaging parents after the techniques were videoed and shared with families and duplicate resources provided for use at home.

For Atelier, as well as informal everyday exchanges, an annual exhibition seeks to engage parents. Through sharing documentation and installations, the staff present the work undertaken by the children throughout the previous year. The underpinning theoretical concepts are highlighted and subtle links to the characteristics of effective learning illustrated. Taking this untied approach in analysing and reflecting on children's learning develops the co-operative and reciprocal approach between staff, children and parents thus strengthening the partnerships held across the learning community.

For any setting seeking to embed a lifelong learning community, there should be a drive to develop and continually improve the professional understanding held through dialogue with parents.

The exchange of information needs to be strong, with relationships being responsive and supportive. Routes of engagement need to be accessible and meet the needs of both families and practitioners, for the benefit of the children (Whalley 2007).

Key messages of this chapter

- Within the changing landscape of early years provision, the lifelong learning skills associated with engagement, motivation and creative and critical thinking are key to maintaining and facilitating the learning communities we belong to and lead within the early years sector.
- For lifelong learning to be effective, the setting must be a place of trust. A learning community requires a culture of open and constructive dialogue, allowing a culture in which the safe and respectful challenging of the working practice of others is acceptable.
- As early years educators we need to reflect upon the elements of our practice that require development in order to truly facilitate a learning community that embraces the partnership between the setting and parents.

References

Atelier Nurseries (2021) Available at: www.ateliernursery.co.uk/about-us-who-are-we-atelier-nursery (accessed 20 February 2021).

Athey, C. (1990) *Extending Thought in Young Children: A Parent-Teacher Partnership.* London: Paul Chapman Publishing.

Athey, C. (2004) Pedagogical leadership in *Pedagogical Leadership.* Nottingham: NCSL.

Bell, J. (2005) *Doing Your Research Project.* Maidenhead: McGraw-Hill.

Butler, H., Krelle, A., Seal, I., Trafford, L., Drew, S. and Hargreaves, J. (2011) *The Critical Friend: Facilitating Positive Change in School Communities.* Australia: Acer Press.

Childcare Act (2016) Available at: www.legislation.gov.uk/ukpga/2016/5/enacted (accessed 20 March 2021).

DfE (Department for Education) (2021) *Statutory Framework for the Early Years Foundation Stage: Setting the Standards for Learning, Development and Care for Children from Birth to Five*. Available at: https://assets.publishing.service.gov.uk/government/uploads/system/uploads/attachment_data/file/974907/EYFS_framework_-_March_2021.pdf (accessed 20 March 2021).

Early Years Workforce Commission (2021) *A Workforce in Crisis: Saving Our Early Years*. Available at: www.cache.org.uk/media/1863/a-workforce-in-crisis-saving-our-early-years.pdf (accessed 20 March 2021).

Elfer, P., Goldschmied, E. and Selleck, D. (2003) *Key Persons in the Nursery: Building Relationships for Quality Provision*. London: David Fulton Publishers.

Frew, B. (2009) Valuing heterarchy in the public sector, *People & Strategy*, 32(1): 11–12.

Goldschmied, E. and Jackson, S. (1994) *People Under Three: Young Children in Daycare*. London: Routledge.

Kolb, D.A. with Osland, J. and Rubin, I. (1995) *Organizational Behaviour: An Experiential Approach to Human Behaviour in Organizations*. Englewood Cliffs, NJ: Prentice Hall.

Laevers, F. (2000) Forward to basics! Deep-level learning and the experiential approach, *Early Years*, 20(2): 20–29.

Law, S. and Glover, D. (2000) *Educational Leadership and Learning: Practice, Policy and Research*. Maidenhead: Open University Press.

Malaguzzi, L. (1993) History and ideas and basic philosophy, in C. Edwards, L. Gandini and G. Forman (eds) *The Hundred Languages of Children: The Reggio Emilia Approach to Early Childhood Education*. Norwood, NJ: Ablex Publishing.

Nutbrown, C. and Page, J. (2008) *Working with Babies and Children from Birth to Three*. London: Sage.

Robbins, A. (2001) *Awaken the Giant Within*. London: Simon and Schuster.

Stanton, P. (2018) *Conscious Creativity*. London: The Ivy Press.

Sullivan, S. and Glanz, J. (2005) *Supervision that Improves Teaching: Strategies and Techniques*. Thousand Oaks, CA: Corwin Press.

Sylva, K., Melhuish, E., Sammons, P., Siraj-Blatchford, I. and Taggart, B. (2004) *The Effective Provision of Pre-school Education*. London: DfES Publications.

Vygotsky, L.S. (1978) *Mind in Society: The Development of Higher Psychological Processes*. Cambridge, MA: Harvard College.

Wenger, E., McDermott, R.A. and Snyder, W. (2002) *Cultivating Communities of Practice: A Guide to Managing Knowledge*. Boston, MA: Harvard Business Press.

Whalley, M. (2006) Leadership in integrated centres and services for children and families – a community development approach: engaging with the struggle, *Childrenz Issues*, 10(2): 8–13.

Whalley, M. (2007) *Involving Parents in their Children's Learning*, 2nd edn. London: Paul Chapman Publishing.

Building for the future – building on the early years

Elaine Bennett and Kim Porter

Chapter summary

- As we have seen in all the other chapters, the characteristics of effective learning are fundamental dispositions, attitudes and skills for life and yet they are often absent in planning and assessment later in primary schools.
- This chapter looks beyond the early years. Smooth transitions for children which build on their learning abilities need to take account of the different roles of the adult, resourcing the environment appropriately and the structure of the day.
- Recommendations and practical suggestions are made for continuing the focus on how children learn into Key Stage 1.

Beyond the early years

Let us begin by thinking about what our children will need as they grow into the adults of tomorrow. The truth of the matter is that we do not know the jobs they will one day be doing; perhaps these roles have yet to be created. The World Economic Forum (2016) shared these predicted top 10 skills for the workforce in 2020:

- complex problem solving
- critical thinking
- creativity
- people management
- co-ordinating with others
- emotional intelligence

- judgement and decision making
- service orientation
- negotiation
- cognitive flexibility

This list is a thought-provoking read for many reasons. First, in the age of a global pandemic, many of these 'softer' skills are the exact things keeping us moving towards solutions in a time of great uncertainty: creativity, critical thinking, decision making, problem solving and working with others.

Second, if we reflect upon these predicted top 10 skills and consider which aspects of the Early Years Foundation Stage (EYFS) they relate to, the links to the prime areas of communication, personal, social and emotional development and the effective learning characteristics are impossible to ignore.

We are living in a time where the world has changed forever: things can quite simply not go back to business as usual. Whether it is the highlighting of engrained racism and inequalities through the Black Lives Matter movement, the Covid-19 pandemic or the challenges we face keeping our planet alive, there can be no doubt the world is an uncertain place. Now is the time to take stock and consider what it is that is really going to matter for our world as we look to the future. Of course, being literate and numerate matter alongside other curriculum knowledge such as science, geography and art. However, is the knowledge of facts enough? As this book has shown the 'how' of learning is as important if not more important than the 'what' of learning. A recent evidence review concluded that:

> There is clear evidence that the Characteristics of Effective Teaching and Learning should be given more prominence as a key focus in the EYFS framework and statutory guidance. (Pascal et al. 2019:25)

Unfortunately, this evidence was ignored and there is now in England no statutory requirement to report on them at the end of the EYFS to parents and Key Stage 1 colleagues. Alongside this, a subtle change to the wording around the characteristics of effective learning means instead of being focused on learner attitudes and dispositions, as a foundation for lifelong learning, they are now focused around rates of development (DfE 2021). With the focus on the characteristics marginalised instead of prioritised, the decision to take them beyond the EYFS and into Key Stage 1 (and perhaps beyond) requires strength in pedagogical leadership and vision.

So, as we prepare to begin this brave, bold and essential journey, we need to ask ourselves the following questions:

- What is the typical Key Stage 1 experience today and what shapes it?
- Is there still a place for play and exploration in Key Stage 1?
- What would active learning in primary school look like?
- How can practitioners provide opportunities for creating and thinking critically in Year 1 and beyond?

Pushing down or building up? A brief history

Despite the fact that many of the values central to the EYFS are also core to post-16 learning, with independence, critical thought and self-reliance strong elements of both further and higher education, something altogether different shapes the experiences of pupils in the vast majority of our primary and secondary schools. Unfortunately, there is now an outcome-driven, knowledge-focused agenda eroding further into our early years settings, and particularly Reception classes – despite the most recent evidence review strongly arguing against this move (Pascal et al. 2019).

A brief look back through recent educational history reminds us of the continuing search for better ways to raise standards of educational achievement. Since former Prime Minister Jim Callaghan's ground-breaking Ruskin College speech of 1976, which is widely regarded as having begun 'The Great Debate' about the nature and purpose of public education, governments of all parties have accepted that education should seek to improve outcomes and prospects for all children. However, Callaghan's criticism that the education system in the mid-1970s was 'fitting a so-called inferior group of children with just enough learning to earn their living in the factory' (Callaghan 1976) has continuing resonance today. Despite (or perhaps because of) all of the reforms and changes, including the National Curriculum, targets, testing, the 'creative' curriculum, as well as a current government agenda which leans towards formal learning in the form of things like times tables and grammar, the overall experience of pupils in primary schools remains firmly about what they learn not how they learn. This risks fitting them with nothing more than an updated modernised version of 'just enough learning'.

Simultaneously, with the top-down curriculum and target-driven approach, which has been pursued by successive governments, there have been other strong voices, demanding the recognition of child development and the child's voice, and some schools are full of initiatives designed to raise the child's profile – Student Councils, Investors in Pupils, Pupil Voice – as well as support social and emotional well-being (Public Health England 2021), for example.

Practitioners in primary schools have been remarkably resilient in the face of changes that have often made little sense to them in terms of classroom practice. Keeping a firm grip on child development and pedagogy is a constant challenge and is sometimes portrayed as oppositional to government reforms. Dame Claire Tickell's review of the Early Years Foundation Stage (2011) led to EYFS reforms (DfE 2012) which gave prominence to prime areas of learning, specific areas and the characteristics of effective learning. However, in 2021, the most recent reforms signify a step backwards from the earlier changes based on evidence and research, and developed with involvement from the sector.

All this may sound gloomy, but we are currently at a moment of great opportunity and possibility for systemic change. On social media, in blogs, webinars, online discussions, articles and research pieces, many are now speaking out about the shape that education needs to take in the future ... and not just in the early years. Crucial issues such as how to decolonise the curriculum, the importance of transition and extending play into Key Stage 1, and visions for a recovery curriculum with well-being at the core, are currently resulting in connections between organisations and individuals who may not have been previously connected and shared voices. One such example has been the *#rightfromthestart* campaign, a grassroots movement challenging the top-down EYFS reforms through a film made during lockdown and online petition. The Early Years Coalition of 16 sector organisations in partnership with over 100 early years experts has developed alternative non-statutory curriculum guidance *Birth to 5 Matters* with the strapline 'by the sector, for the sector' in light of the latest rewrite of *Development Matters* (DfE 2020). So, perhaps ironically, could some of the darkest days in recent history be the turning point for a top-down education system obsessed with testing and results?

Painting the picture: Key Stage 1 in 2021

In recent years, two key trends have been shaping the landscape of teaching in Key Stage 1. The first is the continued drive to raise standards through the preparation for and testing of children through SATS and the phonic screening check in Year 1. The second is the view that many children are not Year 1 ready often judged according to whether they have achieved an arbitrary government measure known as a Good Level of Development. For many children this means they have not met goals in specific areas such as literacy and mathematics. Many of these children will be summer-born children who are measured against the same goals as their autumn-born peers, with no allowance given for perhaps almost a year less of development. In 2005 the Qualifications and Curriculum Authority produced a professional development programme entitled *Continuing the Learning Journey* (2005), which aimed to support schools to build on Early Years practice into Year 1 and ensure seamless transitions. Yet just 16 years later the idea of continuing and building on seems to have changed to pushing down. The current pathway for the Early Years curriculum in England, according to the DfE (2021) and supported by Ofsted (2017) is largely focused on aligning the EYFS to the National Curriculum and the preparation of Reception-aged children for increased formality.

With all of the above in mind, it is perhaps no surprise that the transition between the Reception year and Year 1 has become central to school conversations. This acknowledges the gulf between phases that challenges all but the most resilient of our children. This has led schools in several very different directions, often dependent on the philosophy and EYFS understanding and experience (and often bravery) of leadership and the reality of the school's situation; for example, current data sets and inspection judgements. Some schools have pushed what they perceive to be a 'school readiness' agenda into an increased formalisation in the final term of the Reception year. This usually involves more time on the carpet or at tables and a greater emphasis on adult-led activities, to enable children to 'hit the ground running' when they enter Year 1. Playful play-based, child-initiated and outside learning is reduced as the timetable shifts to a reduction in free-flow opportunities and more of a literacy- and mathematics-driven day, with children working with teachers on teacher-led tasks, often recorded in books or on worksheets to make sure children are ready for what is ahead.

In other schools, the first term of Year 1 has become the key transition point. Classrooms have been reorganised to include some continuous provision and children are encouraged to use these at certain times. All too often in these schools an uneasy and well-intended compromise is reached, whereby a nod is given to the importance of the continuation of EYFS pedagogy. Environments look familiar to children and 'playing' is allowed at certain times, generally after 'work' has been finished or during 'golden time' or the equivalent – which may be very time restricted. It is rare to see the areas of continuous provision being used as a base for teaching activities due to the lack of understanding of play as a powerful vehicle for learning. In an ironic twist, the higher attaining children who do finish 'work' are those most likely to access the areas, even though the provision has been placed in class with lower attainers in mind. It is often the perceived 'lower attaining' children who are removed from this environment to receive intervention teaching – frequently driven by pressure to pass the phonics screening test.

In yet other schools, EYFS pedagogies and principles are fully embraced and continue throughout Year 1, sometimes even into Year 2 and beyond. These schools have the challenge of ensuring the National Curriculum is covered whilst children operate in this environment, which is in opposition to the approach the current knowledge-led National Curriculum steers teachers towards. In these classrooms, there is a careful blend of adult-led, child-led and adult-initiated learning taking place, an approach recently referred to as a hybrid pedagogy by Pascal et al. (2019).

Fisher (2020) provides many examples of how this blended approach can be organised and refers to case studies of schools taking this journey, addressing myths such as suggesting this approach does not support progress or high standards. Unfortunately, many teachers working outside the EYFS do not have the knowledge of child development and early learning to make this approach work fully. For any school to truly take a child-centred approach to Year 1 and beyond, the training of the adults working in the environment must be a priority. Many schools spend a great deal of money on resources but unless the staff working in this environment understand child development, and feel confident to teach in this way, the money is wasted.

Ready for Year 1?

UNICEF identifies three dimensions of the complex concept of 'school readiness':

1 Ready children, focusing on children's learning and development.

2 Ready schools, focusing on the school environment along with practices that foster and support a smooth transition for children into primary school and advance and promote the learning of all children.

3 Ready families, focusing on parental and caregiver attitudes and involvement in their children's early learning and development and transition to school.

(UNICEF 2012:7)

Whitebread and Bingham (2012) provide critical research evidence that children are always ready to learn rather than necessarily being ready for school. The focus, they argue, should be about life preparation rather than school preparation, and they are entirely in tune in this respect with the Confederation of British Industry who maintain that education should be about 'developing a pattern of behaviour, thinking and feeling based on sound principles, integrity and resilience' which 'involves broadening our traditional expectation ... to help bring out those qualities in young people' (CBI 2012).

All too often, the focus is on what the children cannot do and not on how ready the school is for them to demonstrate their abilities. How often do Reception teachers hear the chorus of 'This new bunch can't even ... sit still/get dressed/write their names/count' and so on? More often than not, the children can do all of the above and much, much more. So why aren't they showing it? Perhaps the environment isn't right and doesn't feel safe and familiar enough. Perhaps they don't feel they have the relationship with their teachers yet. Perhaps they are just not feeling settled and confident. Perhaps they are not interested or engaged in what is being offered. Perhaps they miss their families after a wonderful break with them or perhaps they are hungry or worried about things at home.

What is it that happens to children over the summer holidays (when many will finally turn) that means that they no longer require a pedagogy which is focused on their unique development, high-quality, back and forth teaching interactions with tuned-in adults and enabling environments where play is the vehicle for learning and autonomy is an essential feature? When does the switch suddenly flick that means they now need to return to a completely different set-up, with a teacher at the front, where there is little physical movement, no choice, no outside access and a day filled with completing set tasks usually in books or on worksheets? The answer is simple. There is no such switch between Reception and Year 1. In fact, as Fisher (2020:28) points out: 'there is very little to discriminate the five-year-old learner from the seven-year-old learner. Largely because, in terms of human development, nothing very spectacular happens between those birthdays.'

Being a teacher in Key Stage 1, and especially Year 1, can feel like spinning plates (and often dropping a few!). Pressure comes from above to make sure children are ready for Year 2, make sure they will get though the phonics test and make sure gaps are filled from their Reception year. There may be whole school ways of working, such as marking policies, number of exercise books, working walls and learning walks – often built around a model of upper Key Stage 2 practice for those in primary schools and led by leaders with little if any understanding of the complexities of the young child. Moreover, whilst practitioners are spinning these plates, children are asking when it will be home time, when they can play, why they cannot go outside and when they can go back to Reception. In an ideal world, and as proposed in the Cambridge Review (Alexander 2009), the EYFS would extend to Year 1 or even Year 2, as Kindergarten stages around the world do. Under the current government, this is a pipe dream so we have to find ways to put the child back at the heart of practice.

Practitioners talk of being stuck between the proverbial rock and a hard place; they may value the early years pedagogy but they are worried that their children will not make sufficient progress. And opposition from senior leaders and increased parental demands are also cited as the basis of adopting a formal approach.

The importance of effective transition

Researcher: Is there anything you don't like about being in year 1?

First Boy: Being on the carpet for a long time.

Second Boy: Neither do I because it's very boring.

First Boy: And it wastes our time playing.

Second Boy: It wastes your life.

(Sharp et al. 2006:22)

Do we really want to be the adults who waste children's lives? Do we want a class of 5- and 6-year-olds who wish to be 4 again? With two very different curriculums to navigate, smooth transition becomes of fundamental importance. Ideally, children would move into Year 1 with their enthusiasm for learning intact and progress would ensue without the regression so often seen. Certainly, the systems in place do not help, especially those around assessment. The continuing search for a straight line of progress and attainment from the end of Reception to the end of Key Stage 1 (then to the end of Key Stage 2 and onwards to GCSE grades) has spawned a veritable industry of tracking systems. Teachers in Year 1 have to contend with tracking systems, school leaderships and advisors who want EYFS data smoothly correlated to National Curriculum figures. We have to explain that it cannot be done. Common sense tells teachers that those already achieving well at the end of EYFS should go on to achieve well throughout their school career. However, as Barry Hymer asserted at the North of England Conference 2012, 'no one knows his or her own potential let alone anyone else's … potential is different from ability' (Hymer 2012).

How theory and research can support the characteristics in Key Stage 1

Laevers (1994) describes the importance of assessing levels of well-being and involvement when judging the quality of education in any context. The Leuven Scales he developed are used in many educational settings around the world and provide an excellent starting point for any education setting wanting to judge their effectiveness for learners.

Anna Ephgrave (2015) in her work on 'In the moment planning' (which spans from birth into Key Stage 1) recommends using the Leuven Scales when observing individuals, large and small groups of children. She states that: '… it is vital to be able to spot when children are engaged and when they are not, in order to be reflective of the practice on offer and in order to be able to evaluate any changes that are made' (Ephgrave 2017: 4). High levels of engagement indicate brain activity, synaptic connection and thus, Ephgrave concludes, progress. If we refer back to the example earlier of a child in Year 1 stating that being on the carpet 'wastes your life' what progress is being made by this child during these times when he is still and silent and the teacher is speaking?

There is considerable research from the UK and further afield that supports the positive impact of taking active learning, play, exploration and creating and thinking critically beyond the EYFS. Donaldson (1978: 17) concluded that humans have a fundamental urge to 'be effective, competent and independent, to understand the world and to act with skill'. Building on children's natural thirst for skill and knowledge which links to their own interests is central to early years principles, yet often absent in Year 1 and beyond, so external motivation becomes necessary: stickers, certificates and credits become core to everyday classroom practice. Children are motivated to behave through traffic light systems, keeping 'on the sun not in the cloud', being 'good to be green'. Behaviours that were not an issue in EYFS could easily become so in Year 1 with children being asked to switch from a curriculum with them at the heart to one with abstract facts at the centre.

The Rose Report (DCSF 2009), the Cambridge Primary Review (Alexander 2009) and more recently Pascal et al. (2019) have all suggested that active, interactive and collaborative learning experiences would be of benefit beyond the pre-school years. England is out of kilter with much of the world and even the rest of the UK. Northern Ireland, Wales and Scotland all define early years as lasting to at least 6 years of age.

However, research also suggests that if schools move to a model which takes early years principles into primary school, they need to do so in full understanding of the different role of the teacher. Stephen et al. (2010) followed five teachers in four Scottish primary schools where there was a commitment to active learning for a year and concluded that 'while there have been innovations in practice, these may perhaps best be described as changes in degree rather than revolutionary departures' (Stephen et al. 2010: 8). Although the researchers saw many examples of planned purposeful play, and of alternative resources to pen and paper being used, they did not see anything they could describe as spontaneous play. The observed activities did not arise from the children's everyday experiences, and the researchers felt that teachers' training did not engage them with thinking about their role as a teacher.

More recently, Fisher's research with over 500 EYFS and Key Stage 1 teachers (2021) found the most frequently reported barriers to play-based pedagogy in Year 1 was senior leaders' lack of understanding of early years and the role of play.

How the revised Ofsted inspection framework can support the characteristics in Key Stage 1

'Ofsted will not advocate a particular method of planning (including lesson planning), teaching or assessment; it is up to schools to determine their practices and it is up to leadership teams to justify these on their own merits rather than by referring to this handbook' (Ofsted 2019:13).

The recent changes made to the English inspection framework are significant, and present increased possibilities for creative and innovative practice in Key Stage 1 classrooms. Inspectors have been directed to leave their own subjective views on styles of teaching at the door and observe the learning in lessons. There are no prescribed methodologies, so the structure of the day is no longer relevant and the teacher as transmitter is not the desired status quo. Children need to be able to discuss and describe their learning, and practitioners who keep the characteristics central to planning and provision will be rewarded with pupils who are able to work independently, to think about their learning and to articulate that learning. The current inspection regime supports practitioners to develop a 'how you learn' in addition to 'what you learn' approach as it values key characteristics of learning skills.

In their 2015 report *Teaching and play – a balancing act?* Ofsted shared its definition of teaching in the early years; this is included in the 2019 Inspection framework.

Teaching should not be taken to imply a 'top down' or formal way of working. It is a broad term which covers the many different ways in which adults help young children learn. It includes their interactions with children during planned and child-initiated play and activities: communicating and modelling language, showing, explaining, demonstrating, exploring ideas, encouraging, questioning, recalling, providing a narrative for what they are doing, facilitating and setting challenges. It takes account of the equipment they provide and the attention to the physical environment as well as the structure and routines of the day that establish expectations. Integral to teaching is how practitioners assess what children know, understand and can do as well as take account of their interests and dispositions to learning (characteristics of effective learning), and use this information to plan children's next steps in learning and monitor their progress.

(Ofsted 2015:11)

Schools need to embrace this definition and use it beyond the early years. The simple question for headteachers, school leaders, Key Stage 1 and EYFS teachers is: If our children's needs as learners don't change, why is our teaching changing? Why are our environments changing? Why is our pedagogy changing so dramatically? Who are these changes for and with what aim? School leaders also need to feel they have the autonomy to decide what is right for the children in their school, given this this statement:

Ofsted will judge fairly schools that take radically different approaches to the curriculum. They will assess any school's curriculum favourably when leaders have built or adopted a curriculum with appropriate coverage, content, structure and sequencing and implemented it effectively.

(Ofsted 2019: 12)

Case study from Elaine's practice

Year 1, Friars Primary School and Nursery, Shoeburyness, Essex

Friars is a two-form entry primary school on the Essex coast. I was employed as EYFS leader in 2013. Several years later, I was asked to move into Year 1 – to develop practice in a very formal environment – focusing on the same things as I addressed when I worked in EYFS. This time there was the added challenge of implementing a child-centred pedagogy whilst meeting National Curriculum expectations and working towards the phonic screening check as well as preparation for a formal Year 2 approach. Below are some of the changes made along the journey:

Environment

- A dividing wall was removed making the room an open plan base for children to move between – mirroring the EYFS provision.
- Most tables were removed and large rugs were purchased.
- Areas of provision were established, including a large art area.
- An outside area was set up.
- Display backings were changed from bold colours to more neutral ones.
- The display policy (double mounting) was relaxed so that learning was displayed immediately and with/by children.
- The characteristics of effective learning were displayed on the wall – alongside photos and speech bubbles from the children illustrating the 'how' of learning.
- Children were not put in ability groups.

- Exercise books were introduced gradually – children were encouraged to use them in free-flow time to record learning and observations were kept in them too.
- A confidential diary was provided which children could access freely to draw and write in throughout the day.

Timetable

- The day was no longer split into subject specific time in the autumn term.
- Children did not go to every assembly.
- Children had long periods of free-flow daily including outside.
- The timetable was reflected on half termly and new elements gradually added, e.g. adult-led focus groups, more assemblies.
- Staff were rotated to move between inside and outside environments – including across the inside space so children did not stay in one area.

Teaching and learning

- All adults in Year 1 had recent experience working in Reception classes.
- Observations were recorded electronically.
- The first few weeks focused on getting to know the children, building relationships.
- Ofsted's teaching definition was displayed on the door, surrounded by photos of adults 'teaching'. This built up over time and towards the end of the year included more formal examples in preparation for children moving into a formal Year 2 environment
- The school signed up to the Centre for Literacy in Primary Education (CLPE) resource 'Power of reading'. Instead of topics through the year, books provided starting points and learning was clearly linked to the National Curriculum.
- As the year progressed, 'challenges' were provided for children to complete, often linked to the current Power of Reading text, which linked to the National Curriculum.
- Helicopter stories were continued into Year 1 (Lee 2015).
- Although as the year progressed the teaching became more formal, there were always opportunities for children to access continuous provision and initiate their own activity each day. By the summer term this was in the afternoons.
- A scrapbook was set up where 'in the moment' learning episodes were shared; these were referenced to the National Curriculum. The easiest way to do this was to set up an imaginary child on the 2Simple app called *In the Moment* – by doing this and tagging spontaneous group activities to this 'child' many examples quickly grew!

Transition

- Parents and children completed simple surveys about their transition to Year 1 and were 100% positive.
- Transition stopped being a one-hour event in summer, and instead the Reception children and current Year 1 free-flowed between the EYFS and Year 1 inside and outside environments every week for one afternoon in the summer term. The EYFS children got to meet their new teachers, and the Year 1 children got to go back and visit their much-loved Reception teachers.
- Parents/carers were invited to a Year 1 transition meeting. These meetings had not ever happened before. Parents found them reassuring.
- Children were excited about Year 1. Tears were minimal and children seemed completely at home in their new environments and with their new teachers from day one.

Some examples of learning

Some of these examples were adult initiated; some were adult guided and others child initiated. A clear example of how to work towards this model is explained comprehensively by Fisher (2020).

Games and playing cards were constantly on offer in the classroom, along with a selection of dice (including some that were a smaller dice inside a larger dice and dice with more than six sides), spinners, counters, timers and blank board games with different types of tracks. The children were taught how to play simple games such as snakes and ladders, Ludo, pick-up sticks, and simple track games. They would then choose to play these with friends. Adults also modelled how to make up board games, considering various positive and negative consequences of landing on spaces. Children learned how to make their own board games, writing the rules and explaining these to others.

After Remembrance Day, a child brought in his great-grandfather's war medals to show the class. The children were fascinated by them and had the opportunity to hold them, look at them, ask questions and draw them. A few days later and another child bought her great-grandfather's military papers and photographs. The children handled these with great respect, making comments and asking questions.

As part of our geography work, we used Google maps to look at our local area. The children were fascinated by how we could zoom in and out from space. The adult modelled looking at local places of interest, such as the supermarket and beach, before suggesting looking at places further afield. The children began to share their interests and we looked at their home addresses, those of family members elsewhere in the country and famous landmarks such as the Eiffel tower, Buckingham Palace and the Pyramids in Egypt. Google maps was often on the whiteboard and the children would explore it throughout the year. It was also used to connect learning, for example looking at the Great Wall of China when learning about Chinese New Year or the Monument in London after studying the Great Fire of London, and learning about Space when looking at the Power of Reading text *Beegu*. Large rolls of paper were always available for children to use and mapping featured heavily.

In history, we started learning about the Great Fire of London by watching an episode of *Magic Grandad* (BBC available online). The children became fascinated and were able to remember details such as dates, places and how Samuel Pepys buried his cheese! The learning was brought to life by a visit from a firefighter with some artefacts the children could hold as they re-enacted a bucket chain and used the squirter. In preparation for his visit the children wrote questions and then asked them during his visit. A Forest School teacher also came in and taught the children how to build a fire, toast bread and how to keep safe around fire. This was also connected to a fire poem from one of the Power of Reading texts (*Out and About*, Shirley Hughes) and the children explored vocabulary to describe how the fire felt, looked, smelt, sounded and tasted. These words were then used to create word banks and were used in writing. Following this work, several of the children went to London with their parents to visit the scene of the fire and the Monument.

A parent donated some large plastic boxes with various-sized compartments. The teacher provided them along with a range of money and sticky notes. The children sorted the coins, labelled the compartments and set up their own bank. These boxes were then stored in the maths area and children returned to them. The paper notes provided quickly ripped, so the teacher showed images of some real notes and the children made their own, looking at the size, colour, patterns and markings.

The Power of Reading text *Out and About* by Shirley Hughes, featured seasonal poems. Each season, the children studied one of the poems, and the intricate illustrations. The class (and any parents who wanted to come) visited the local park for a seasonal walk. Before the walks, predictions were made about what would be experienced and changes since the last walk. During the walks, photos were taken, observations made of the seasonal changes, and the children drew and wrote what could be seen, heard, smelled and felt. These lists were then used on our return in writing and to create simple poems and recounts.

An academy-wide art exhibition was held and moved around the schools. It included work from each school across the Primary age range from Nursery to Year 6. When it visited Friars, each class had the chance to visit. The Year 1 children were fascinated and excited by the range of work from the other children and they photographed their favourite pieces. These photos were then printed for the art area to inspire them in their work and shared on the whiteboard so children could discuss why they liked them and focus on skills and techniques.

A child came in after the holidays with her foot in a boot cast because she had broken a bone. The other children decided they wanted to make boots so she did not feel different. They spent the afternoon in the art area rummaging through the junk modelling materials to find what was needed to make their own boots. The children wore them home and came back with them for several days.

As part of the National Curriculum, the children needed to learn the names of birds. The children helped to build a bird table and a bird-watching station was set up by the large window. Posters and clipboards were provided, as well as non-fiction books from the library. The children helped to feed the birds and made their own binoculars from kitchen roll tubes and became avid bird watchers, often adding to the tallies of which birds had been seen. Children were able to identify them – the magpie became the class favourite! They used these skills and knowledge on our park walks.

A teacher took in a recorder from home and the children were interested in it; one child especially wanted to learn how to play. The school provided several and children learned to play some simple songs and wrote some of their own. The child who showed the initial interest is now in Key Stage 2 and is in the school orchestra.

Practical solutions: How to take the characteristics into Year 1 and Year 2

Although many practitioners may be inspired by these examples from Elaine's practice, some may wish to begin with a less radical approach to ensuring that engagement, motivation and thinking are key elements to their practice. The following are some suggestions available to all Key Stage 1 practitioners.

Playing and exploring – Engagement

- When the children first join Year 1, take at least the first week to play alongside and get to know them. Building relationships is essential if you want them to learn from you and make progress in your care.
- Make sure there is floor space for children to use to play.
- If space is limited, consider which areas of provision are essential – perhaps small world to support language and literacy, maths and writing areas to enable children to apply skills and a well-resourced art area.
- Ask to sometimes share the outdoor space used by the EYFS children if you have none of your own to use or try to find some around the school you could develop.
- Set up areas of provision, which feature authentic resources that promote exploration, such as a science area with magnifiers, non-fiction texts, kaleidoscopes, torches; maths area with open-ended resources such as dice, timers, spinners and counters and a small-world area with fabric and loose parts to encourage children to create their own worlds.
- Build up collections of objects for children to explore, sort, count, match and create with such as buttons, keys, stones and beads.
- Plan for speaking and listening activities which link into role play and allow children to explore feelings and thought such as hot seating, conscience alley, role on the wall.

- Welcome guests to your classroom connected to topics and themes and work with the children to create lists of questions they'd like to ask them, and perhaps write thank-you letters to post after the visit.
- It may be hard to achieve uninterrupted time but it may be possible to do projects which run across sessions and days and allow for pupils to follow particular interests, for example the classic Year 1 'toys' topic could be planned in this way with children engaged with an aspect that they find interesting and want to investigate further.

Active learning – Motivation

- Make time to celebrate photos of children engaged in play and discuss them – reflecting on how children were feeling, what they were thinking and where they think they will go next! Encourage children to take their own photographs and share them in school and with families.
- Read and tell stories to children of those who have bounced back, encouraging them to see the benefit of persistence. Celebrate this within the class using stories about your own children.
- Consider developing a mud kitchen outside. The free *Mud Book* (White and Edwards 2018) resource is a great starting point. Some pots, pans, utensils, working areas and mud are the only essentials!
- Consider developing block play in your classroom both inside and out.
- Consider starting woodwork. Moorhouse (2019) is a fantastic free guide to get you started!
- Ensure outside offers opportunities for children to be physical and take risks – again the use of loose parts such as crates, planks and tyres is great for this (Casey and Robertson 2019)!

Thinking creatively and critically thinking

- Model self-talk: give time and value to sustained shared thinking; give time to feedback; model the plan, do, review process. Respect effort and ideas (see Chapter 7).
- Give opportunities to explore and manipulate materials before a specific 'learning' activity.
- Use mind mapping when suitable; plan themes and projects – noting children's ideas and recording names next to their contributions.
- Start topics and themes with a list of children's queries and questions, which the learning community of the class will then find out about.
- Encourage staff to ask questions, so that children are reminded that we are all learners.
- Provide opportunities to create art and music on large and small scales inside and out, using a range of resources. Look at and listen to other people's art and music as springboards for discussion and questions.

- Ensure that in the outside environment there are science/maths resources for children to use, such as magnifiers, measuring equipment, non-fiction books, resources for identifying nature and weather stations, alongside writing materials to encourage children to record their observations.
- Provide PE equipment outside so that children can create their own games and challenges, again along with maths resources to help them measure and record scores/times.

Getting started

As you begin on this journey, remember to take small steps. There will be successes and perhaps occasional disasters, but every day will be a learning experience for you and the children.

Reflect honestly about what transition means in your school and consider these six key principles as you move to improve it.

1 Transition is a process and not an event.
2 Transition is a whole school issue.
3 Transition should be viewed as positive and exciting.
4 Transition should be a smooth and seamless journey for all children.
5 Transition relies on joint working between all staff involved in the process.
6 Effective transition will only be achieved after genuine consultation with children and parents.

(Fisher 2020:49)

For those with jam-packed timetables of Key Stage 1 subjects, it may perhaps involve going off timetable once a week to work on a project likely to engage children, or providing sessions for children to play and for you to engage with them. Remember that playing may not come naturally to children who have become conditioned to being given set activities and the resources they need – so let them see you playing, trying things out, being creative and making mistakes! There may be children who need to rediscover the joy of play.

Make some time to visit your colleagues who work in early years. Observe their interactions with the children and look at the environment. How can you ensure that the resources you offer build on and extend their learning?

It is vital that you are clear about what you are doing, why you want to do it and the evidence behind it, in order to convince colleagues and particularly senior leaders whose support you will need. Build up evidence through the year of learning through play, perhaps in a scrapbook with sections for each month or a wall display. This will provide great evidence of progression in learning.

Observation is part of your pedagogical toolkit. Do not feel that this means you are not teaching! Consider using the Leuven scales to assess the children's (and perhaps staff's) levels of well-being and involvement. If you notice patterns of low levels reflect and address this!

> **Key messages**
> - In order to support children in Key Stage 1 appropriately, practitioners need to be aware that when young children are encouraged to follow their natural instincts to play and explore, allowed to concentrate on self-chosen challenges and supported to plan and review their own learning, they become self-regulated learners who are more likely to achieve socially and academically than children who have been more passive in their learning.
> - Practitioners will need to think differently about transition, the role of the teacher and learner, the structure of the day and the learning environment.

And finally ...

The world has changed and now it is time for education to change. That change starts with you. Together we can do this!

References

Alexander, R. (ed.) (2009) *Children, their World, their Education. Final report and recommendations of the Cambridge Primary Review*. Abingdon: Routledge.

Callaghan, J. (1976) 'A rational debate based on the facts' (The Ruskin College speech), available at: www.educationengland.org.uk/documents/speeches/1976ruskin.html (accessed 22 April 2021).

Casey, T. and Robertson J. (2019) *Loose parts play toolkit*. Available at: www.inspiringscotland.org.uk/publication/loose-parts-play-toolkit-2019-edition/ (accessed 3 September 2020).

Confederation of British Industry (CBI) (2012) *First Steps, a new approach for our schools* https://issuu.com/the-cbi/docs/first_steps_a_new_approach_for_our_ (accessed 20 April 2021).

DCSF (Department for Children, Schools and Families) (2009) *Independent Review of the Primary Curriculum: Final Report (Rose Report)*. Nottingham: DCSF Publications. Available at: www.educationengland.org.uk/documents/pdfs/2009-IRPC-final-report.pdf (accessed 20 April 2021).

DfE (Department for Education) (2021) *Statutory framework for the early years foundation stage: Setting the standards for learning, development and care for children from birth to five*. Available at: www.gov.uk/government/publications/early-years-foundation-stage-framework–2 (accessed 21 April 2021).

DfE (Department for Education) (2020) *Development Matters: Non-statutory curriculum guidance for the early years foundation stage* (updated July 2021). Available at: https://assets.publishing.service.gov.uk/government/uploads/system/uploads/attachment_data/file/971620/Development_Matters.pdf (accessed 1 October 2021).

DfE (2012) *Statutory Framework for the Early Years Foundation Stage*. Available at: www.foundationyears.org.uk/files/2014/05/eyfs_statutory_framework_march_2012.pdf (accessed 8 October 2021).

Donaldson, M. (1978) *Children's Minds*. London: Fontana Press.

Ephgrave, A. (2015) *The Nursery Year in Action: Following Children's Interests through the Year*. Oxford: Routledge.

Ephgrave, A. (2017) *Year One in Action: A Month-by-Month Guide to Taking Early Years Pedagogy into KS1*. Oxford : Routledge.

Fisher, J. (2020) *Moving on to Key Stage 1: Improving Transition into Primary School*. Maidenhead: Open University Press.

Fisher, J. (2021) *An Early Years qualification for primary school headteachers?* Available at: https://early-education.org.uk/news/guest-blog-julie-fisher-early-years-qualification-primary-school-headteachers (accessed 20 March 2021).

Hymer, B. (2012) *Passion, potential, performance*. Paper presented at the North of England Education Conference, Leeds, January 2012.

Laevers, F. (ed.) (1994) *Defining and Assessing Quality in Early Childhood*. Leuven: Leuven University Press.

Lee, P. (2015) *Princesses, Dragons and Helicopter Stories: Storytelling and Story Acting in the Early Years*. London: Routledge.

Moorhouse, P. (2019) *Woodwork in the Early Years*. Available at: https://cdn.communityplaythings.co.uk/-/media/files/cpuk/library/training-resource/woodworking-booklet-early-ed.pdf?d=20210106T232059Z (accessed 12 December 2020).

Ofsted (2015) *Teaching and play in the early years – a balancing act?* Available at: https://assets.publishing.service.gov.uk/government/uploads/system/uploads/attachment_data/file/936086/Teaching-and-play-in-the-early-years-a-balancing-act.pdf (accessed 10 August 2020).

Ofsted (2017) *Bold beginnings: The Reception curriculum in a sample of good and outstanding primary schools*. Available at: https://assets.publishing.service.gov.uk/government/uploads/system/uploads/attachment_data/file/663560/28933_Ofsted_-_Early_Years_Curriculum_Report_-_Accessible.pdf (accessed 10 October 2021).

Ofsted (2019) *School Inspection Handbook*. Available at: https://assets.publishing.service.gov.uk/government/uploads/system/uploads/attachment_data/file/843108/School_inspection_handbook_-_section_5.pdf (accessed 10 September 2020).

Pascal, C., Bertram T. and Rouse L. (2019) *Getting it right in the Early Years Foundation Stage: a review of the evidence*. Available at: www.early-education.org.uk/sites/default/files/Getting%20it%20right%20in%20the%20EYFS%20Literature%20Review.pdf (accessed 3 July 2020).

Public Health England (2021) *Promoting children and young people's emotional health and wellbeing A whole school and college approach*, available at: https://assets.publishing.service.gov.uk/government/uploads/system/uploads/attachment_data/file/958151/Promoting_children_and_young_people_s_emotional_health_and_wellbeing_a_whole_school_and_college_approach.pdf (accessed 20 March 2021).

Qualifications and Curriculum Authority (2005) *Continuing the learning journey-training package* Norwich: QCA. Available at: https://dera.ioe.ac.uk/9147/1/12729_Continuing_the_Journey_web.pdf (accessed 5 May 2021).

Sharp, C. White, G., Burge, B. and Eames A. (2006) *Making a successful transition to year 1*. Available at: https://nfer.ac.uk/nfer/PRE_PDF_Files/06_35_04.pdf (accessed 1 August 2020).

Stephen, C., Ellis, J. and Martlew, J. (2010) *Taking active learning into the primary school: A matter of new practices?* Available at: www.researchgate.net/publication/233260044_Taking_active_learning_into_the_primary_school_A_matter_of_new_practices (accessed 7 August 2020).

Tickell, C. (2011) *The Early Years: Foundations for life, health and learning*. Available at: https://assets.publishing.service.gov.uk/government/uploads/system/uploads/attachment_data/file/180919/DFE-00177-2011.pdf (accessed 1 July 2020).

UNICEF (2012) *School Readiness: A conceptual framework.* Available at: www.unicef.org/earlychildhood/files/Child2Child_ConceptualFramework_FINAL(1).pdf (accessed 10 October 2020).

White, J. and Edwards, L. (2018) *Making a mud kitchen* 2nd edn. Available at: https://muddyfaces.co.uk/content/files/Mud-Book-2nd-edition.pdf (accessed 3 September 2020).

Whitebread, D. and Bingham, S. (2012) *School Readiness: A Critical Review of Perspectives and Evidence.* TACTYC Occasional Paper 2. Available at:
https://tactyc.org.uk/occasional-papers/ (accessed 20 April 2021).

World Economic Forum (2016) https://www.weforum.org/agenda/2016/01/the-10-skills-you-need-to-thrive-in-the-fourth-industrial-revolution/ (accessed 1 August 2020).

Index

Page numbers in italics are figures; with 't' are tables.